Political Automation

Political Automation

*An Introduction to AI in Government and
Its Impact on Citizens*

EDUARDO ALBRECHT

OXFORD
UNIVERSITY PRESS

Oxford University Press is a department of the University of Oxford.
It furthers the University's objective of excellence in research, scholarship,
and education by publishing worldwide. Oxford is a registered trade mark of
Oxford University Press in the UK and in certain other countries.

Published in the United States of America by Oxford University Press
198 Madison Avenue, New York, NY 10016, United States of America.

© Oxford University Press 2025

All rights reserved. No part of this publication may be reproduced, stored in a retrieval system, transmitted, used for text and data mining, or used for training artificial intelligence, in any form or by any means, without the prior permission in writing of Oxford University Press, or as expressly permitted by law, by license or under terms agreed with the appropriate reprographics rights organization. Inquiries concerning reproduction outside the scope of the above should be sent to the Rights Department, Oxford University Press, at the address above.

You must not circulate this work in any other form
and you must impose this same condition on any acquirer.

Library of Congress Cataloging-in-Publication Data
Names: Albrecht, Eduardo Zachary, author.
Title: Political automation : an introduction to AI in government and its impact on citizens / Eduardo Albrecht.
Description: New York : Oxford University Press, 2025. | Includes bibliographical references and index.
Identifiers: LCCN 2024038482 (print) | LCCN 2024038483 (ebook) | ISBN 9780197696958 (paperback) | ISBN 9780197696941 (hardback) | ISBN 9780197696972 (epub) | ISBN 9780197696989
Subjects: LCSH: Public administration—Automation. | Public administration—Technological innovations. | Artificial intelligence—Political aspects. | Artificial intelligence—Government policy.
Classification: LCC JF1525.A8 A392 2025 (print) | LCC JF1525.A8 (ebook) | DDC 351.0285/63—dc23/eng/20241228
LC record available at https://lccn.loc.gov/2024038482
LC ebook record available at https://lccn.loc.gov/2024038483

DOI: 10.1093/9780197696989.001.0001

Paperback printed by Integrated Books International, United States of America
Hardback printed by Bridgeport National Bindery, Inc., United States of America

For Fab, Zoe & Zac

Contents

Preface	ix
Acknowledgments	xii
1. Political Machines	1
2. California	16
3. The Informatized Body	28
PHOTO SECTION: VITALS	
4. Europe	55
5. Mechanics of Expression	69
PHOTO SECTION: EMOTIONS	
6. Africa	97
7. Digitized Biographies	113
PHOTO SECTION: RELATIONS	
8. India	141
9. The Eye of Nations	158
PHOTO SECTION: CONTEXT	
10. Kenya	185
11. A Third House	195
Appendix I Further Reading by Scholars	212
Appendix II Further Reading by Organizations	257
Index	277

All photography by Nicholas Albrecht

https://nicholasalbrecht.com/

Preface

Vindica te tibi
Seneca

Please be warned, this book will travel into uncharted territory. As such, there will be plenty of mistakes along the way and we will encounter questionable phenomena that we cannot, or will not wish to, acknowledge. The least I could do is try to justify why I have taken you there. The reason is that I am concerned that AI technologies will introduce a level of division the likes of which humanity has rarely experienced before. The gap between the upper and lower strata, across nations and within them, will soon become so wide that the two groups may become quite unrecognizable to each other, and to whom we are today.

You may note this will not be the first time society becomes radically polarized. Certainly, such a thing undulates with the tides of history. This time, I fear it may be a more fundamental matter. AI will have differential *physiological* consequences for humanity. To countenance this, we must dig past history and into our prehistory. Through the mega-annums, dramatic environmental or technological factors occasionally emerged and drove wedges into our evolutionary lineages.

I believe that one such technological factor is occurring today. Like the discovery of fire, AI is unlocking a basin of unknown potential that is transformative for our species. Like fire, we will depend on it to live and as such it will change the shape of our bodies and the contours of our minds. But not all of us will depend on it in the same way. Some will control it while others will be controlled by it. This distinction is not trivial. Depending on where one lands, it will determine the kind of reshaping of the body and recontouring of the mind. Similar to those hominids that learned to control fire versus those that did not.

Those who control AI will be able to reinvent themselves. They will be augmented in extraordinary new ways. They will direct and control that augmentation. In other words, their human agency will increase. On the other hand, those controlled by AI will be affected in ways that they do not fully know or control. In many aspects of their lives they will be making decisions that are not entirely their own. They will think, act, buy, and love through AI—and in the process be reinvented in its image. It is not an exaggeration to say that how we design AI today will determine how we design humans in the future.

What is the image of AI? What will the bodies and minds of those shaped by AI look like? The answer to this question lies in the nature of the technology itself. AI without agency is reductionist. Every measure that it takes toward a person reduces the person to a narrower and narrower scope of possibilities. This is because AI decisions are based on the *likelihood* of a person thinking, acting, buying, or loving in a certain way. Take, for example, algorithmically produced music, food, or mating partner suggestions. Those suggestions that are acted upon in turn further shape that person's tastes, proclivities, and affections through exposure to that experience. Over time this restricts the scope of experience. People become less capable to surprise with thought and action that is not expected, that is not *likely*. Once reduced in this way they become predictable and therefore programmable. Indeed, just like AI.

This has consequences we have not fully realized. Let us return to the example of the algorithmically produced music, food, or mating partner suggestions. There are certain suggestions that the AI will never make. Whoever or whatever programmed it decided a priori that certain things or people are unacceptable, and therefore they simply will not appear on the menu of doable things or likable people. This amounts to an evolutionary pressure akin to natural selection. Quite literally, certain music will not be danced to, certain foods will not be eaten, and certain partners will not be mated with. Conversely, other types of music, foods, and partners will be promoted. Those types of human bodies that are most adaptable to interacting with the promoted suggestions (or indeed of being promoted) will thrive, others will fade out.

At some deep preverbal level, I don't like this. It is as if whoever or whatever is programming AI is also programming the persons that use it—and I use it quite a lot. I wrote this book as a call to collectively participate in the programming of AI before we are programmed by it beyond the point in which we no longer care to be involved.

If we do nothing, AI will slowly, quietly, indefatigably curate the social norms of large portions of the population, deciding what entire subcultures look like. It will make its own ethical calculations regarding what people should and should not do. What is safe and not safe. What is hurtful or dangerous and what instead is permissible and preferable. What is most efficiently conducive today to a vaguely defined social good tomorrow. It is silly to believe it will by default promote traits like love of freedom, eagerness to question authority, or capacity to surprise. Those may not be on the menu of doable or likable things; unless, of course, we insist they are.

Acknowledgments

This book would not have been possible without the research, editorial, emotional, and creative support of the following people, whom I list in alphabetical order: my brother and photographer Nicholas Albrecht, my parents Carl and Lucia Albrecht, my research associate for over ten years Apna Balgobin, OUP senior acquisitions editor Angela Chnapko, friend and comparative literature scholar Alex Enderle, Global TechnoPolitics Forum leadership Pari Esfandiari and Gregory Treverton, UNU-CPR's Eleonore Fournier-Tombs and Adam Day, Mercy University colleagues Alberto Manzi, Rebecca Trenz, and Julia Zavala, as well as Mercy University's Faculty Development Grants 2020–2022, and research assistants Aurora Ruud, Davina Resto, and Anne Valentino. I would be remiss if I did not mention the many students at Mercy University, City College, and Columbia University who have contributed insights and ideas through many semesters of engaging classroom discussion, as well as the scholars, researchers, and activists that agreed to be interviewed for this work contributing their valuable time and understanding. Finally, a special thank you goes to room 209 on the second floor of Mahoney Hall, especially the south- and east-facing windows, and to Providence, that guides all.

Chapter 1
Political Machines

Governments today use artificial intelligence (AI) to gather information about our lives and decide how to allocate resources. These political machines determine, for example, who gets policed and who receives economic benefits. As AI edges up the ladder of cognitive skills, it will take over increasingly complex government functions from human supervision.[1] Machines may soon decide—as they already do in some parts of the world—the level of privacy a citizen can enjoy, how far they can travel, or what they can and cannot say publicly. Taken together, this amounts to a phenomenon of political automation that is rapidly materializing across the globe.

Political machines will be incredibly consequential for everyone, yet few understand how they work. Even fewer understand the changing role of humans in interacting with them. What decisions *do* we make? Some argue that our job now is to provide the machines with a sense of morality. We may not make all the decisions, but we do calibrate the ethical parameters that bind those decisions.[2] Essentially, we will tell the machines the difference between good and bad decisions.

This may be so, yet there is no guarantee that citizens will have equal access to this process of ethical calibration. Groups will compete for privileged admission to the discussion over AI ethics. Some may gain the right to contribute their preferences, i.e., their views on what constitutes a good or a bad decision, while others will simply inhabit systems under the authority of the political machines.

A new class division will become apparent between these two categories of people. Those with access to the machines will determine how wealth, prestige, and power are distributed in a community, while excluded groups will become increasingly less participant.[3] The effects will be agglutinative

---

[1] See Roose, Kevin (2021) *Futureproof: 9 Rules for Humans in the Age of Automation*, Penguin.
[2] Hijlkema, Fabian, "Political Automata," *Personal Blog*, accessed March 25, 2022, https://fabianhijlkema.nl/political-automata/.
[3] See Eubanks, Virginia (2018) *Automating Inequality: How High-Tech Tools Profile, Police, and Punish the Poor*. St. Martin's Press; and O'Neil, Cathy (2016) *Weapons of Math Destruction: How*

for elites and fissiparous for civil society. Groups with access will see their ethics converge alongside the alignment of their interests through cooperation. Those without will be the new barbarians at the gates, competing among each other for privileges and resources distributed in ways they do not quite fully understand.

Conditions will change for many as they find themselves on the far side of a new frontier of citizenship—a metaphorical location where they are citizens in some ways but no longer in others.[4] The central theme and substantive argument of this book is that if we want to be on the inside of this border, if we wish to have rights and representation in a future increasingly characterized by the use of political machines, then we, as the public, must gain access to their calibration. Two tasks follow.

First, we need to have a lucid understanding of what these political machines do and how they operate. One way to describe political machines is via an analogy with self-driving cars. These cars rely on data about the environment to drive safely. Similarly, "driverless government" relies on data about citizens to work efficiently. Recent decades have seen an unprecedented boom in information about peoples' physiological, psychological, and sociological activity, as well as data about activity in their broader surrounding environment.

Indeed, we can only understand these machines by recognizing the civilizational shift that has occurred with the availability of massive amounts of information about our everyday lives.[5] Data repositories have burgeoned, containing information about our lives far beyond what we know about ourselves. A novel "quantified citizen" has emerged whose identity can no longer be confined to a body in space.[6] Political machines use these data repositories to automatically inform (partially or entirely) any course of action (small or large) adopted by a government (individually or in concert with other governments and/or private companies). Uncovering

---

Big Data Increases Inequality and Threatens Democracy, Crown, for a description of the current interplay between technology and inequality.

[4] Throughout the book, readers may note the use of terms such as citizen as opposed to denizen, or government as opposed to governance. This choice stems from the need to ground analysis in a historical trajectory of state–citizen relations and is used here in the most inclusionary way possible to encompass all people in a government's charge, including international protection applicants as well as irregular border-crossers. Similarly, the term automation is used as opposed to AI, for despite the proliferation of the latter term what it does at root is the automation of cognitive work.

[5] This shift has led to a "new order" where human experience is the raw material for the production of power, away from previous eras governed by land, capital, or labor. See Zuboff, Shoshana (2019) *The Age of Surveillance Capitalism: The Fight for a Human Future at the New Frontier of Power*, Public Affairs Books.

[6] See Taylor, Mark (2020) *Intervolution: Smart Bodies Smart Things*, Columbia University Press, for a discussion on the increasingly blurred distinction between self, technology, and the other.

these political machines and how they work is the subject of chapters 3, 5, 7, and 9.

Second, we must learn to mobilize differently than in the past. The objective is to find ways to formally include the public in discussions guiding the programming of the machines. How? New institutions will be needed to mediate access. For reasons that will be made clear, it will not suffice to reapportion legislatures and institutions founded before the arrival of algorithmic governance. This book proposes that a "Third House" be created to address the deployment and operation of political machines within a polity. Democracies typically have a higher house (e.g., the Senate) and a lower house (e.g., the House of Representatives). They now need an additional chamber that legislates exclusively on AI in government decision-making.[7]

Citizens will use such an institution to decide on the ethical parameters guiding the political machines, collectively defining what constitutes a good and a bad decision. They may green-light projects or deliberate on the values they want to see prioritized in their machines' thinking. They may leverage AI technology themselves, *as citizens*, in order to better interact with this institution—using it to augment their reach and amplify their preferences. "Digital citizens," AI powered replicas of real citizens, could engage in deliberation on their behalf and act as personal emissaries to the Third House.

Undoubtedly, this institution will take decades to emerge and one can hope it is achieved without the bloodshed that has accompanied the birth of new democratic institutions in the past. The broad outlines of such a chamber, however, may already be forming today. Revealing these budding contours is the subject of interview-based chapters 2, 4, 6, 8, and 10.

These even-numbered chapters will showcase a series of conversations with individuals active in civil society groups that are engaging with the political machines described in the adjacent odd-numbered chapters. Interviews will span several geographic contexts and seek to achieve a fuller understanding of citizens' attempts to interact with this novel form of algorithmic governance—and highlight their efforts to contribute to the political machines' configurations.[8] Their insights will link with ideas developed

---

[7] Additionally, given the transnational nature of the technologies behind the political machines, national Third Houses must be networked internationally to work effectively. Over the long term, a United Nations governance institution will be indispensable in this regard, linking initiatives horizontally across countries and vertically between regulatory frameworks, rising from the local to interoperably connect with the national, regional, and global levels.

[8] Interviews will utilize an anthropological framework and critical perspective that transcends the strictly applied aspects of the technologies, avoids atomizing solely political or legal challenges, and does not confine issues as being unique to one geographic area. For references to this comprehensive

in the odd-numbered chapters and help shape the conclusions put forth in chapter 11, in which the idea of a Third House is explored in more detail.

This interlocking methodology is designed to address a dilemma that will become increasingly central to discussions around AI in government decision-making: Are political machines so efficient at governing that they lessen opposition to the existing distribution of power in a society? In other words, are political machines neutralizing conventional popular checks on power? Is a more efficient government also less democratic, allowing power to circumvent legacy representative institutions? This book will address these questions head-on.

Readers should also note that odd-numbered chapters are organized according to the type of data used, the domain of application, and the level of governance. Chapter 3 will focus on technologies that collect data about our physical bodies, such as our biometrics, used by policing agencies operating at the local level. Chapter 5 will examine attempts to gather information about our psychological dispositions using techniques like personality profiling and sentiment analysis in national security matters. Chapter 7 progresses to data collected about our social networks and looks at uses at the national and intergovernmental levels. Finally, chapter 9 reviews endeavors by multilateral organizations like the United Nations that collect information about peoples' wider environment to predict, and potentially prevent, collective violence such as armed conflict.

This progression will take us through various government types and geographies, allowing us to compare and contrast developments in western liberal democracies with Asian nations like China and India and a variety of countries in Africa. Gazing so far afield requires that we stay committed to the book's main focus: How highly automated policing, national security, and peacekeeping systems function within existing political power structures—and emerging civil society responses to that. It also requires clarity on the strategy for identifying algorithmic governance technologies in considerably diverse cultural and political contexts. The strategy employed will be twofold: First, chapters will seek to identify common (or at least similar) historical roots for different political machines, and second, the narrative will try to emphasize (where possible) their likeness across

---

and critical approach see, for example, Serres, Michel (2015) *Thumbelina: The Culture and Technology of Millennials*, Rowman and Littlefield; Smith, Gary (2018) *The AI Delusion*, Oxford University Press; and Smith, Gary and Jay Cordes (2019) *The 9 Pitfalls of Data Science*, Oxford University Press.

regime type and geography, as well as level of governance and domain of application.

Throughout the book, it will emerge that while political machines may increase efficiency from a purely administrative perspective, they are far from perfect in other significant ways. Indeed, they are beset with major limitations.[9] The first comes from the somewhat mystifying nature of the technology itself. Most nonexperts have a vague idea of what these machines do and how they do it. It is often difficult for policymakers to fully understand what happens within the "black box" of the technology, which has created a kind of "invisibility of algorithmic infrastructures."[10] A second limitation is the difficulty of implementing policy based on what is, at most, an approximation of accuracy compared to real-world events. The existence of incorrect assessments, or "false positives," can seriously harm individuals. This occurs, for example, when withholding asylum benefits from a deserving family due to a machine error. A third limit is the matter of the "perverse incentives" that motivate governmental actors to utilize the technologies in ways that may be contrary to principles of open governance. These limitations, taken together, are making it challenging to develop standard ethical guidelines,[11] find satisfactory regulatory frameworks,[12] redress power disparities,[13] and reduce human and civil rights violations.[14]

To better illustrate the effects of these limitations, we may turn to the example of political machines that monitor public speech. It is generally agreed that new online communication platforms have facilitated the delivery of individual political expression. This expression can lead to forms of

---

[9] For examples of these issues, see work conducted by researchers at Cardiff University's Data Justice Lab (www.datajusticelab.org) and the University of Toronto's Citizen Lab (www.citizenlab.ca).

[10] Berry, David (2019) "Against Infrasomatisation: Towards a Critical Theory of Algorithms," in *Data Politics: Worlds, Subjects, Rights*, Didier Bigo, Engin Isin, and Evelyn Ruppert, eds., Routledge.

[11] West, Darrell (2005) *Digital Government: Technology and Public Sector Performance*, Princeton University Press; and Raymond, Nathaniel (2017) "Beyond 'Do No Harm' and Individual Consent: Reckoning with the Emerging Ethical Challenges of Civil Society's Use of Data," in *Group Privacy: New Challenges of Data Technologies*, Linnet Taylor, Luciano Floridi, and Bart van der Sloot, eds., Springer.

[12] Carayannis, Elias, David Campbell, and Marios Efthymiopoulos, eds. (2014) *Cyber-Development, Cyber-Democracy and Cyber-Defense: Challenges, Opportunities, and Implications for Theory, Policy and Practice*, Springer; Taylor, Linnet, Luciano Floridi, and Bart Van Der Sloot, eds. (2017) *Group Privacy: New Challenges of Data Technologies*. Springer; Kello, Lucas (2017) *The Virtual Weapon and International Order*, Yale University Press; and Shackelford, Scott (2020) *Governing New Frontiers in the Information Age: Toward Cyber Peace*, Cambridge University Press.

[13] Langlois, Ganaele, Joanna Redden, and Greg Elmer, eds. (2015) *Compromised Data: From Social Media to Big Data*, Bloomsbury; and Bigo, Didier, Engin Isin, and Evelyn Ruppert, eds. (2019) *Data Politics: Worlds, Subjects, Rights*, Routledge.

[14] Wagner, Ben, Matthias Kettemann, and Kilian Vieth, eds. (2019) *Research Handbook on Human Rights and Digital Technology: Global Politics, Law and International Relations*, Edward Elgar Publishing.

collective action, some of which may turn violent. Therefore, in different parts of the world, state or state-funded bodies (often with private partners) are deploying machines that automatically parse through online dialogue to censor speech that might lead to violence.

Of course, there is the problem of the black-box nature of the technology. How exactly do these filters work, and are we assured that they are fair? Can they understand context, frame things within an abstract notion of past and future, perceive others' intentions correctly, and deem one worthy of empathy based on attenuating circumstances?[15] There is also the issue of the many likely false positives. Consider the difficulty in using automated systems when parsing speech related to radical political ideologies, either on the left or the right. Subscribers to radical views often use evolving narratives that demand action against similarly evolving sets of institutions or outgroups. These changing narratives spread across human social networks that are also continually fluctuating. Participation in these conversations is fluid, making the identification of true believers and their intention, or capacity, to incite violence an arduous task.

Yet, the bigger complication this book will tackle is that the definition of "lead to violence" is, in reality, not automated. It is an ethical parameter that partly depends on the type of violence one prefers to avoid. Are structural or state-sponsored types of violence and expropriation included, for example? Government-funded systems may have an incentive to exclude these. Behind every quantitative model, there are qualitative definitions. These tools are contingent on the value systems of the persons that build them, and we cannot expect them to be any more objective than those persons. The idea that we may acquire more objective and precise judgment by outsourcing decisions to a device, known as automation bias, is one of the main challenges to equitably deploying political machines.

This example is one of many. However, it does illustrate the substantive argument described above, which is as follows: Conditions are forming where political machines continuously assess citizens' behavior (e.g., what they say online). Rights in matters of public governance are then allocated based on those calculations (e.g., speech is allowed). Most people will have little to no understanding of the rules that guide that assessment; conversely, the select few that set the machines' ethical parameters (e.g., definitions of

---

[15] See Zarkadakis, George (2015) *In Our Own Image: Will Artificial Intelligence Save Us or Destroy Us?*, Rider Books, for a description of how, throughout history, we have always sought to produce artifacts that somehow mirror our human qualities, like empathy.

what counts for violence) will enjoy sizable levels of influence in the public sphere.[16]

Where does this argument fall within the general academic debates on the topic? Recent years have seen an extraordinary increase in book publishing on AI in public decision-making and related themes. Authors tend to focus on a variety of areas, such as predictive policing, the impact on democracy, the ethics of algorithmic technologies, or various legal aspects like privacy. Therefore, a review of this literature requires a somewhat extended perusal of a diverse set of fields. For convenience, the debates below are organized by thematic area and proceed in the following order: privacy, politics, media, policing, law, culture, and ethics. Each will describe the main contributions from the literature and where the arguments made in this book stand in relation to them. It will emerge that few have attempted a holistic approach that encompasses both a review of the technologies *and* the experiences of citizen recipients of automated decisions. None have compared uses of automation in political systems and emergent conditions of citizenship in the West, East, and South.

Let us start with the growing body of literature dealing with the challenges to privacy resulting from automation. Goldenfein's *Monitoring Laws*[17] explores how automated systems continually classify citizens. Government profiling—especially with computer vision—can even assess previously abstract qualities such as our personality. Goldenfein correctly observes that this is changing the meaning of our interaction with governance and asks the vital question: What aspects of our identity should be known by the government and what elements should not? Furthermore, we should be wary of reaching a point where what governments know about us surpasses what we know of ourselves. Goldenfein's argument is very similar to the one in this book in that we agree that automation is changing the nature of governance. A general difference is that *Monitoring Laws* focuses on defining new legal structures, while this book will attempt broader connections to the cultural

---

[16] We can see the balance between citizen and group levels of rights tipping in favor of the latter: public order over privacy; group security over speech. For a debate over the need for new definitions of privacy and related rights, see Mantelero, Alessandro (2016) "From Group Privacy to Collective Privacy: Towards a New Dimension of Privacy and Data Protection in the Big Data Era," in *Group Privacy: New Challenges of Data Technologies*, Linnet Taylor, Luciano Floridi, and Bart van der Sloot, eds., Springer.

[17] Goldenfein, Jake (2019) *Monitoring Laws: Profiling and Identity in the World State*, Cambridge University Press.

and political shifts occurring in society at large. Another distinction is that Goldenfein spotlights the government's intrusive knowledge of our intimate "identities," while we will also focus on its understanding of our supposed future actions. Nevertheless, Goldenfein's book is a strong foundation from which to launch this inquiry.

DeBrabander's *Life after Privacy*[18] makes the case that we, as "digital citizens," are the main threat to democracy, as we willingly surrender our biodata to the government. He asks the pointed question: What is the nature of freedom in a state without privacy? The answer *Life after Privacy* provides is controversial as the author notes that it is the "vitality of the public realm" and not privacy that is central to a democracy. He argues that while important and often repressed, privacy is a relatively new value and not a requirement for democracy. This book disagrees and will engage in philosophical conversation with DeBrabander's thesis on this point.

The position put forth here is closer to Véliz's in *Privacy is Power*.[19] For Véliz, the privacy ship has not yet sailed, and we can and should fight for it. Our books agree that it is essential that people maintain some basic form of unknowability. To that end, Véliz recommends banning machines that can draw "surreptitious information" about us. Just because a particular type of progress is technologically possible, she argues, does not make it politically inevitable. The interview-based even chapters in this book, in particular, will provide additional research on the current balance, or tension, between what technologists envision and what civil society would ultimately like to allow.

Literature in political science and economics is heavily solutions-oriented. In *Humans Need Not Apply*,[20] Kaplan notes that automation can usher in a golden era for humanity. However, the path there is fraught with political dangers, particularly social unrest resulting from mass unemployment. Kaplan recommends that these dangers be kept at bay with adequate social policy and freer markets. Similarly, Howard's *Pax Technica*[21] examines how the evolution of the Internet of Things (IoT)—the invisible network of

---

[18] DeBrabander, Firmin (2020) *Life after Privacy: Reclaiming Democracy in a Surveillance Society*, Cambridge University Press.
[19] Véliz, Carissa (2020) *Privacy Is Power: Why and How You Should Take Back Control of Your Data*, Melville House.
[20] Kaplan, Jerry (2016) *Humans Need Not Apply: A Guide to Wealth and Work in the Age of Artificial Intelligence*, Yale University Press.
[21] Howard, Philip (2015) *Pax Technica: How the Internet of Things May Set Us Free or Lock Us Up*, Yale University Press.

everyday consumer objects that communicate with us and each other via the internet—is poised to propel society into a future state of global stability. He also suggests policy adjustments, for example around privacy issues and the threat of political manipulation, to ensure that we avoid the many perils along the way. Acemoglu's edited volume *Redesigning AI*[22] also addresses how economic and social justice issues can be redressed by appropriate policy, funding, and regulation.

These books are part of a format that laces long-term optimism with short-term caution. One could argue that suggestions like these do not consider the structural shifts occurring in the distribution of power and new dynamics of class conflict. In this sense, this book is more akin to Crawford's *Atlas of AI*[23] and Lingel's *The Gentrification of the Internet*.[24] Crawford posits that AI is a "technology of extraction," by which she means, among other things, that it pulls value out of every aspect of our human experience. In doing this, it centralizes power and challenges democratic governance. In *The Gentrification of the Internet*, Lingel describes how corporate interests have transformed the internet—despite its democratizing potential—into a divided and divisive space organized along class lines of exclusion and privilege, much like cities undergoing gentrification processes. Both these titles are part of a new genre of books that critically assess the impact of digital technologies on shifting power dynamics, and vice versa. We will build on the insights emerging from this output by adding an account of citizens' experiences with these changes.

Other similar works in the political space are Zerilli's *A Citizen's Guide to Artificial Intelligence*[25] and McGinnis' *Accelerating Democracy*.[26] Zerilli argues that automation requires an analytical approach "whose sweep is necessarily political rather than technical" and provides some questions that will help frame many of the issues investigated in the following chapters, for example: Why do we assume that machines are better at making decisions? Can these processes ever be truly transparent? What is our role as humans in them? McGinnis puts forth an intriguing thesis that can help answer the last

---

[22] Acemoglu, Daron, ed. (2021) *Redesigning AI: Work, Democracy, and Justice in the Age of Automation*, MIT Press.
[23] Crawford, Kate (2021) *Atlas of AI: Power, Politics, and the Planetary Costs of Artificial Intelligence*, Yale University Press.
[24] Lingel, Jessa (2021) *The Gentrification of the Internet: How to Reclaim Our Digital Freedom*, University of California Press.
[25] Zerilli, John et al. (2021) *A Citizen's Guide to Artificial Intelligence*, MIT Press, p XXI.
[26] McGinnis, John (2015) *Accelerating Democracy: Transforming Governance Through Technology*, Princeton University Press.

question. He notes that automation may lead to better governance, but only if it is concomitant to a decentralization of power. New information technologies could increase the general public's contribution to policy-making by allowing input from a wider variety of channels. This is a correct observation; this book will explore the efforts of citizen groups engaged in what are essentially attempts to decentralize power.

Several books look at how new digital media technologies are influencing political processes. The trend in this literature seems to follow an arc from optimism (like Bock's *The Technology of Nonviolence*,[27] which looks at how social media can help prevent violence and empower citizens) to distrust (like Persily and Tucker's edited volume *Social Media and Democracy*,[28] which sees social media as a potential tool of foreign influence and dangerous misinformation campaigns) to outright concern (like Howard's *Lie Machines*,[29] which explains how to "save democracy" from what is increasingly portrayed as a kind of existential threat).

Most authors on the topic find themselves on one point or another along this arc, but *Retooling Politics*[30] by Jungherr, Rivero, and Gayo-Avello is more nuanced. Their book attempts an approach that transcends an inflated sense of optimism on the one side and an excessive pessimism on the other to ask what structural changes have occurred to our political systems. Similarly, this book will dig into these foundational shifts by moving the focus onto how political power interacts with this specific type of newly generated data about citizens to gain unprecedented leverage upon their behavior.

In this regard, there is an affinity to Gillespie's *Custodians of the Internet*,[31] Feldstein's *The Rise of Digital Repression*,[32] Han's *Contesting Cyberspace in China*,[33] and Rendueles' *Sociophobia*.[34] All of these books question

---

[27] Bock, Joseph (2012) *The Technology of Nonviolence: Social Media and Violence Prevention*, MIT Press.

[28] Persily, Nathaniel and Joshua Tucker, eds. (2020) *Social Media and Democracy: The State of the Field and Prospects for Reform*, Cambridge University Press.

[29] Howard, Philip (2020) *Lie Machines: How to Save Democracy from Troll Armies, Deceitful Robots, Junk News Operations, and Political Operatives*, Yale University Press.

[30] Jungherr, Andreas, Gonzalo Rivero, and Daniel Gayo-Avello (2020) *Retooling Politics: How Digital Media are Shaping Democracy*, Cambridge University Press.

[31] Gillespie, Tarleton (2018) *Custodians of the Internet: Platforms, Content Moderation, and the Hidden Decisions that Shape Social Media*, Yale University Press.

[32] Feldstein, Steven (2021) *The Rise of Digital Repression: How Technology is Reshaping Power, Politics, and Resistance*, Oxford University Press.

[33] Han, Rongbin (2018) *Contesting Cyberspace in China: Online Expression and Authoritarian Resilience*, Columbia University Press.

[34] Rendueles, César (2017) *Sociophobia: Political Change in the Digital Utopia*, Columbia University Press.

assumptions about the purportedly democratizing power of new technologies. Gillespie looks at how powerful tech companies use automation to "police" what is posted online, thus shaping the public debate in ways that have very real political consequences, with little to no public scrutiny as to the rationale behind what to censor and what to promote. Feldstein examines the changing "nature of how governments counter dissent" and describes the wide range of powers that governments have developed to monitor online citizen activity, creating new forms of repression and endangering democracy around the globe. Han looks at how citizens often happily collude with government initiatives to enforce censorship and generate obedience. Rendueles points out that new communication technologies, taken together, have lowered our overall expectation of what we can contribute politically as citizens.

This book will add to each of these arguments above by: providing research on the role of government agencies and different types of public–private partnerships to complement Gillespie's work on the private sector; conducting comparative analysis in the US and EU to complement Feldstein's and Han's work in Africa and Asia; and, evaluating nascent forms of citizen engagement to further Rendueles' reflections on the future role of the public in the digital age.

There are also similarities between this book and Owen's *Disruptive Power*.[35] Both our books examine how digital communication technologies have changed the global balance of power. However, where Owen argues that new non-state actors are disrupting established power structures and diminishing the state's role, creating a "radically decentralized international system," it will be posited here instead that the state has increased its power. The position is, therefore, closer to that of Tucker in his book *The End of Intelligence*.[36] Tucker argues that the international system is seeing power coagulate around state actors with advanced surveillance capacities.

Let us now turn to the literature on matters of public order. Brayne's *Predict and Surveil*[37] explains how data are used in predictive policing and helps demystify many popular misconceptions. It is methodologically similar in that it uses ethnographic observation and interviews. Another similarity is

---

[35] Owen, Taylor (2015) *Disruptive Power: The Crisis of the State in the Digital Age*, Oxford University Press.
[36] Tucker, David (2014) *The End of Intelligence: Espionage and State Power in the Information Age*, Stanford University Press.
[37] Brayne, Sarah (2020) *Predict and Surveil: Data, Discretion, and the Future of Policing*, Oxford University Press.

the focus on the consequences of algorithmic control for ordinary people. The author argues that algorithmic technologies "reproduce and deepen" patterns of inequality and erode civil liberties. She also criticizes the claims to objectivity of these systems. Brayne's work serves as an inspiration to look at the role of these technologies in state decision-making processes more widely, not only in policing.

Ashworth and Zedner's *Preventive Justice*[38] documents the tools used to prevent anticipated future harm. These tools identify pre-criminal conduct, reduce the liberties of suspected future criminals, and extend prison sentences based on predicted recidivism. Their book questions the justification of these practices in the name of public security and highlights the increasingly blurred boundary between criminal and civil law. Here, too, we will problematize uncritical applications of the public security justification—but will also seek to further unpack how this justification is utilized within evolving systems of power and ideology.

Within the field of criminal justice, McQuade's *Pacifying the Homeland*[39] stands out as it addresses broader systemic shifts occurring in the role of the state. The author brings attention to the transition away from mass incarceration (prison populations in the US have been decreasing since 2010) and toward technologically sophisticated forms of mass surveillance and policing of citizens generally. New digital technologies, he argues, are making possible new systems of social control that make mass incarceration in some ways redundant. McQuade makes this compelling argument by examining the activity of the Department of Homeland Security's intelligence fusion centers. The odd-numbered chapters in this book, in which we review surveillance technologies in various contexts globally, may aid in a comparative assessment across nations of the trend outlined by McQuade in the US.

A related field of inquiry focuses on human rights and other legal aspects. Land and Aronson's edited volume *New Technologies for Human Rights Law and Practice*[40] looks at how new technologies can both promote and jeopardize human rights. The authors recognize that this process is starting to change "what we mean by human rights." Consider, for example, the human

---

[38] Ashworth, Andrew and Lucia Zedner (2015) *Preventive Justice*, Oxford University Press.
[39] McQuade, Brendan (2019) *Pacifying the Homeland: Intelligence Fusion and Mass Supervision*, University of California Press.
[40] Land, Molly and Jay Aronson, eds. (2020) *New Technologies for Human Rights Law and Practice*, Cambridge University Press.

rights repercussions of developing autonomous lethal weapons. We agree that what we are experiencing is a definitional shift in the meaning of human and civic rights— but this book also argues that these new definitions do not fit within existing political paradigms or institutional arrangements, requiring an investigation into emergent notions of citizenship and the potential development of a Third House of governance, as maintained above.

This argument for a Third House is informed by the same premise— that to democratize AI, technology should partner with, not replace, human judgment—that also informs Pasquale's *New Laws of Robotics*.[41] In his book, Pasquale asks some key questions: When should a robot replace a human? What is the optimal mix of robot–human interaction? Pasquale correctly recognizes that autonomous systems cannot supplant all aspects of work, socialization, and public decision-making. We must not forget that some characteristics of human intelligence are simply irreplaceable by the artificial alternative.

Let us now look at the literature dealing with the cultural aspects of algorithmic technologies. An intriguing book in this space is Bucher's *If . . . Then*.[42] The book describes how we increasingly live in what the author calls "algorithmic lives," even though life itself is not algorithmic. This creates a disconnect in which algorithmic technologies have become "powerful brokers of information," but the cultural forms they engender go beyond the technology itself, as we are not the passive recipients of a "this-or-that" way of thinking. The author, therefore, invites us to look at the discursive dimensions of the technology and how it shapes our social and cultural life, not just our economy or institutions.

AI Narratives,[43] edited by Cave, Dihal, and Dillon, explores the history of human thinking about intelligent machines. Its main strength is the emphasis on the fact that contemporary thinking about these technologies is embedded in historical processes developed over centuries. Narrative, imagination, and discourse about a thing matter as they define what we do with it. How we think about technology shapes the way it is developed and deployed. Likewise, the inverse is also true: The technologies we use shape

---

[41] Pasquale, Frank (2020) *New Laws of Robotics: Defending Human Expertise in the Age of AI*, Harvard University Press.
[42] Bucher, Taina (2018) *If... Then: Algorithmic Power and Politics*, Oxford University Press.
[43] Cave, Stephen, Kanta Dihal, and Sarah Dillon, eds. (2020) *AI Narratives: A History of Imaginative Thinking about Intelligent Machines*, Oxford University Press.

how we think. Besteman and Gusterson's edited volume *Life by Algorithms*[44] demonstrates how our culture has been changed by what they call "roboprocesses." They note that the models of algorithmic "thinking" used by computers shape how we think about the world and inform our interactions in various fields, from medicine to the public space. While purportedly rational, these roboprocesses can, in certain circumstances, be entirely out of place and, in some cases, have harmful societal consequences. This book adds to both these books by comparing how experts and citizens conceptualize the technology—and are conceptualized *by* the technology—in matters of governance more specifically.

Larson's *The Myth of Artificial Intelligence*[45] discusses how overreliance on an ideological view of AI thwarts innovation by taking the focus off the only form of intelligence that does exist: the biological one. The main difference between these two types of "thinking" is that AI works by formal reasoning while humans make conjectures based on a perception of context ultimately irreducible to data. This conjecture, Larson argues, cannot be emulated by machines. Indeed, it is a mistake to equate automation with human intelligence. In this book, we will further note that financial and political interests are often behind that mistake; for example, when claims of AI objectivity hide particular ideological preferences baked into the machines' coding.

Finally, there is a growing body of literature on the ethics of AI. Liao's edited volume *Ethics of Artificial Intelligence*,[46] Abbas' *Next-Generation Ethics*[47] collection, and *The Oxford Handbook of Ethics of AI*[48] edited by Dubber, Pasquale, and Das, offer wide-ranging reflections on issues that would have seemed science fiction only a few years ago. For example, what are an AI system's potential rights and duties stemming from its status as not just intelligent but now also possibly conscious? Could an AI tool predicting future crime or social unrest for a government, say, have a series of duties and obligations and, like a civil servant in breach, face a penalty (perhaps reprogramming) for violating those duties?

---

[44] Besteman, Catherine and Hugh Gusterson, eds. (2019) *Life by Algorithms: How Roboprocesses Are Remaking Our World*, University of Chicago Press.
[45] Larson, Erik (2021) *The Myth of Artificial Intelligence: Why Computers Can't Think the Way We Do*, Harvard University Press.
[46] Liao, S. Matthew, ed. (2020) *Ethics of Artificial Intelligence*, Oxford University Press.
[47] Abbas, Ali, ed. (2019) *Next-Generation Ethics: Engineering a Better Society*, Cambridge University Press.
[48] Dubber, Markus, Frank Pasquale, and Sunit Das, eds. (2020) *The Oxford Handbook of Ethics of AI*, Oxford University Press.

In *The Machine Question*[49] Gunkel investigates this issue and challenges the assumption that machines have no moral responsibilities. Is there a boundary that, when crossed, constitutes a tool or instrument into a "legitimate moral agent"? Is that boundary reached when that "tool" embarks on independent actions that have consequences for humans? While sharing some of these concerns may be tempting, it is necessary to avoid the risk of over-anthropomorphizing new technologies. To that end, this book will specifically embed them within emergent political dynamics and contestations of power.

Kearns and Roth's *The Ethical Algorithm*,[50] like other books reviewed above, argues that algorithmic technologies are starting to violate the civil rights of individuals in undeniable ways. They say that addressing this issue head-on is one of the most important responsibilities of our generation. The usual regulatory approaches are proving to be ineffectual, so the authors propose a new approach that embeds "human principles" into machine code. While quite defensible, this view obscures the fact that human principles are themselves in flux and that the contest currently unfolding over *whose* principles are coded into the machines needs to be examined just as critically.

In conclusion, the following chapters will join the debates and ideas considered above by adding a comparative review of political machines in different continents and a series of interviews with citizen groups on the receiving end of the machines' decisions. These groups have essentially been crash-testing various forms of driverless government, and we should weave their voices into the conversation alongside the logic and ethos of the technology's designers. The aim is to develop a more nuanced idea of where we may be getting it right and where we are not. If a driverless car has an accident, the damage is easy to assess. The consequences are much harder to see when political machines get it wrong, but they are no less real. To this end, the book will differ from much of the current literature in being diagnostic rather than descriptive or prescriptive. In chapter 11, however, we will break from the diagnostic approach and turn to the more creative exercise of envisioning what an ideal political institution—here termed the Third House—may look like in the age of political automation.

---

[49] Gunkel, David (2012) *The Machine Question: Critical Perspectives on AI, Robots, and Ethics*, MIT Press.
[50] Kearns, Michael and Aaron Roth (2019) *The Ethical Algorithm: The Science of Socially Aware Algorithm Design*, Oxford University Press.

Chapter 2
California

As the use of surveillance technology and artificial intelligence becomes more pervasive, many would argue that there has been a corresponding decline in the transparency of these systems and our right to privacy. A number of civil society organizations have been fighting to overturn this trend. In the US, Oakland Privacy, a citizens' coalition with the tagline "I've been watching you watching me," has been advocating for the right to privacy and increased transparency and oversight concerning surveillance tools and techniques since 2016. Operating across the state of California, they have conducted research and numerous investigations into the ubiquitous technologies, engaged with lawmakers to improve legislative programs, and campaigned to raise awareness and increase civic engagement. The Advocacy Director for Oakland Privacy, Tracy Rosenberg, was instrumental in the group's formation when it was known as the Occupy Oakland Privacy Working Group. Rosenberg was part of a team that discovered the Department of Homeland Security's citywide covert surveillance program, the Domain Awareness Center (DAC), the implementation and existence of which was shrouded in secrecy. After this small group of activists' effective campaign against the DAC, they evolved into Oakland Privacy and have since been successful in hindering the rollout of surveillance programs all over California.[1]

Rosenberg and Oakland Privacy have also collaborated with the nonprofit American Civil Liberties Union (ACLU) Northern California to develop a "Fighting Local Surveillance" toolkit, designed to support local communities across the nation with best practices for advocating for facial recognition bans or surveillance transparency ordinances. The toolkit was developed after the historic legislative win in 2019 in San Francisco when government facial recognition was banned and "public oversight for local decisions related to the acquisition and use of other surveillance technologies such as cameras, drones, and more" was made a requirement. This win, led by

---

[1] Oakland Privacy, "About," accessed November 9, 2023, https://oaklandprivacy.org/about/.

Political Automation. Eduardo Albrecht, Oxford University Press. © Oxford University Press (2025).
DOI: 10.1093/9780197696989.003.0002

the ACLU, with support from Oakland Privacy and other grassroots groups, was important in bringing communities and the democratic process to the forefront of the surveillance and AI debate in San Francisco.[2]

Another community organization that is based in California and is pushing back against surveillance and biased algorithms, particularly those that target immigrants, is NorCal Resist. Since 2017, they have been advocating for a more just and equitable society, and providing resources and support to those fighting immigration injustice.[3] In 2021, together with another immigrant rights group, Mijente, and four other activists, they took legal action against facial recognition company Clearview AI. Their suit alleged that Clearview AI's database of three billion human faces scraped from social networks and provided to law enforcement agencies, even in states where facial recognition was banned, violates privacy laws and disproportionately harms immigrants and people of color due to the inaccuracies of facial recognition technology.[4] Jeremy Rud is a volunteer with NorCal Resist who assisted with the press in the lawsuit against Clearview AI. He is a PhD candidate at the University of California, Davis, and his research interests include sociocultural linguistics, anthropology, migration, and political asylum. He has studied sentiment analysis from a sociolinguistic perspective and published on the subject of AI in the context of immigration and asylum.[5]

In her interview, Tracy Rosenberg makes the key point that AI is automating and mechanizing judgments that used to be made by human beings. This can have a number of negative consequences, including the incorporation and normalization of bias in decision-making. It is also becoming harder for humans to catch errors before they manifest, with potentially harmful consequences to vulnerable individuals. She also argues that AI-based surveillance systems can be opaque and difficult to understand, making it difficult for citizens to hold these systems accountable and to protect their privacy. She advocates for citizens to educate themselves about these systems

---

[2] "Fighting Local Surveillance: A Toolkit" (2020) *American Civil Liberties Union*, May 14, www.aclunc.org/publications/fighting-local-surveillance-toolkit.

[3] NorCal Resist, "Who We Are," accessed November 9, 2023, www.norcalresist.org/who-we-are.html.

[4] Metz, Rachel (2021) "Clearview AI Sued in California by Rights Groups, Activists," *CNN*, March 9, https://amp.cnn.com/cnn/2021/03/09/tech/clearview-ai-mijente-lawsuit/index.html.

[5] UC Davis Department of Linguistics, "Jeremy A. Rud," accessed November 9, 2023, https://linguistics.ucdavis.edu/people/jarud. See also Rud, Jeremy (2023) "Asylum Text Analytics as an Algorithmic Silver Bullet: The Impossible Quest for Automated Fraud Detection," *Talking Politics*, January 20, https://talkingpoliticsonline.blogspot.com/2023/06/asylum-text-analytics-as-algorithmic.html.

and to support organizations that are working to protect civil liberties in the digital age.

In Jeremy Rud's interview he discusses his concerns about the use of AI at the borders to surveil and evaluate asylum narratives, as it can lead to the exclusion of legitimate asylum seekers. He also explains that there is evidence that AI-based surveillance is being used to monitor activists and critics of the government in the Bay Area, and believes that it is important to involve communities in the development of AI technology to ensure that it is used in a transparent and responsible manner. Below follow more detailed replies to specific questions posed during the interviews.[6]

Tracy, what are some of the ways that you've seen AI-based surveillance being used in the Bay Area?

In the Bay Area and across the United States, there has been a significant shift in surveillance technology toward AI-enabled or "smarter" versions of traditional equipment. These advanced gadgets, akin to smart home appliances, possess capabilities far beyond their predecessors. This technological leap presents a challenge to existing regulatory policies, which were designed to address the limitations of older, "dumber" versions of surveillance tools.

A key development in this area is the integration of AI with unmanned devices, including drones and what were formerly known as robodogs. Recently, the Bay Area has seen intense public discourse on what have been termed "killer" robots. While somewhat hyperbolic, this term refers to AI-enabled bomb robots that are far more advanced than their predecessors, verging on the capability to perform autonomous lethal actions.

Another area of concern is the potential installation of facial recognition technology on police body cameras. This proposal represents a significant escalation in surveillance capabilities, transforming a tool initially designed for accountability and transparency into a far more invasive device. This adaptation not only distorts the original purpose of these devices but also renders existing policies and regulations obsolete, as they fail to address these new functionalities.

---

[6] Interviews held via videoconferencing technology on February 23, 2023; replies paraphrased by author.

The use of facial recognition technology, particularly in police operations, is a contentious issue. In the Bay Area, there has been a historical resistance to facial recognition, leading to its ban in major Northern California cities. However, other regions in the state and the country might consider its implementation. The introduction of facial recognition in police body cameras and other surveillance tools raises significant privacy and civil liberties concerns.

The rapid advancement of AI in surveillance technologies challenges existing regulatory frameworks, pushing the boundaries of privacy and ethical use. These developments necessitate a re-evaluation and update of policies to address the capabilities and implications of modern AI-enabled surveillance tools. The debate over these technologies, especially concerning facial recognition and autonomous capabilities, is critical in shaping the future of surveillance, privacy rights, and public safety.

What are your thoughts regarding the impact of AI-based surveillance on civil liberties?

AI's integration into various decision-making processes, while offering speed and efficiency, amplifies existing biases present in the data it processes. This automation of judgments, previously made by humans, results in rapid decision-making that often does not allow for timely human intervention to correct errors or biases.

One key advantage of human decision-making is its pace, which allows for the consideration and correction of mistakes or biases. However, AI operates at a much faster rate, making it difficult for humans to identify and address issues before they fully develop. This is particularly problematic given that many common AI applications are prone to bias and discriminatory outcomes.

The source of data fed into AI systems significantly influences their decisions. For example, in financial or credit-related AI, the input data may carry historical biases like redlining, and the AI lacks the capacity to filter out these biases. Consequently, the AI perpetuates them in its decision-making. Similarly, in law enforcement, AI often relies on data reflective of over-policing in certain areas and that underemphasizes white-collar crimes. This data bias informs the AI's operations, leading to decisions that mirror and potentially exacerbate these existing inequalities.

Current AI systems generally lack a corrective mechanism to address these biases. As a result, the automation facilitated by AI not only speeds up but also intensifies the inherent problems within our law enforcement and surveillance systems. This situation calls for a critical examination of AI's role in decision-making processes and the development of mechanisms to mitigate its tendency to perpetuate existing societal and systemic biases.

What are ways citizens can better understand these mechanisms at play in a society?

In our research, we've observed that citizens generally have a keen understanding of AI systems and their potential issues when they are aware of these systems' existence. For instance, the concept of "killer robots"—unmanned robots equipped with AI and lethal force—was quickly grasped by the public. People easily comprehended the risks associated with giving autonomous entities analytical capabilities and lethal force under minimal human supervision.

Similarly, public perception of facial recognition technology reveals an understanding of its implications. Historically, people have recognized the value of anonymity in public spaces. The prospect of police or anyone else instantly identifying individuals just by their presence on a street is intuitively concerning for many, highlighting privacy issues. However, the application of AI in more covert areas, like the transformation of traditional surveillance cameras into AI-enhanced versions, often goes unnoticed. The public may not be fully aware of the extent to which these systems have evolved and the implications of such advancements. Moreover, AI's role in decision-making processes, particularly in sectors like financial services, housing, and health, remains largely hidden and obscure. These algorithms operate behind the scenes, significantly impacting people's lives without their knowledge or understanding.

While the public can readily grasp the potential problems of more conspicuous AI applications, like autonomous lethal robots and facial recognition technology, the subtler uses of AI in surveillance and decision-making remain largely invisible. These hidden applications, despite their significant impact, are not as apparent to the public, underscoring the need for greater transparency and awareness regarding AI's role in various facets of everyday life.

Who should be able to access the design of these technologies and the data they use?

AI systems operate on algorithms, a set of formulas processing data flows from various sources to generate outcomes. However, the specifics of these algorithms, including their data sources and manipulation methods, are often unknown to the public. This lack of transparency is primarily due to private vendors protecting their algorithms as proprietary trade secrets. This secrecy poses a significant challenge in addressing AI's civil rights implications, as these algorithms frequently use data marked by historical patterns of discrimination and bias.

This issue of proprietary technology hinders any meaningful attempt to correct or even understand the biases within these systems. As a result, AI often becomes a civil rights disaster, with its workings resembling an impenetrable black box. Any efforts to address the biases and injustices within these systems are severely limited by this lack of transparency.

There is growing discourse about the need for algorithmic audits, particularly in California and other places discussing privacy protection. These audits aim to make algorithmic formulas transparent. However, the challenge lies in overcoming the barrier posed by the proprietary nature of these technologies. Since most AI products are operated by private vendors, an audit can only scratch the surface unless it penetrates this layer of secrecy.

The core of the issue lies not only in the sources of information, which may be less guarded, but also in how the data is manipulated before it is fed to the algorithm. Understanding this manipulation is critical to comprehending how biases, discrimination, and historical inequities are ingrained in AI systems. Until a solution is found to navigate the proprietary technology argument effectively, efforts to audit and reform these algorithms will likely remain superficial. Addressing this challenge is crucial for ensuring that AI systems operate equitably and justly, free from embedded biases that perpetuate societal disparities.

What are the obstacles to informing citizens about how their data is being used?

The phenomenon of "privacy fatigue" is a significant issue in the context of data usage and consumer rights. People are increasingly aware of the misuse of their data but often feel helpless to control it. Existing systems for data privacy, typically involving opting out, are cumbersome, unclear, and place an unreasonable burden on the individual. The effort required to opt out from each company collecting personal data is overwhelming and impractical for most people. This leads to a sense of resignation: acknowledging the problem's severity but feeling powerless to effect change, which can be both distressing and demotivating.

Another barrier is the deliberate complexification of privacy issues by companies and law enforcement. These entities often use technical jargon and overly complicated explanations to obscure the reality of data practices, deterring public scrutiny. This strategy is particularly evident in presentations to elected officials and political bodies. By framing these issues in complex, jargon-laden terms, vendors and law enforcement create an impression that these matters are too intricate for nonexperts to understand, thereby dissuading further investigation or questioning.

This approach effectively shields problematic data practices from thorough examination and critique, as it convinces decision-makers, like city council members and supervisors, to refrain from delving deeper. The misconception that these issues are beyond comprehension serves to maintain the status quo, leaving problematic data practices unchallenged and misunderstood. Overcoming these obstacles requires simplifying the conversation around data collection practices and empowering individuals and officials with clearer, more accessible information. This change is crucial for fostering an environment where citizens and policymakers can make informed decisions and take meaningful action.

Jeremy, can you speak about your research on the use of AI at borders for migration purposes?

In my work, I investigate and shed light on the often unspoken yet rigid expectations surrounding credible asylum narratives. This involves studying how organizations like NorCal Resist, along with advocates and attorneys, assist asylum seekers in crafting their stories to be favorably received by governments evaluating their cases. This complex process involves navigating a myriad of formal and informal rules and expectations.

The advent of AI technologies introduces new dimensions to this narrative evaluation process. Countries, including the United States, are increasingly incorporating AI in managing and directing migrant flows. This application ranges from facial recognition and social media scraping to enhanced interagency connectivity regarding biometric data. The use of AI in this context raises significant concerns. Government agencies, both in the US and elsewhere, have a history of misunderstanding or underestimating linguistic differences and their impact on how stories are told and perceived. This issue is compounded by the exclusionary approaches these governments often take, leveraging available tools to deny people access to rights and entitlements, like asylum.

AI's involvement in evaluating asylum narratives is particularly worrying because these technologies, just like human adjudicators, may not adequately account for cultural and linguistic nuances. Furthermore, the historical tendency of governments to use bureaucratic processes as a means of exclusion could be exacerbated by AI, making it harder for asylum seekers to access their legal rights. The incorporation of AI in asylum evaluations underscores the need for a better understanding of the biases inherent in these technologies and the importance of ensuring that they are employed in a manner that upholds the rights of individuals.

Can you tell us more about how automated language analysis is used in this process? How does the calibration of these software tools create the sort of filter you were talking about for asylum seekers?

The use of AI by governments in evaluating asylum narratives is a murky area, with specific methods and practices largely unknown. Current policy documents suggest that such evaluations are indeed happening, but the details of these processes remain unclear. A likely method being experimented with is language sentiment analysis, particularly relevant in asylum cases where the crux of the application hinges on proving a credible and well-founded fear of persecution. Given that fear is a crucial element, algorithmic technologies designed to detect emotions in narratives could theoretically be employed by governments to assess the legitimacy and credibility of expressed fear.

Corporate entities have developed technologies with the ability to identify emotions in content, making them potential tools for governments to use in asylum evaluations. However, concrete evidence about the specific algorithms, methods, or training data used, especially in the United States, is not readily available. The situation is similar globally, with scant details about the application of such AI systems in various countries.

Despite this lack of transparency, there are indications that these AI systems are beginning to be implemented in parts of Europe, Canada, and possibly other regions. This emerging trend raises significant concerns about the fairness of using AI in such sensitive and life-altering decisions. The implications of employing AI for sentiment analysis in asylum cases are profound, necessitating thorough scrutiny and transparency to ensure that such technologies do not undermine the rights and protections owed to asylum seekers.

Can you explain more about the convergence of different data streams about different aspects of someone's life? How are patterns found in these disparate data sets about someone?

The increasing interconnectedness of surveillance systems, particularly in the context of asylum, poses significant concerns. My insights, partly drawn from assisting in the Clearview AI lawsuit, highlight how this connectedness could adversely affect asylum seekers and the broader public. One major issue is the potential creation of a surveilled underclass, especially in asylum cases. If obtaining asylum necessitates relinquishing the right to privacy, it could lead to a new societal caste constantly subjected to surveillance, including biometric monitoring. The Clearview AI case exemplified this, revealing that not just individuals directly searched in the database are surveilled, but also anyone they've appeared with in online photos, expanding the surveillance network exponentially. This pervasive surveillance risks not only creating a segregated class but also chilling free speech and public discourse.

Asylum processing presents another major issue. The US faces a significant backlog in handling asylum applications, with processing times ranging from two to ten years. In the pursuit of efficiency, the US government has established a singular asylum vetting center to streamline the process. This centralization includes the development of AI technologies for mass pre-screening of applications to detect fraud and consolidate agency data.

This process seeks to integrate data from multiple agencies like USCIS, FBI, NSA, and CIA into a centralized system for algorithmic analysis. This comprehensive data collection on individuals inside and outside the US and their cross-border movements, including those applying for asylum, indicates a shift toward ubiquitous surveillance. Such a system could have adverse effects on the rights and freedoms of individuals, impacting not just asylum seekers but also the general public.

The evolving landscape of AI-enabled surveillance and data connectivity, particularly in the realm of immigration and asylum, raises profound concerns. It threatens to create a heavily monitored underclass, compromises privacy rights, and potentially infringes on freedoms, including the freedom of speech. These developments necessitate careful consideration and regulation to protect individual rights and maintain the integrity of public discourse and civil liberties.

How have you personally experienced or perceived AI-based surveillance in the Bay Area?

The Clearview AI lawsuit reveals a concerning use of AI facial recognition technology, particularly in surveilling activists and critics of organizations wielding this technology. Clearview AI's system can associate any individual with every photo of them available on the internet, along with related information. This capability arises from the company's practice of scraping billions of photos from the internet without the consent of the individuals or the platforms hosting these images.

By accumulating such vast data, Clearview AI has created a powerful identification tool. This tool is not only accessible to law enforcement but also potentially available to any entity with access to their technology. The lawsuit provides substantial evidence that activists, watchdogs, and other critics have been, and potentially continue to be, surveilled using this technology, often illegally.

This situation highlights significant concerns and raises questions about the ethical use of facial recognition technology, especially regarding consent and the right to privacy. The ability of organizations like Clearview AI to gather and use such expansive personal data without permission represents a troubling infringement on individual rights and a potential tool for unwarranted surveillance.

While certain technologies may be banned in certain states, may they still be used by other agencies at a federal level or in other states?

Despite a technology being illegal in a specific jurisdiction, like some counties in California, the interconnected nature of these systems poses a challenge. Due to this connectivity, anyone with access to these technologies, such as a facial recognition database, can still effectively surveil individuals. They could look up a photo in the database and use that information for surveillance purposes, or even share it with others. This situation underscores a significant issue where geographic legal boundaries are rendered less effective by the widespread and interconnected nature of modern surveillance technologies, leading to potential violations even in areas where such practices are prohibited.

What are some ways to involve communities in the development and deployment of AI technologies?

The significance of public awareness and involvement in the development and application of technologies like AI is immense, primarily because many of these processes remain hidden from the public, both intentionally and unintentionally. This lack of transparency means that people are often unaware they are being subjected to these systems. A notable example is the Clearview AI lawsuit, where individuals and organizations had their photos collected and used without consent.

The development of these technologies by private companies further complicates the issue. These technologies are often created with corporate interests in mind and then applied to public or governmental settings. The public is left in the dark about the technology's original intention, whose interests it protects, the data used for its training, and the criteria for determining what patterns are considered "good" or "bad."

Pattern recognition in itself is not inherently problematic—it is a common scholarly practice. However, the use of these patterns as evidence of fraud or participation in a protest, for instance, involves critical decisions. These decisions, which in the past were made publicly by judges or officers, are now embedded in algorithms. The issue is compounded by automation bias, where machine-produced results are trusted more than human-generated ones, and quantitative information is seen as more credible than qualitative.

The public has a right to know the factors contributing to these algorithmic decisions. Despite efforts to shield this information under the guise of proprietary secrets or to prevent bad actors "gaming the system," transparency is crucial. Communities deserve to understand how the technologies affecting their lives and futures operate. This understanding is not just about ensuring fairness but also about preventing harm that can arise from decisions made by these hidden algorithms.

Involving the public in the development of AI and other data collection systems is crucial for ensuring that these technologies are not only accurate but also equitable and just. Transparency in how these systems operate, the data they use, and the decision-making criteria they employ is essential for maintaining public trust and safeguarding individual rights in the increasingly digital world we inhabit.

Chapter 3
The Informatized Body

How do you make sure you caught the right criminal? This was the question inconveniencing the *Préfecture de Police* in Paris circa 1882. Name changes among criminals attempting to circumvent the authorities were common, and providing aliases upon arrest was the norm. However, while a felon might evade the authorities by changing their name, it was impossible to change "certain elements of their bodies," according to French criminologist Alphonse Bertillon. This idea was the impetus behind the development of the Bertillon system, a method of classifying people based upon measurements occurring in their physical bodies (versus more traditional and mutable factors like name and profession). It marks a significant leap forward in law enforcement history, effectively creating a form of judicial memory reliant upon indexed bodily identifiers. There were eleven measurements in total, including hair and eye color and skull and foot sizes.[1]

During the late nineteenth and early twentieth centuries, Bertillonage spread throughout Europe and the US. Lauded as the more accurate way of authenticating criminals, especially recidivists, the practice also sometimes coincided with the theories of those eager to attribute biological determinants for criminal behavior. Despite the emphatic implementation of this approach, there were apparent limitations. Criticisms of this anthropometric protocol—later labeled signaletics—began to abound. A significant drawback lay in the human error factor. Looking at the eleven measurements comprising the basis for Bertillon's system, there were 177,000 possible combinations. The amount of time needed to measure, record, cross-reference, and later correctly identify a person was not always available. Also, there was the matter of variations in the procedures used and calibration of the

---

[1] About, Ilsen, James Brown, and Gayle Lonergan, eds. (2013) *Identification and Registration Practices in Transnational Perspective: People, Papers, and Practices*, Palgrave; and Mayhew, Stephen (2018) "History Of Biometrics," *Biometric Update*, February 1, www.biometricupdate.com/201802/history-of-biometrics-2.

Political Automation. Eduardo Albrecht, Oxford University Press. © Oxford University Press (2025).
DOI: 10.1093/9780197696989.003.0003

equipment. From place to place, standards changed; this made the system even more vulnerable to human error.[2]

In an attempt to improve Bertillon's anthropometric system, fingerprinting took center stage. The rise of forensic fingerprinting began in part with the scientific efforts of Francis Galton. Among the first to scientifically posit that no two fingerprints were alike and that they remained constant for life, Galton helped establish the inaugural fingerprint recording system used to authenticate a criminal's identity in the UK.[3] Fingerprinting was considered a far more accurate method of classifying and identifying individuals and quickly gained popularity among police investigators. Jonathan Finn, professor of communication at Wilfrid Laurier University, notes that governments quickly co-opted this law enforcement practice for other uses. According to Finn, this and other types of identification like the mug shot, were really about the construction of identity and issues of power.[4]

We may look at the use made by the British in South Africa for a telling example. Historian Keith Breckenridge points out that while initially employed for purposes of criminal identification, by the 1920s, fingerprinting became a widely used form of recognition for African men—and a method for curtailing their rights.[5] Fingerprinting enabled the state to codify and store unique information on individuals quickly, thereby providing a tool for closely monitoring one's employment status, place of residence, and movement. African men were required to carry an identity card on them at all times bearing their prints which had, in essence, come to symbolize their personhood within the context of their public existence. This authentication system continued to expand in the following decades, eventually extending to African women and European colonial settlers as well. Protests frequently erupted at every new expansion.[6]

---

[2] Cole, Simon A. (2009) *Suspect Identities: A History of Fingerprinting and Criminal Identification*, Harvard University Press; see also Kaluszynski, Martine (2001) "Republican Identity: Bertillonage as Government Technique," in Caplan, Jane and John Torpey, eds., *Documenting Individual Identity: The Development of State Practices in the Modern World*, Princeton University Press; and Kittler, Friedrich (2010) *Optical Media*, Polity.

[3] There is a debate regarding who is the "father of fingerprinting," with Henry Faulds and William Hershel claiming paternity in addition to Galton.

[4] Finn, Jonathan (2009) *Capturing the Criminal Image: From Mug Shot to Surveillance Society*, University of Minnesota Press.

[5] Breckenridge, Keith (2016) *Biometric State: The Global Politics of Identification and Surveillance in South Africa, 1850 to the Present*, Cambridge University Press.

[6] While the unpopular Pass Laws in South Africa ended in 1986, and the country had a brief respite from surveillance, South Africa has since developed their surveillance capabilities significantly to include a DNA database and extensive use of CCTV; see D'Amico, Alex (2013) "Fingerprints of Apartheid Residual Effects of the Former South African Government on Current DNA

Japan is another example. First introduced in 1908, the goal of fingerprinting was initially that of enhanced criminal identification. Indeed, fingerprinting became an indispensable part of the Japanese criminal justice system in the technology's early years. It was used most notably in Tokyo to aid in organized crime investigations. However, new applications for the technology were not hard to find. In the 1930s, the empire had a flourishing coal industry, particularly in Manchuria, and insufficient labor to keep pace with production. This coal mining boom hastened a large influx of Chinese workers to the mines. Fingerprinting protocols were instituted to track Chinese laborers. Soon, firms in other Japanese industries began to integrate similar forms of biometric monitoring so that the system became a de facto means of migrant labor population management.[7]

Fingerprinting, in some ways the more successful little brother of Bertillonage, began to help curb crime but would eventually expand to serve purposes well beyond those concerning constabulary matters alone. The practice ended up enabling governments to keep tabs on targeted parts of their populations, and tended to grow step by step with the state's awareness of the power inherent in collecting data of this nature. Also, such developments were not always immediately recognized by the wider population as they tended to concern those on the margins. Interviews in chapters 2 and 4 confirm the continuation of this trend, as the most advanced AI governance systems today are being implemented in the areas of migration, border control, and asylum adjudication.

It was just a matter of time before practices of biometric monitoring found a new focus. By the mid twentieth century, trained on criminals and colonial subjects, the assessing eye was now ready to gaze upon the entire nation.

Legislation," *Fordham International Law Journal*, 36/2, 505–544; Jili, Bulelani (2020) "The Spread of Surveillance Technology in Africa Stirs Security Concerns," *Africa Center for Strategic Concerns*, December 11, https://africacenter.org/spotlight/surveillance-technology-in-africa-security-concerns/; Kwet, Michael (2023) "Surveillance in South Africa: From Skin Branding to Digital Colonialism," in *The Cambridge Handbook of Race and Surveillance*, Michael Kwet, ed., Cambridge University Press; Cooper, Fredrick (2016) "Review of Biometric State: The Global Politics of Identification and Surveillance in South Africa, 1850 to the Present," *African Studies Review*, 59/2, 251–252; Savage, Michael (1986) "The Imposition of Pass Laws on the African Population in South Africa 1916–1984," *African Affairs*, 85/339, 181–205; and Shear, Keith (2013) "At War With The Pass Laws? Reform and the Policing of White Supremacy in 1940s South Africa," *The Historical Journal*, 56, 205–229.

[7] See Wetherall, William (2008) "History of Fingerprinting in Japan," *Yosha Bunko*, January 1, www.yoshabunko.com/fingerprinting/Fingerprinting_Japan.html; and Fujimoto, Hiro (2016) "Review of Fingerprinting and Modernity: Control of Moving Bodies and Technology of Governance," *Harvard-Yenching Institute*, November 3, www.harvard-yenching.org/research/fingerprinting-and-modernity-control-moving-bodies-and-technology-governance/.

Eugenics, at first a backroom theory in elite circles, ballooned into a highly publicized platform with widespread support from physicians and intellectuals. The practice whereby desirable genetic characteristics are encouraged and, inversely, undesirable traits eradicated, promised the betterment of the human race.[8] The trouble, of course, is how to define that betterment. As eugenics' popularity grew in Western nations, so too did "the othering of those deemed biologically 'unfit' and 'degenerate.'" It became essential to draw up "a new, biological map of the body of the nation" with clarity regarding those inside and outside its borders. Most chillingly, those on the outside, those considered below certain physical and mental standards, were to be regarded as enemies of the state.[9]

Under the influence of prominent eugenicists, scientists, and doctors, state bureaucracies were soon enlisted to serve the cause. They were, after all, the perfect tool to collect and store data on "the body of the nation"—and to do something about it. Thus the state began to sort, categorize, and rank citizens' characteristics via tests conducted in schools, hospitals, prisons, and mental health facilities. These institutions, often alongside private foundations, began collecting many different forms of data, including genealogical information such as details about one's parents and grandparents, and personal information like epilepsy, dwarfism, and physical and mental disabilities. Less obvious characteristics were also registered, such as sexual promiscuity, poverty, alcoholism, and criminality.[10]

Bearing the lowest scores on these would deny one the right to procreate. Beginning in the 1930s, Sweden, Denmark, Norway, Germany, Switzerland, Canada, and thirty-four US states passed sterilization laws for the unfit. The most notorious was Germany's 1933 Hereditary Health Law. One of the disabilities designated in the ordinance was "hereditary feeblemindedness," a dubious diagnosis that today would include a variety of learning disabilities, some of which are quite mild.

Medical professionals, including doctors and midwives, were now obliged to report patients with these illnesses or disabilities in the exercise of their

---

[8] Chaulin, Charlotte (2020) "'Improving the Human Species': Eugenics in Europe, Nineteenth–Twentieth Century," *Encyclopédie d'Histoire Numérique de l'Europe*, June 22, https://ehne.fr/en/node/12517.

[9] Turda, Marius (2010) *Modernism and Eugenics*, Palgrave, pp 65–67.

[10] Rivard, Laura (2014) "America's Hidden History: The Eugenics Movement," *Nature Forum*, September 18, www.nature.com/scitable/forums/genetics-generation/america-s-hidden-history-the-eugenics-movement-123919444.

duties. Directors of hospitals, mental institutions, schools, prisons, work houses, and concentration camps also proposed candidates for sterilization, as did teachers, social workers, and public welfare agencies. Denunciation by ordinary citizens—by employers, employees, neighbors, and even family members—was not uncommon ... Paragraph 12 of the legislation sanction the use of force on unwilling victims. Those attempting to circumvent the procedure might be escorted by police guard to the facility in question ... From 1934, when the legislation took effect, until the end of World War II, some 400,000 Germans were forcibly sterilized under the auspice of the Hereditary Health Law.[11]

Some countries would conceal their eugenics-inspired programs under the guise of social welfare even well after WWII. There are documented cases of the Canadian and Swedish government's compelling sterilization of "undesirables" as recently as the 1970s.[12]

Bertillonage, fingerprinting, and eugenics were just the beginning; these rudimentary measures were implemented to identify and collect information on those deemed criminal, colonial subjects, or inadequate. The drive to organize and manage those on the edge of society is not a novel one; what is novel is the biometric nature of the knowledge gathered, the increasingly expedient methods of gathering it, and its ability to dictate specific terms of citizenship. Of particular interest is how the already fine lines between labor management and racial differentiation, or between social stigma and biological determinism, became even finer with the introduction of each new technology. As Norman Smith, professor of history at the University of Guelph, explains, having the ability to identify people via their fingerprints made it that much easier to discriminate against them.[13] However, two more subtle novelties will impact states' orientation toward their citizenries.

The first is the way these initiatives were often motivated by a desire to serve a very narrowly defined and, in some instances, a very catastrophically defined, "greater good." In the case of late nineteenth-century police forces, it was to stem crime. In the case of early twentieth-century British

---

[11] Heberer, Patricia (2011) *Children During the Holocaust*, AltaMira Press, pp 194–195.

[12] "Here, of All Places" (1997) *The Economist*, August 28, www.economist.com/europe/1997/08/28/here-of-all-places; and Kevles, Daniel (1999) "Eugenics and Human Rights," *British Medical Journal*, 319/7207, 435–438, p 437.

[13] Smith, Norman, ed. (2017) *Empire and Environment in the Making of Manchuria*, UBC Press, p 36.

and Japanese industry, it was the outward expansion of their empires. To the mid twentieth-century eugenicists, it was to protect against the propagation of weaker traits. Whatever the case, the presence of this emotive element influenced the approach taken to the method of data collection—and to the living persons providing it.

The experience with eugenics in particular will leave a mark, for it introduced a type of thinking among institutional experts that is fundamentally deductive. According to the eugenicist and statistician David Heron, different practitioners defined the ideal race differently. Evidence, he found, would often be selectively generated to support favored definitions, and it was common knowledge that "the conclusions reached [were] not always justified by the data."[14] We may identify the deductive reasoning at work behind this kind of confirmation bias. In deductive reasoning, the truth of the premise guarantees the truth of the conclusion. The collection of evidence does not threaten the validity of the premise.

In the context of state institutions, a deductive process is safer. So long as the state can control the premise—via reference to the greater good, for example—it can control the conclusions provided by the data. Gathering large amounts of information on citizens can bring advantages in terms of capacity to administer the population; all the while, these new data do not threaten the premises upon which they were collected, nor the decisions made. The adoption of this approach made the state data-hungry, for more information only provides more support to whatever premise motivated the initiative.

The second novelty is that these programs hastened a reconceptualization of individuals as two-dimensional numbers on a page, instead of ultimately irreducible multidimensional phenomenon. This shift, of course, mirrored a broader movement toward positivist frameworks and away from religious ones that was well afoot, but it also had more long-lasting effects. It would enable the construction of what scholars Joseph Pato and Lynette Millett term the "informatized body," a type of body that sidelines characteristics and features that may be observed by human means and foregrounds instead information about the body that can be housed in massive databases. This, they say, has important implications for how societies conceive of individuals. For example, the informatized body blurs the boundary between a

---

[14] Heron, David (1913) "Mendelism and the Problem of Mental Defect: A Criticism of Recent American Work," *Questions of the Day and the Fray*, 7, p 12.

person's private and public information."[15] Are the data stored on a person's bodily features public or private property? If public, does using them as a government resource impact that person's rights?[16]

> Another implication is that the informatized body is also a radically delocalized body. As a person's physiological traits gradually become the central part of the conversation with state authorities, that person's actual body is less and less involved. Irma Van der Ploeg, senior research fellow at Maastricht University, notes that this type of rendering ... allows forms of processing, of scrolling through, of datamining peoples' informational body in a way that resembles a bodily search. Beyond mere data privacy issues, integrity of the person, of the body itself is at stake here ... This issue is of particular relevance with regard to a curious aspect of this new body, namely that it has become (re-)searchable at a distance ... [It] can be transported to places far removed, both in time and space, from the person belonging to the body concerned. Databases can be remotely accessed through network connections; they are built to save information and allow retrieval over extended periods of time. A bodily search or examination used to require the presence of the person involved—a premise so self-evident that to question it would be quite ridiculous. Moreover, this requirement rendered the idea of consenting to any bodily search at least a practicable possibility. Today, however, these matters are not so obvious anymore.[17]

These two developments together, deductive state thinking plus the birth of the informatized body, set the stage in the late twentieth century for an explosion of data collection programs run by the state on peoples' bodies.

---

[15] Pato, Joseph and Lynette Millett, eds. (2010) *Biometric Recognition: Challenges and Opportunities*, The National Academies Press.

[16] Critics note that governments often use these kinds of data without any meaningful informed individual consent, to the detriment of individual rights. Some suggest that state efforts to "protect the public" via such technologies may, ironically, actually risk *undermining* the rule of law—which, of course, is predicated upon individual rights. See Raymond, Nathaniel (2016) "Beyond 'Do No Harm' and Individual Consent: Reckoning with the Emerging Ethical Challenges of Civil Society's Use of Data," in Taylor, Linnet, Luciano Floridi, and Bart van der Sloot, eds., *Group Privacy: New Challenges of Data Technologies*, Springer; and Korff, Douwe (2019) "First Do No Harm: the Potential of Harm being Caused to Fundamental Rights and Freedoms by State Cybersecurity Interventions," in Wagner, Ben, Matthias Kettemann, and Kilian Vieth, eds., *Research Handbook on Human Rights and Digital Technology: Global Politics, Law, and International Relations*, Edward Elgar Publishing.

[17] Van der Ploeg, Irma (2007) "Genetics, Biometrics, and the Informatization of the Body," *Annali dell'Istituto Superiore di Sanità* 43/1, 44–50, p 48.

Automation accelerated this process. The shift from purely human efforts to much more efficient and theoretically more accurate, machine-assisted ones meant that governments could access the biometric information of their booming populations with increasing ease. Governments could now do more, and more they did. One technology in particular contributed to this acceleration: facial recognition systems.

This technology was in part developed in 1993 by the US Department of Defense to assist law enforcement, security, and intelligence personnel in the performance of their duties.[18] The Face Recognition Technology Program (FERET), helmed by scientists at the Army Research Laboratory in Maryland, aimed to make the technology more reliable than existing prototypes and thus more useful. Soon after, in 1997, researchers at the University of Bochum in Germany further refined the technology, which resulted in the ZN-Face system. This commercially available software was "robust enough to make identifications from less-than-perfect views ... seeing through such impediments to identification as mustaches, beards, changed hairstyles, and glasses—even sunglasses."[19]

Facial recognition technology (FRT), improved upon continuously by computer vision experts and paralleling the ubiquitous unfurling of closed-circuit television camera networks (CCTV), became immensely popular in the first two decades of the millennium. The adoption of FRT spread from one country to another in the same way as we have seen with fingerprinting. Proving successful in one country, other countries are quick to follow. China has been perhaps the most prolific "pusher" of FRT, exporting their version of the surveillance technology to numerous countries, especially those with authoritarian regimes, including Bahrain, Belarus, Cuba, Egypt, Ethiopia, Iran, Kazakhstan, Myanmar, Russia, Saudi Arabia, Sudan, Syria, Thailand, the United Arab Emirates, Uzbekistan, Venezuela, and Vietnam.[20]

In China itself, FRT became a part of everyday life beginning in 2013 with the development of Skynet. What began as a policing initiative installing thousands of cameras soon became one of the world's most sophisticated and comprehensive centralized databases of human characteristics. Today,

---

[18] "Face Recognition Technology (FERET)" (2017) *National Institute of Standards and Technology*, July 13, https://www.nist.gov/programs-projects/face-recognition-technology-feret.

[19] University of Southern California (1997) "'Mugspot' Can Find a Face in the Crowd—Face Recognition Software Prepares to Go to Work in the Streets," *Science Daily*, November 12.

[20] Gallagher, Ryan (2019) "Export Laws: China is Selling Surveillance Technology to the Rest of the World," *Index on Censorship*, 48/3, 35–37.

there are an estimated 415 million surveillance cameras in the country.[21] Chinese tech firms and sponsoring government agencies enjoy the ability to create FRT systems that are more advanced than their Western counterparts because they are unrestricted by privacy laws and can mine training data (camera footage) at previously unattainable rates.

Perhaps unsurprisingly, the target of surveillance has expanded alongside the technology to surveil. Chinese authorities have adopted a more broadly defined approach to policing that encompasses a wider assortment of offenders. The list now includes ideological wrongthinkers, whistleblowers, and those who engage in the cultural practices of targeted ethnic groups, most notably Muslim Uyghurs from Xinjiang.[22] Indeed, the Chinese surveillance apparatus in the province has reached a level of sophistication few would have deemed possible.

After facing years of discrimination and forced land confiscations, the Uyghurs started protesting. Mass protests and suicide bombings led to a crackdown that has resulted in over a million Uyghurs being sent to concentration camps. The "China Cables," documents obtained by the International Consortium of Investigative Journalists, demonstrate how an automated analysis system deployed in Xinjiang can, almost entirely without human supervision, identify individuals for detention on a mass scale. Data fed into this system, the Integrated Joint Operations Platform (IJOP), is collected through police checkpoints, CCTV cameras with facial recognition, spyware installed forcefully on phones, social media apps, and Wi-Fi sniffers. Combinations of certain activity thresholds, many of which are publicly unknown, prompt deportation to the camps: growing a beard, leaving the house via a back door, visiting a mosque, or buying too many books. In June 2017, police rounded up more than 15,000 Xinjiang residents based upon recommendations from an IJOP automatically generated offender list.[23]

---

[21] Bischoff, Paul (2021) "Surveillance Camera Statistics: The World's Most-Surveilled Cities," *Comparitech*, May 17, www.comparitech.com/vpn-privacy/the-worlds-most-surveilled-cities/; and Gershgorn, Dave (2021) "China's 'Sharp Eyes' Program Aims to Surveil 100% of Public Space," *OneZero*, March 2, https://onezero.medium.com/chinas-sharp-eyes-program-aims-to-surveil-100-of-public-space-ddc22d63e015.

[22] Denyer, Simon (2018) "China's Watchful Eye," *The Washington Post*, January 7, www.washingtonpost.com/news/world/wp/2018/01/07/feature/in-china-facial-recognition-is-sharp-end-of-a-drive-for-total-surveillance/.

[23] "Read the China Cables Documents" (2019) *International Consortium of Investigative Journalists*, November 24, www.icij.org/investigations/china-cables/read-the-china-cables-documents/ ; for a detailed review of the situation, see Cain, Geoffrey (2021) *The Perfect Police State: An Undercover Odyssey into China's Terrifying Surveillance Dystopia of the Future*, Public Affairs Books.

Maya Wang from Human Rights Watch says China has waged war on individual privacy, while the anthropologist Adrian Zenz notes the project—a global first for this degree of political automation—has "given the government a sense that it can finally achieve the level of control over people's lives that it aspires to."[24] This potential may be the reason states around the globe are clamoring for it. Kenya, for example, has turned to China for FRT equipment (as well as the loans to buy it). The Safe City project in the country is ostensibly designed to help reduce violent crime in urban areas.

As part of this project, Huawei [the Chinese multinational technology corporation] deployed 1,800 HD cameras and 200 HD traffic surveillance systems across the country's capital city, Nairobi. A national police command center supporting over 9,000 police officers and 195 police stations was established to achieve monitoring and case-solving ... With Huawei's HD video surveillance and a visualized integrated command solution, the efficiency of policing efforts as well as detention rates rose significantly.[25]

Smart city initiatives in Kenya and elsewhere in Africa have, however, raised quite a few eyebrows. Khwezi Nkwanyana, writing for *The Strategist*, finds that in Africa, "there is no indication that the mass deployment of [Chinese] facial recognition technology results in meaningful protection of citizens from crime" and suggests "that surveillance diminishes individual privacy and can be used to silence dissent." In many African states, this has been quite undeniably the case. There are reports of African states using Huawei's FRT for electoral purposes. In 2020, hundreds of opposition party supporters in Uganda were detained after being identified through FRT.[26]

In Africa, like elsewhere, the technology has been observed to be prone to "function creep."[27] Myanmar is a revealing example of this function creep

---

[24] Wang, Maya (2017) "China's Dystopian Push to Revolutionize Surveillance," *Human Rights Watch*, August 18, www.hrw.org/news/2017/08/18/chinas-dystopian-push-revolutionize-surveillance; Adrian Zenz quoted in Denyer, "China's Watchful Eye."

[25] Feldstein, Steven (2020) "Testimony Before the U.S.-China Economic and Security Review Commission: Hearing on China's Strategic Aims in Africa," *United States—China Economic and Security Review Commission*, May 8, www.uscc.gov/sites/default/files/Feldstein_Testimony.pdf, p 5.

[26] Nkwanyana, Khwezi (2021) "China's AI Deployment in Africa Poses Risks to Security and Sovereignty," *The Strategist*, May 5, www.aspistrategist.org.au/chinas-ai-deployment-in-africa-poses-risks-to-security-and-sovereignty/.

[27] Allen, Karen (2020) "Future of Facial Recognition Technology in Africa," *Institute For Security Studies*, July 6, https://issafrica.org/iss-today/future-of-facial-recognition-technology-in-africa; Arthur Gwagwa, a researcher at Kenya's Strathmore University, notes that China, too, benefits in

dynamic at work. In 2020, the country launched its own Safe City initiative using surveillance equipment purchased primarily from Huawei. The purpose of the project was, as usual, to deter crime. A total of 335 cameras were placed throughout Naypyidaw, enabling authorities to identify wanted individuals in Myanmar by facial scans. However, after the February 2021 military coup, law enforcement uses were sidelined in favor of a different agenda. A report from Human Rights Watch explains that the technology allowed the newly installed government to crack down on protests and track the movements of those citizens considered a threat. To do this, the report states, the "junta suspended sections of the Law Protecting the Privacy and Security of Citizens, removing basic protections, including the right to be free from arbitrary detention and the right to be free of warrantless surveillance, search, and seizure."[28]

Huawei's reach in the surveillance sphere extends to areas in the western hemisphere as well. In 2019, Brazil announced a bill that would mandate FRT in all public spaces. Over thirty-seven cities in Brazil have implemented Chinese technology for public safety, transportation, and border control. Critics argue that in Brazil, young, Black, and not formally educated men, who are already disproportionately overrepresented in the criminal justice system, may be particularly vulnerable to the system's potential for bias.[29] Indeed in almost all of the cases recounted above, we see that FRT, like previous biometric techniques, disproportionately affects political and ethnic minorities. This has also been the case in the US, where the technology is not Chinese.

When Detroit's Green Light Project, a collaboration between law enforcement and local business using FRT systems, was launched in 2016, only eight

---

various ways from the arrangement. He suggests that China uses developing countries as a giant research lab to improve upon and expand their own surveillance and facial recognition programs. See also Gallagher, Ryan (2019) "Export Laws: China is Selling Surveillance Technology to the Rest of the World," *Index on Censorship*, 48/3, 35–37.

[28] "Myanmar: Facial Recognition System Threatens Rights" (2021) *Human Rights Watch*, March 12, www.hrw.org/news/2021/03/12/myanmar-facial-recognition-system-threatens-rights.

[29] Canineu, Maria (2020) "High-Tech Surveillance: From China to Brazil?" *Human Rights Watch*, October 28, www.hrw.org/news/2019/05/31/high-tech-surveillance-china-brazil. See also Kemeny, Richard (2020) "Brazil is Sliding into Techno-Authoritarianism," *MIT Technology Review*, August 19, www.technologyreview.com/2020/08/19/1007094/brazil-bolsonaro-data-privacy-cadastro-base/; Ionova, Ana (2020) "Brazil Takes a Page From China, Taps Facial Recognition to Solve Crime," *The Christian Science Monitor*, February 12, https://cacmb4.acm.org/news/242783-brazil-takes-a-page-from-china-taps-facial-recognition-to-solve-crime/fulltext; and "The Controversial Use of Facial Recognition in Brazil and Europe" (2021) *Leaders League*, August 12, www.leadersleague.com/en/news/the-controversial-use-of-facial-recognition-in-brazil-and-europe.

stores subscribed. By early 2021 more than 1,700 had opted in. Images from surveillance cameras in participating businesses stream to the city's real-time crime center. While theoretically a solution to crime, many point out the racial biases. The particular software used in Detroit (DataWorks Plus, the most popular among law enforcement in the US) performed relatively poorly in tests run by the National Institute of Standards and Technology. It was revealed that the algorithms were considerably less accurate for women and people of color. In fact, in 2018, a false match led to the arrest of the wrong Black man for shoplifting. Similar incidents occurred in the same city in 2019 and 2020.[30]

The technology is less able to accurately identify darker and female faces because algorithms are typically trained on databases consisting of primarily white, male faces.[31] Fixing this problem would require gathering more data on darker and female faces, but this is in tension with privacy concerns as the places where this data is most available is from social media accounts on the web or public CCTV networks. This highlights a trade-off that is seldom realized in public debate: To obtain more accuracy and redress biases we must all give up more privacy.

Class biases are at work in Detroit's Green Light Project, too. For a business to participate it must pay to install the technology. Those who are members of this network receive a faster police response time. The American Civil Liberties Union has noted the "pay-to-play" logic that operates to the detriment of businesses in poorer neighborhoods.[32] It is also likely that these systems disproportionately target types of crime that are not typical to persons living in more affluent areas.

Detroit is not a unique case. The New York Police Department (NYPD) has access to over 15,000 cameras, and apparently used a special fund to experiment with novel biometric surveillance tools. Today, the NYPD possesses technology that processes photos of people's faces and compares their

---

[30] See Kaye, Kate (2021) "Privacy Concerns Still Loom Over Detroit's Project Green Light," *Smart Cities Dive*, February 21, www.smartcitiesdive.com/news/privacy-concerns-still-loom-over-detroits-project-green-light/594230/; Rivero, Nicolás (2020) "The Little-Known AI Firms Whose Facial Recognition Tech Led to a False Arrest," *Quartz*, June 26, https://qz.com/1873731/the-unknown-firms-whose-facial-recognition-led-to-a-false-arrest/; and Hill, Kashmir (2020) "Wrongfully Accused by an Algorithm," *The New York Times*, June 24, www.nytimes.com/2020/06/24/technology/facial-recognition-arrest.html.

[31] Najibi, Alex (2020) "Racial Discrimination in Face Recognition Technology," *Science in the News, Harvard University Graduate School of Arts and Sciences*, October 24, https://sitn.hms.harvard.edu/flash/2020/racial-discrimination-in-face-recognition-technology.

[32] Kaye, "Privacy Concerns Still Loom Over Detroit's Project Green Light."

precise measurements and symmetry to a large database of images to find potential matches.[33] FRT use in New York has led to some questionable practices that again highlight matters of political and racial inequality. In 2020, a Black Lives Matter activist's apartment was surrounded by officers, some dressed in riot gear; the officers requested that he voluntarily surrender. He was accused of unlawful conduct during a protest that occurred one month earlier. The NYPD admitted to using FRT to identify the activist, seeming to have matched surveillance images with those taken from his Instagram page.[34] Matt Mahmoudi, artificial intelligence and human rights researcher at Amnesty International, says these and related FRT practices have created a distinctly Orwellian atmosphere in the city. "You are never anonymous" he notes, "whether you're attending a protest, walking to a particular neighborhood, or even just grocery shopping—your face can be tracked by facial recognition technology using imagery from thousands of camera points across New York."[35]

Today, FRT systems are more ubiquitous than ever, and their spread has intensified public debate among researchers and rights advocates concerned about usages that unfairly target persecuted groups.[36] Gillian Tett, journalist and social anthropologist, accurately sums up a substantial part of the debate when she notes, "the key point is this: what makes facial recognition and AI technology so emotive is that it challenges us to think about what it means to be human and to have human agency."[37] We are, in a sense, forced to reimagine the range of our agency on this planet. What we thought was ours is simply no longer so. The informatized body, stored and perennially searchable, is now in its pixelated version also constantly tracked. Our real body is made all the more vulnerable by virtue of the reams of data collected about it.

---

[33] "Surveillance City: NYPD Can Use More Than 15,000 Cameras to Track People Using Facial Recognition in Manhattan, Bronx and Brooklyn," (2021) Amnesty International, June 3, www.amnesty.org/en/latest/news/2021/06/scale-new-york-police-facial-recognition-revealed; Fussell, Sidney (2021) "The NYPD Had a Secret Fund for Surveillance Tools," Wired, August 10, www.wired.com/story/nypd-secret-fund-surveillance-tools; and Ryan-Mosley, Tate (2021) "The NYPD Used a Controversial Facial Recognition Tool. Here's What You Need To Know," MIT Technology Review, April 9, www.technologyreview.com/2021/04/09/1022240/clearview-ai-nypd-emails/.

[34] Joseph, George and Jake Offenhartz (2020) "NYPD Used Facial Recognition Technology in Siege Of Black Lives Matter Activist's Apartment," Gothamist, August 14, https://gothamist.com/news/nypd-used-facial-recognition-unit-in-siege-of-black-lives-matter-activists-apartment.

[35] "Surveillance City," Amnesty International.

[36] See Van Noorden, Richard (2020) "The Ethical Questions That Haunt Facial-Recognition Research," Nature, November 18, www.nature.com/articles/d41586-020-03187-3.

[37] Tett, Gillian (2020) "Facial Recognition: Authoritarian Intrusion or Crime-Fighting Tool?" The Financial Times, January 29, www.ft.com/content/7e6131be-4298-11ea-abea-0c7a29cd66fe.

Given this review of past and present state-sponsored projects, what future biometric technologies may we expect? Let us consider that in the long run, if a technology is available, some state, somewhere, may eventually adopt it. We have seen this typically starts as a way to manage marginalized or criminal sections of the population—for which there is little popular resistance—and then gradually makes its way into mainstream usage. What starts with those on the edge of society soon engulfs all. Let us also recognize that there is generally little public involvement in debating and introducing new practices into society. Mark MacCarthy, senior fellow in governance studies at Brookings, notes that overall, "policymakers are used to letting the marketplace determine the timeline for the deployment of new technology," without much "prior public assessment... fearing that rules will hinder innovation."[38]

So what does the marketplace have in store for us? It seems possible that existing uses of contactless (cameras, sensors) technologies will increasingly merge with significant advances in monitoring using contact (wearables) technology. Using contactless cameras and sensors, automated systems can already accurately recognize individuals and instantaneously assess primary vital signs like body temperature. This information may soon be complemented by a number of other biometric indicators sourced via wearables—particularly if information from wearables that is uploaded to the cloud is made available to public clients. Let us briefly review trends in the wearables biotech market.

Readings captured by smartwatches currently include factors such as heart rate, step count, and electrodermal activity. These can be used to evince physiological issues like anemia, dehydration, and red blood cell count. Researchers from Stanford Medicine, funded by the National Institutes of Health, found that smartwatches were just as accurate as blood draws. Patients may one day no longer need to visit a clinic for another battery of tests to monitor their overall health or post-operation recovery.[39] Soon, however, these types of wearables will be able to measure much more.

---

[38] MacCarthy, Mark (2021) "Mandating Fairness and Accuracy Assessments for Law Enforcement Facial Recognition Systems," *Brookings Institution*, May 26, www.brookings.edu/blog/techtank/2021/05/26/mandating-fairness-and-accuracy-assessments-for-law-enforcement-facial-recognition-systems.

[39] Park, Andrea (2021) "More Than Just a Step Tracker, Smartwatches can Predict Blood Test Results and Infections, Study Finds," *Fierce Biotech*, May 28, www.fiercebiotech.com/medtech/more-than-just-a-step-tracker-smartwatches-can-predict-blood-test-results-and-infections.

Scientists at the University of Glasgow and the Bruno Kessler Foundation have developed a new "stretchable wearable sensor that can measure pH levels from a patient's sweat—potentially replacing blood tests to measure glucose, sodium, and potassium." Data from the noninvasive sensor is sent to a smartphone and monitored in real time. This technology, developed using European Union funds, has the benefit of eliminating the need to breach the skin to administer tests, and in the future will allow patients to also monitor ammonia and urea levels.[40] Another newly developed wearable sensor, created by Nanolab at the Swiss Federal Institute of Technology in Lausanne, could soon detect cortisol levels in a person's sweat. This indicator is purportedly useful in anticipating "burnout," as cortisol is the body's primary stress hormone. Other specialized wearables in existence or under construction measure blood oxygenation, acoustic measurements (coughing, wheezing), and biomechanical measurements (for example, how quickly one starts to walk). These are all inward-looking data, but developments are also underway to include external data, like detection of exposure to UV radiation or harmful biological agents in the atmosphere.[41]

The variety of wearables is expanding, while their size seems to be shrinking. Smart shoes and clothes represent one segment of the market. Brands such as AiQ Smart Clothing, Hexoskin, and OMsignal, for example, can track the same types of health variables that wristbands and smartwatches can, but in a considerably less noticeable way. Another area of attention is jewelry, which provides a more individualized approach to wearable technology. Other devices will go into the ear, where the signal is clearer than in other parts of the body. Efforts are underway to commercialize "microneedles," minuscule electrochemical sensors that can pick up cancer-related enzyme biomarkers. Researchers have also developed ways to print sensors directly onto human skin, or use temporary tattoos with high-tech capabilities that can record and transfer data to devices such as smartphones.[42]

---

[40] Gonzalez, Carlos (2018) "New Wearable Sensor May Soon Replace Blood Tests," *Machine Design*, May 8, www.machinedesign.com/mechanical-motion-systems/article/21836716/new-wearable-sensor-may-soon-replace-blood-tests.

[41] "Detecting Burnout Through Sweat with a Wearable Sensor" (2021) *Health Europa*, February 9, www.healtheuropa.com/detecting-burnout-through-sweat-with-a-wearable-sensor/105742/ ; and Ozanich, Richard (2018) "Chem/Bio Wearable Sensors: Current and Future Direction," *Pure and Applied Chemistry*, 90/10, 1605–1613.

[42] Liao, Yue et al. (2019) "The Future of Wearable Technologies and Remote Monitoring in Health Care," *American Society of Clinical Oncology Educational Book, ASCO Annual Meeting*, 39, 115–121; Lakatos, Megan (2020) "These Biometric Tech Sensors Can Be Printed Directly Onto Human Skin," *World Economic Forum*, October 19, www.weforum.org/agenda/2020/10/tech-technology-human-

In general, the trend in "wearables is going from macro size to micro and, in the future, will go nanoscale to be introduced in the body."[43]

These devices typically communicate wirelessly with smartphones or tablet computers, which in turn transmit data wirelessly to a Wi-Fi router or cell tower, and then on to the cloud for storage and processing. Once here, all these digital biomarkers can be run through machine learning algorithms to identify relevant insights. PhysIQ is one tech startup whose digital analytics platform collects and analyzes data from wearable biosensors. "Real-world sensor data and digital biomarkers are the new frontier of pharma," says Chris Economos, PhysIQ's chief commercial officer. The company has received contracts with the US National Institutes of Health and Janssen Pharmaceuticals.[44]

We must also address the role that new types of generative AI, like large language models (LLMs) and diffusion models for image generation, are set to play in this picture.[45] These tools provide novel ways to extract information from vast amounts of physiological data, whether collected via wearables, sensors, or external storage—for example in hospital and insurance company records. They allow a healthcare provider, or any other authorized authority, to quickly query this treasure trove of data to make a diagnosis. The patient does not even have to be in the room for the models to produce a detailed report of what issues there may be and what course of treatment is recommended. They give language to the informatized body.

Government agencies have been examining how they can leverage these tools to improve healthcare service delivery.[46] The United Kingdom's upper chamber in parliament, the House of Lords, published a report entitled

---

skin-biometric-sensors-wearable-tech; "The Future of Wearable Technology," *GFC Global*, accessed December 11, 2023, https://edu.gcfglobal.org/en/wearables/the-future-of-wearable-technology/1/

[43] Dias, Duarte, and João Paulo Silva Cunha (2018) "Wearable Health Devices-Vital Sign Monitoring, Systems and Technologies." *Sensors*, 18/8, 2414.

[44] Park, Andrea (2021) "Janssen Taps PhysIQ's AI Platform to Make Wearable Sensor Data More Useful," *Fierce Biotech*, April 20, www.fiercebiotech.com/medtech/janssen-licenses-physiq-s-ai-analytics-platform-to-make-data-collected-by-wearable-sensors.

[45] LLMs have dramatically altered the AI space since they became publicly available in 2023 with the launch of a series of high-profile virtual writing assistants, like Anthropic's Claude, OpenAI's ChatGPT, or Google's Gemini. These general-purpose AI tools understand connections between units of written language and other data and predict sequences. Based on these predictions they can create new textual content in response to certain instructions, known as "prompts," or they can be used for a range of other applications including summarization, translation, classification, and semantic searches. Diffusion models for image generation such as Midjourney and Stable Diffusion are also set to significantly change the AI landscape, as are a number of products that can generate audio and video. The combination of these media is termed multimodal.

[46] For a review of LLMs in the public sector more generally, see Kempler, Adam (2023) "Large Language Model Applications for Government," *GovWebworks*, October 31, www.govwebworks.

Large Language Models and Generative AI, and identified public health as one of the main areas set to benefit from LLM-powered technologies. The report notes how these tools may be able to do the heavy lifting in the analysis of patient records and therefore significantly increase efficiency.[47]

The Alan Turing Institute, the UK's national institute for data science and artificial intelligence, supplied evidence to the House of Lords and expressed their support for the introduction of LLMs in healthcare. The institute has for some time advocated for the use of AI to confront the nation's health challenges. They argue that there are many benefits to be had in using LLMs to extract value from the UK's vast amounts of health data.[48] This position is endorsed by other parts of the UK government such as the Director of Data Science in the Office of the Prime Minister and the Secretary of State for Science, Innovation and Technology.[49]

In India, this innovation is already underway. Private firm Vizzhy is set to capitalize on the enterprise data—the totality of digital information flowing through an organization—of two hospital chains in the nation to create a specialized tool called VizzhyGPT. This tool, a multimodal LLM with the capacity to understand text, images, audio, video, X-rays, and MRI scans, is being deployed for use in Indian hospitals to automate processes and facilitate decision-making.[50]

---

com/2023/10/31/large-language-model-applications-for-government/. The author notes that governments should also seek ways to mitigate the risks of these technologies, which include bias and instances where plausible but inaccurate or made-up results are generated, i.e., "hallucinations."

[47] House of Lords Communications and Digital Committee (2024) "1st Report of Session 2023-24: Large Language Models and Generative AI," *House of Lords*, https://publications.parliament.uk/pa/ld5804/ldselect/ldcomm/54/54.pdf.

[48] House of Lords Communications and Digital Committee (2024) "The Alan Turing Institute—Written Evidence (LLM0081)," *House of Lords*, https://committees.parliament.uk/writtenevidence/124407/html/, and "Transformation of Health," *Alan Turing Institute*, accessed June 20, 2024, www.turing.ac.uk/research/transformation-health.

[49] While formal use of LLMs in the UK public sector is still being explored, the government's Director of Data Science, Laura Gilbert, confirmed that LLMs were used internally in the analysis of healthcare reports to identify trends for particular cases, and proposed the implementation of a ChatGPT-style interface for the government's citizen portal "gov.uk" to make information more accessible. Wodecki, Ben (2023) "UK Taps Large Language Models to Reinvent Government," *AI Business*, March 8, https://aibusiness.com/nlp/uk-wants-to-tap-large-language-models-to-reinvent-government. Similarly, the UK Secretary of State for Science, Innovation and Technology, Michelle Donelan, responded to the House of Lords report saying that LLMs "will introduce transformation comparable to the invention of the internet." Donelan, Michelle (2024) "Government Response to the Committee's Report Large Language Models" *Department for Science, Innovation and Technology*, April 17, https://committees.parliament.uk/publications/44576/documents/221444/default/.

[50] Pinnu, Suraksha (2024) "Sharp Companies Leverage Data to Build Out Healthcare LLMs," *Economic Times*, February 15, https://economictimes.indiatimes.com/tech/technology/companies-leverage-healthcare-data-to-create-llms-for-hospitals/articleshow/107698003.cms?from=mdr.

While a hospital's enterprise data includes information from across different internal departments, it is likely that externally generated but health-relevant information—data from insurance companies, data generated via wearables, and data relating to a person's lifestyle habits or mental health—may also find their way into these systems. This will especially be the case if these types of commercially available data demonstrably help the system make better diagnostic decisions and lead to better public health outcomes.

There is a lot of good that these technologies can do, but there are also a lot of open questions. Minna Ruckenstein and Mika Pantzar, at the University of Helsinki's Centre for Consumer Society Research, warn of cultural and technological practices that are "pushing us to rethink life in a data-driven manner." The rise of this "quantified self," they say, is promoting a paradigm that

> reflects and promotes a data-driven world where digital devices and the data they generate have rapidly become a part of commercial, governmental, and academic practices. Various kinds of personal and social initiatives are being imagined and materialized with the aid of data, and self-tracking practices are expanding to new areas as the collection and analysis of personal data are implemented in different social contexts and institutions including insurance companies, schools, work places, and healthcare facilities ... An area meriting investigation is how specific self-tracking devices and the data they generate materialize new forms of sociality and politics.[51]

This area of research will be particularly pressing as private companies commence sharing information in real time with select state agencies. States can currently access a wide variety of records concerning citizens' physical and mental health. As laws around privacy "evolve" and are "interpreted," the list could quickly expand in the interest of public security, for example. Recent decades have witnessed a similar trajectory around citizens' private telecommunications, social media, and internet usage. In many countries around the globe this information is shared with government entities.[52] Will states mine wearables' data alongside that from contactless sensors and facial recognition camera networks (and, indeed, much else) for predictive signals? The

---

[51] Ruckenstein, Minna, and Mika Pantzar (2017) "Beyond the Quantified Self: Thematic Exploration of a Dataistic Paradigm," *New Media & Society*, 19/3, 401–418, p 414.

[52] See Feldstein, Steven (2021) *The Rise of Digital Repression: How Technology is Reshaping Power, Politics, and Resistance*, Oxford University Press.

technology to enact such predictions is already available, inviting serious reflection on what apparatuses may emerge and what forces are arrayed in our societies for or against them.

Additionally, while a lot of the innovation above comes from the private sphere, it is funded directly and indirectly by governments, government-funded research universities, or public and publicly subsidized healthcare facilities. Put simply, the state is where the real market is, for there is a rapidly growing need for biometric solutions in identity, border, national security, and healthcare management. Indeed, according to one study, the most significant single driver in the biometrics market is the public sector.[53] It is not unthinkable that there may come a time (perhaps a future pandemic, major war, or climate crisis) in which governments tie further research grant funding, or public subsidies, to access to citizens' data.

With this in mind, let us look at some hypothetical use cases where the state may use data from contact biometric technologies together with facial recognition. An elevated respiratory rate may indicate that a suspect in confrontation with police officers may try to resist arrest or use a firearm. A higher pulse rate may reveal that a visitor to a residential or commercial complex is unauthorized. Abnormal hormone values may help identify ill intent in a passerby near a critical national facility.

It is worth noting that the same systems may also suggest the optimal mix of interventions to nudge behavior this way or that. In the examples above, an algorithm could trigger specific courses of action. It may instruct law enforcement officers to use low-threat tactics to calm a suspect. Electronic signboards with additional "private property" or "area under surveillance" warnings could appear along the path of the individual whose biometrics give indication of wrongdoing. The system may suggest apprehending the passerby with abnormal cortisol levels near a protected national security facility for interrogation.

It is difficult to imagine any of these scenarios occurring with a citizen's full knowledge of the complex sets of data used, the programming that goes into their analytics, and the often-arbitrary trigger thresholds that activate one course of action rather than another. In other words, to know what is going on. There may be dozens of these interventions occurring throughout

---

[53] See "Facial Recognition 2021 and Beyond—Trends and Market," *I-Scoop*, accessed December 11, 2023, www.i-scoop.eu/facial-recognition/; and "Facial Recognition: Top 7 Trends," *Thales*, accessed December 11, 2023, www.thalesgroup.com/en/markets/digital-identity-and-security/government/biometrics/facial-recognition.

the day, of which the average citizen has little to no knowledge. If historical and current trends in the rate of state adoption of new technologies continue unchecked, these types of political automation systems could proliferate widely in both democratic and non-democratic societies.

In democratic societies, the challenges are uniquely daunting. State agencies could, theoretically, monitor the vital signs of large portions of the population and sponsor initiatives that prod collective behavior in a desired direction. Citizens could find themselves nudged this way or that without their full awareness. Some initiatives may be quite harmless, like nutritional campaigns based on critical levels of sodium, potassium, or glucose in a specific population. Others less so, like promoting contact sports participation among low-paid laborers experiencing higher testosterone and cortisol levels to divert collective action. What would stop the state from using such systems to incentivize citizens to vote a certain way in a local election or referendum—with no doubt some version of the greater good in mind but without necessarily the voters' consent or full comprehension? Such a state of affairs would grant a level of influence that ultimately challenges the viability of democracy itself as a system.

Scholars have begun to query the systemic implications of this new level of possible control. Sarah Brayne's *Predict and Surveil* and Brendan McQuade's *Pacifying the Homeland*, in particular, offer sharp critiques.[54] Brayne, a sociologist at the University of Texas at Austin, makes the central point that the combination of advanced computing with massive amounts of information essentially widens the scope and range of policing, often in ways that perpetuate inequality. McQuade, a criminologist at the University of Southern Maine, is concerned that this is transforming all of society into an open-air prison, reducing the need for actual prisons.

McQuade is in many ways correct. His book describes the function of the Department of Homeland Security's intelligence fusion centers in the US. These seventy-nine inter-agency centers were initially created to conduct counterterrorism operations, but they now have a considerably wider reach. Fusion centers compile data from different sources, including a wide variety of government, criminal justice, and social services records, but also new data types such as that collected via social media scrapers and automated license plate readers. According to McQuade, this network of fusion centers

[54] Brayne, Sarah (2020) *Predict and Surveil: Data, Discretion, and the Future of Policing*, Oxford University Press; and McQuade, Brendan (2019) *Pacifying the Homeland: Intelligence Fusion and Mass Supervision*, University of California Press.

has resulted in governmental agencies conducting extensive surveillance on the general public—in order to "pacify" the population and maintain a flexible labor pool. Because of this new approach, incarceration is no longer as vital to maintain societal control as it once was.

Other societal implications remain to be fully considered by scholars, especially as new forms of biodata (like that sourced via wearables) start making their way into the fusion centers and other government agencies' predictive algorithms, which are then used for nudging behavior as described above. What interests would benefit from the widespread introduction of these new systems? What are the ideological arrangements being made that justify and rationalize them? How is civil society organizing itself in response? Are citizens, activists, and organizers mobilizing to contribute to, shape, divert, or direct the evolution of these systems? What new conditions of subjectivity are occurring in places where unrestrained political automation risks obviating the role of individual agency? This book addresses these questions partly through a series of interviews with digital rights activists and citizen innovators, as in the next chapter.

Yet, there is an additional, more central concern of the interviews. Some of these technologies are designed (or are being designed) to deduce the existence of particular objective or subjective states from physical signals. For example, facial scans alongside sensors may consider one to be sick if they have a high temperature, or stressed if they present a high pulse rate. The list goes on. This approach to biometric signals—where physical traits are taken as unequivocal indicators of a specific condition, has links to the type of deductive thinking outlined above—where particular instances of a condition are inferred by reference to a general rule. Interviews throughout the book will therefore also seek to question these "general rules," or deductive premises, that often underpin the programming of the algorithms.

PHOTO SECTION
VITALS

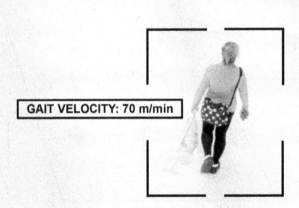

Chapter 4
Europe

In chapter 2 we explored how advocacy groups are defending citizens' rights in the US. We now turn our attention to how organizations in Europe are fighting to safeguard rights. The European Digital Rights (EDRi) organization, based in Brussels, focuses on protecting online and digital freedoms across Europe, and collaborates on campaigns with other advocacy groups such as Access Now.[1] The Senior Policy Advisor for EDRi, Sarah Chander, leads their policy work on the EU's AI Act and related regulations. Named one of *Time* magazine's 100 most influential people in AI for 2023,[2] she focuses on digital rights within the context of discrimination and racial justice and has worked on a project called "Decolonizing Digital Rights" alongside the organization Digital Freedom Fund.[3]

Recent EDRi efforts have opposed regulation that would allow the EU to police communications across the internet and, in particular, laws that would allow authorities to break encryption. An EDRi survey of over 8,000 young people aged 13 to 17 from 13 EU member states, revealed that 66 percent did not want their online communications to be monitored for suspicious content. Fifty-six percent of respondents also considered their online anonymity crucial to their activism and ability to organize politically. Only 2 percent of minors believed that the EU's proposed measures would be effective at protecting them from harm online.[4]

Access Now is a grassroots global digital rights NGO with offices around the world, including in Europe. They engage with a number of key issues that intersect human rights and technology, including AI, data protection, freedom of expression, privacy, transparency, and surveillance.[5] Caterina

---

[1] EDRi, "Homepage," accessed November 9, 2023, https://edri.org/.
[2] Rajvanshi, Astha (2023) "Time 100 AI, Sarah Chander," *Time*, September 7, https://time.com/collection/time100-ai/6308948/sarah-chander/.
[3] "Decolonising Digital Rights," *Digital Freedom Fund*, accessed November 9, 2023, https://digitalfreedomfund.org/decolonising/.
[4] "Poll: Young People in 13 EU Countries Refuse Surveillance of Online Communication" (2023) *EU Business*, March 7, www.eubusiness.com/focus/23-03-07.
[5] Access Now, "Our Work," accessed November 9, 2023, www.accessnow.org/our-work/.

Political Automation. Eduardo Albrecht, Oxford University Press. © Oxford University Press (2025).
DOI: 10.1093/9780197696989.003.0004

Rodelli is an EU Policy Analyst for Access Now. Her main focus is the connection between technology and migrant rights, as well as AI, biometric surveillance, and privacy."[6] She has worked on campaigns that oppose certain elements of the AI Act that would allow lie detectors and drones, among other new technologies, to surveil European borders.[7]

In the interview with Sarah Chander, she explains that digital rights issues are increasingly touching on broader areas like policing, mass surveillance, and privacy, which tend to have a disproportionate impact on marginalized communities. She is critical of the EU's AI Act, arguing that the ban on social scoring is too narrow and that proposed regulation to break encryption to fight crime would be ineffective and constitute a threat to privacy.

In Caterina Rodelli's interview, she explains the purpose of the #ProtectNotSurveil campaign, which is calling for a ban on the use of AI-based individual risk assessments in the context of migration in the EU. She maintains that these automated technologies (i.e., these political machines) are discriminatory and can lead to the exclusion of people who are legally entitled to asylum, which parallels and builds on Jeremy Rud's assessment in chapter 2. Like Jeremy, she also points out that these systems are opaque and that it is difficult to understand how they work. She expresses concern about the EU's use of AI forecasting tools to predict migration flows, believing that they rely on problematic data, and worries that the EU is moving toward a system of surveillance and control rather than protecting the rights of migrants. Below follow more detailed replies to specific questions posed during the interviews.[8]

Sarah, could you describe your work as a Senior Policy Advisor with the European Digital Rights network?

My work primarily involves collaborating with various civil society organizations to influence the AI Act legislation. This effort includes developing

---

[6] Access Now, "Profile, Caterina Rodelli," accessed November 9, 2023, www.accessnow.org/profile/caterina-rodelli/.
[7] #ProtectNotSurveil, "Homepage," accessed November 9, 2023, https://protectnotsurveil.eu/.
[8] Interviews held via videoconferencing technology on April 6, 2023; replies paraphrased by author. Please note, the European Union Artificial Intelligence Act (AI Act), establishing a common regulatory and legal framework for AI, came into force on August 1, 2024. At the time of this interview it was a Commission proposal (2021/206). The conversation has been preserved in its original form to open a window for the reader on the process of civil society engagement with emerging regulations around uses of AI by the state.

a policy stance toward this legislation and engaging with other civil society groups to shape its direction. A key part of this process is organizing meetings with policymakers and politicians to advocate for our position on the legislation. The focus is on ensuring that the legislation effectively protects people from the most immediate and harmful uses of AI, rather than addressing potential future concerns.

I am also involved in a broader, more strategic initiative for decolonizing the digital rights field. This project takes a step back from reactive policy work to reform the digital rights field's composition and functioning. The goal is to better align the field with the needs of communities affected by digitalization and technology trends. This initiative involves looking at how the digital rights field can evolve to more accurately address the issues faced by those most impacted by digitalization trends. This work is crucial for creating a more equitable and representative digital rights landscape that genuinely serves the diverse needs of global communities.

Can you speak about your work linking digital surveillance to other social justice issues?

My work in the field of digital rights began with my antiracism work. While working for an antiracism organization, my focus was on racial profiling. I started exploring how technology, specifically data-driven policing, was being employed by law enforcement and whether its use was discriminatory. This exploration led me to delve deeper into digital rights issues, which intersect with broader themes like policing, mass surveillance, and privacy. These issues have significant implications for various groups, including migrants, racialized communities, LGBTQ+ individuals, and activists across different domains.

It is important to note that discussions around digital rights and surveillance often fail to adequately address how these technologies specifically target and affect marginalized communities. There's a tendency for the discourse to overlook the nuanced ways in which surveillance disproportionately impacts racialized, working-class, and queer communities, as well as activists.

A prime example of this is the debate surrounding facial recognition technology. Our stance goes beyond merely seeking to "de-bias" these technologies; we advocate for their complete cessation. The reason is grounded in the observable trend that facial recognition is disproportionately used against certain groups more than others. Over-targeting and hyper-criminalization based on race are central to our arguments against the use of such technologies. Thus, our work in digital rights isn't just about addressing mass surveillance in general, but more specifically about highlighting and combating the racialized and discriminatory nature of how these surveillance technologies are deployed.

Does EU regulation address this type of social profiling?

The European Commission's AI Act, for instance, proposes a ban on "social scoring." This initiative seems to be a geopolitical response to the perceived practices in China, where various social data—consumer behavior, government interactions, etc.—are compiled into a single score that influences public life decisions. The Commission's attempt to ban social scoring is noteworthy, but it has been critiqued for being too narrow and specific.

The ban's wording focuses on the "scoring of the trustworthiness of a person," which is a very particular aspect of social scoring. However, there are many other scoring systems that can be equally, if not more, harmful. For instance, risk scoring systems used in areas like welfare benefits, policing, and immigration can be detrimental to a person. These systems don't necessarily aim to measure an individual's trustworthiness or compile a single, all-encompassing score. Yet, they still have significant impacts on people's lives.

Civil society organizations have been working to modify this legislation to make it more comprehensive. However, as it stands, the ban in the AI Act might not effectively address the more prevalent types of scoring systems used in Europe, such as predictive policing, welfare benefits scoring, and individual risk assessments in migration.

The current form of the ban is somewhat simplistic and may not be effective against the types of scoring systems that are actually being implemented in Europe. It overlooks the nuanced and varied ways in which these systems operate and affect individuals. The challenge lies in broadening the scope of this legislation to encompass a wider range of harmful scoring practices beyond the limited definition of social scoring as it is currently understood in the AI Act. This broadening is essential for the legislation to be truly effective in protecting individuals from the adverse impacts of social profiling techniques.

How can government monitoring of online conversations affect civil rights?

In the European context, a growing trend among government actors is the pursuit of "backdoors" into private communications, often justified by security-related concerns. One particularly alarming development is the EU Commission's proposal for a regulation on child sexual abuse material. This proposal uses the fight against child sexual abuse as a rationale to break encryption of private communications.

While this is not my direct area of expertise, our organization's stance is clear: breaking encryption for specific purposes is technically unfeasible and fundamentally undermines the principle of privacy. This current proposal to break encryption leverages a highly emotive issue—protecting children—which has not been proven as an effective strategy in this context. The proposed measure risks compromising encryption for everyone under the guise of addressing a specific concern.

This issue is central to the broader debate on privacy. The proposed measure suggests a surveillance-adjacent approach, where governments could potentially scan private communications in the name of public safety. Our position challenges this notion, emphasizing that surveillance does not inherently equate to safety. Any measures proposed that threaten privacy and freedom of expression must be effective, proportionate, and necessary.

The current proposals at the EU level fail to meet these criteria. They are neither proven effective nor proportionate in addressing the issues they claim to tackle. The implications for privacy are significant, as these measures could lead to widespread surveillance, infringing on individual rights and freedoms. Our advocacy is focused on ensuring that responses to security concerns respect and uphold the principles of privacy and freedom, and do not resort to invasive surveillance tactics under the pretext of safety.

Would this entail breaking encryption for everybody without a warrant, or would it break encryption just for a few after the due process of obtaining a judicial warrant?

In recent discussions with various experts, including Meredith Whittaker, the president of Signal, a consensus has emerged that creating a selective backdoor in encryption, as proposed by some governments, is technically unfeasible. The idea that encryption can be partially compromised for specific cases while maintaining its integrity for others is a misconception. Experts affirm that encryption is binary in nature; it's either secure for all or broken for all. This understanding debunks the notion of a limited threat to encryption that governments are advocating for.

Civil society organizations are currently engaged in dispelling this myth at both national and European levels. They are countering claims that a limited loophole or backdoor into encrypted systems is technically possible. The stance of technical experts worldwide is that any compromise in encryption inevitably affects all users, leading to a slippery slope where everyone's privacy is at risk. This challenge underscores the crucial role of civil society in advocating for the maintenance of robust encryption standards to protect the privacy and security of all individuals.

Seems like a Trojan horse tactic?

The trend of leveraging vulnerabilities, such as those of children or people with disabilities, to justify the use of invasive AI systems, including emotion recognition technologies, is increasingly prevalent. This approach co-opts the concept of vulnerability or marginalization to advocate for invasive surveillance technologies. However, this strategy is problematic for several reasons.

For example, these justifications do not always genuinely reflect the perspectives and needs of the people directly affected, and this is particularly noticeable in the disability justice arena. Second, the emotive nature of such policy arguments often allows for technically inaccurate claims to be made to rationalize unnecessarily high level of surveillance. These claims, driven more by emotion than fact, can lead to the implementation of surveillance technologies under the guise of necessity, without proper scrutiny of their effectiveness or impact.

In the digital rights field, effective collaboration with oppressed and marginalized communities is essential. Such collaboration could provide a more grounded and authentic perspective on the needs of these groups. Furthermore, working closely with these communities can enable the digital rights field to more effectively challenge and debunk the false claims and narratives used to justify invasive surveillance technologies.

A more inclusive approach in the digital rights field, involving genuine engagement with marginalized groups, can lead to better policies. It can help ensure that the deployment of surveillance technologies is critically examined and ensure that they are not imposed under misleading pretenses.

Governments currently engage in monitoring of non-private online communications. This is a lot of information that has to be parsed by AI systems. How does that work and what are the main issues?

The debate surrounding copyright law offers a useful parallel to understand the implications of AI systems used for online content moderation. This debate centers around the use of automated filters to scan online activity and determine what content should be banned based on its infringement of copyright law. Such filters essentially perform an automated scanning of a wide variety of user-generated content, making decisions on what is permissible. However, as highlighted by the digital rights community, these automated filtering systems have proven to make numerous errors and can even be harmful to certain communities.

The reason for this is twofold: first, these systems are based on data sets that are inherently flawed, often containing innumerable inaccuracies. Second, they tend to embed existing cultural norms and discriminatory patterns, thereby perpetuating and sometimes exacerbating these issues.

Even if one sets aside the significant privacy concerns associated with automated content moderation, the issue of accuracy and fairness in these systems remains a major challenge. The parallel with automated filtering for copyright infringement highlights the broader implications of relying on AI systems for decision-making in content moderation. It underscores the need for cautious implementation of such technologies, considering their potential for errors and the perpetuation of discriminatory practices.

What other kinds of data are collected by government agencies that may affect people's rights?

At the EU level, there is a significant expansion of the framework governing the types of information collected in police databases such as the Eurodac.[9]

---

[9] European Dactyloscopy (Eurodac) is the European Union fingerprint database for identifying asylum seekers and irregular border-crossers.

This database was initially established to monitor the Dublin Regulation, which determines that an asylum seeker must remain in the EU country they first claim asylum in. For example, if someone claims asylum in Greece, they are expected to stay in Greece. This expansion involves not just the volume of data but also the increased interoperability of these databases, enhancing the ease with which law enforcement and immigration control can access them.

This expansion raises serious concerns regarding data protection and human rights. A key principle of data protection is purpose limitation, ensuring that data, especially sensitive personal information, is used only for its original intended purpose. However, with interoperability, this data could potentially be accessed by various actors, including police in different member states, far beyond its initial collection purpose.

This situation is not just a privacy issue in the traditional sense but also pertains to privacy vis-à-vis the state. It concerns the control individuals have over their data and the far-reaching consequences this data can have on their interactions with state agents like the police and immigration officials. The lack of control over who accesses this data can significantly impact individuals' lives.

Certain demographic groups, such as people of color and the Roma community, are likely to be overrepresented. This overrepresentation is evident in both policing and immigration information systems, making these legal reforms not just a matter of expanding databases but also a racial justice issue. The technical aspects of legal reforms often obscure their deeper implications: the increasing reach of the state into the private lives of specific populations and the potential for increased criminalization and coercive measures against these individuals.

The expansion and increased interoperability of EU-level databases raise critical concerns about data protection, privacy, racial justice, and discrimination. These developments extend the state's reach into individuals' private information, disproportionately affecting certain groups and potentially leading to greater criminalization and coercive state actions against them.

Caterina, can you describe Access Now's #ProtectNotSurveil campaign?

The #ProtectNotSurveil campaign is a collaborative effort led by Access Now, alongside migrants' rights organizations like the Platform for International Cooperation on Undocumented Migrants and the

Refugee Law Lab. It now includes ten other organizations spanning the digital rights, migration rights, and broader human rights fields. The campaign's primary focus is to highlight the role of AI-based systems for migration and border control within the framework of the EU's AI Act. The aim is to ensure that the regulation adequately addresses the use of AI systems already operational in these contexts. The campaign has formulated specific recommendations for the regulation, targeting the European Parliament in particular.

The campaign seeks to raise awareness of these recommendations, and for them to be acknowledged and incorporated by relevant institutions. The #ProtectNotSurveil campaign represents a concerted effort to influence policy and advocate for the responsible use of AI in migration and border control, ensuring that these technologies do not infringe on the rights and dignities of individuals, especially those in vulnerable situations like refugees.

How are AI-based systems used in the context of migration and border control in Europe?

The trend toward utilizing automated risk assessments is growing in these contexts, with plans for their widespread implementation. These systems are being integrated into various procedures, and I can provide some examples to illustrate their use.

One such example is the European Travel Information and Authorisation System (ETIAS), which is yet to be implemented. This system will affect non-European citizens who do not need a visa to enter Schengen states. In the future, these individuals will be required to undergo a travel authorization, submitting information through a form. This form will include an automated risk assessment, providing authorities with a score based on the likelihood of the person presenting various risks, such as overstaying the travel authorization or posing a threat to public security. The system will also cross-reference the individual's information with other databases to check if they have been previously flagged.

Our primary concern is that such systems, while theoretically nondiscriminatory, can lead to discriminatory outcomes, both directly and indirectly. Despite the design intentions, inherent problems with these systems can result in biases that are difficult, if not impossible, to eliminate. The power to decide what indicators are used in defining risk is significant. For instance, should risk indicators include country of origin or level of education, with different values assigned based on these factors? This could result in certain countries receiving higher risk scores, or individuals with less formal, or perhaps religious educational backgrounds being assessed differently.

The UK's visa streaming algorithm provides another relevant example. The UK Home Office's automated risk assessment system used a color-coding method to assign risk levels to different nationalities. It was found that people from certain countries were systematically flagged as carrying a higher risk factor. This system was eventually halted following strategic litigation, and it was deemed racist due to its indirect discrimination based on nationality.

Currently, many of these systems, including ETIAS, are still under development, but their implementation is imminent. The critical concern is that without careful oversight and consideration of potential biases, these automated risk assessments could perpetuate discrimination and have real consequences for individuals seeking to migrate or travel. It underscores the need for rigorous evaluation in the development and deployment of such systems to ensure they are fair, nondiscriminatory, and respect the rights of individuals.

Can you describe in more detail what types of information goes into these automated risk assessment scores?

In the initiatives I've researched there's a significant focus on cross-referencing different databases. For example, an asylum seeker's details would be checked against police databases containing crime-related information. The purpose is to ensure an individual hasn't been previously flagged in these systems. But there is also another purpose. Data from these policing databases, in turn, play a crucial role in shaping the rules that inform the risk indicators. For example, they are used for determining the risk categorization of countries of origin. Based on data from various policing contexts, the system assesses which countries of origin pose a higher or lower security risk.

Recently, in partnership with other organizations, Access Now submitted a response to a proposal from the European Commission to establish a new IT infrastructure to facilitate the exchange of "security-related data" between European border guards and non-European countries. The objective is to enhance security measures by allowing the exchange of criminal records between these entities. However, this exchange raises concerns, especially considering the different approaches to criminal law, due process, and civil rights safeguards in various countries of origin. For instance, an innocent person flagged as a terrorist in their home country for reasons of political persecution might seek asylum in a European country but not be able to get it because this information negatively impacted their risk score. This scenario illustrates the complexities and potential issues with such data exchange.

These initiatives are in the early stages, but they indicate a clear direction for European institutions: expanding the scope of information exchange within the EU and with countries outside the EU. This trend necessitates careful consideration because the implications for individual rights and international human rights standards are serious. As European institutions move forward with these initiatives, it's crucial to balance security measures with the need to protect fundamental rights and freedoms.

Sarah, it seems like your point earlier about increased interoperability of systems can be extended beyond the EU?

In discussing interoperability, Caterina provided an excellent overview. The primary focus here is not solely on how specific algorithms function but more broadly on the framework within which these AI systems operate. Our main concern regarding the AI Act is that it fails to fully recognize that our apprehensions extend beyond just the application of AI systems in matters of migration. Instead, we're worried about a growing, all-encompassing framework that increasingly captures information in EU databases. This framework is expanding both in terms of the scope of the databases and the range of actors with access to them. The introduction of AI systems to process information within this wide-ranging interoperability framework could result in a vast labyrinth of data aimed specifically at managing certain categories of people.

In Europe, such expansive data collection with minimal safeguards would be contested under the General Data Protection Regulation (GDPR), especially for ethnic Europeans. Yet, for migrants, the proposal leans toward maximum data capture with the least protection. This approach represents a stark contradiction to the principles of GDPR.

It's essential to acknowledge therefore the colonial history of these surveillance technologies. The debate around AI often focuses on its novelty and the new forms of discrimination it might introduce. However, what we're actually seeing is the embedding discrimination, oppression, and criminalization. The roots of these technologies trace back to colonial administrations with fingerprinting and even further to the transatlantic slave trade. Understanding these technologies as a continuation of historical extractivist trends is crucial, not just for historical accuracy but to recognize them for what they are today.

Therefore, our policy recommendations are framed with this historical context in mind, viewing AI systems not as a novel, innocuous development but as part of a long-standing tradition of discriminatory practices. This perspective is vital for comprehensively addressing the issues presented by these technologies and advocating for more equitable applications.

Caterina, how have you seen predictive analytics being used in the EU?

In my area of focus there are several developments in the use of predictive analytics. For instance, we are advocating against the use of predictive analytics to forecast migration flows. Such systems are often justified as tools for preparing reception facilities. However, they can just as easily be transformed into instruments that inform and justify punitive migration policies. By predicting where people might arrive, these tools can lead to the reinforcement of border guards and increased border control in specific areas.

One notable project in this context is the ITFLOWS project, which aims to build a forecasting tool. A significant aspect of this project involves social media scraping to gather data. The tool incorporates various types of information, including historical data on migration flows and arrivals. In some cases, due to a lack of information for certain routes or countries, the project has resorted to extracting data from social media accounts of individuals in transit, such as in Libya or Niger. This data then feeds into the system for migration forecasting.

Another example involves a forecasting tool being developed by the European Union Agency for Asylum. This agency is also investing in social media monitoring to track migration routes outside Europe and infer the intentions of people on the move. The tool utilizes language detection to identify potential routes, country names, or specific verbs that might indicate a person's direction or destination.

These examples illustrate the growing use of information from social media for producing migration forecasting tools. However, there are significant concerns about the implications of such practices, especially regarding privacy and the potential for these tools to be used for purposes other than aiding asylum seekers. The use of these predictive systems raises critical questions about data protection, human rights, and the ethical use of technology in managing migration. For example, if such analytical methods are employed to shape migration policies, their impact on people's lives can be profound. Enhanced border surveillance, more challenging border crossings, and potentially more violent encounters with border guards are likely outcomes.

Additionally, there's a distinction to be made between the persons providing the data upon which the tools are based, and the persons who feel the subsequent impact of decisions made using those data and tools. In these scenarios, the individuals whose data is utilized might not be the ones directly affected. Instead, their information contributes to a system that impacts others. This indirect effect raises ethical concerns about using personal data in migration policy and border control strategies.

Sarah, what is the input of populations into the calibration of these systems? How can people contribute to the definitions, thresholds, and objectives of these governance tools?

From my perspective, I think that it is ultimately a question of power. It doesn't really relate to any AI system, but rather relates to the accessibility of public decision-making processes. One of the hardest challenges in discussing AI is recognizing that it is not an isolated technological concern, but a phenomenon that is deeply integrated into public service delivery and enforcement mechanisms, impacting society in various ways.

Areas like policing, welfare, and migration—which can be viewed as a collective category—are among the least democratically accessible of all public services. Our societal structure grants these institutions a mandate that is difficult to interrogate and modify, especially for the marginalized communities most affected by them. The barriers in altering public decision-making processes in these domains are significant, and the introduction of AI systems only exacerbates these barriers.

AI systems add layers of opacity and complexity, further distancing democratic control over decisions made in these areas. This distance is primarily because these systems are often developed by private companies. Even when public institutions use them, their understanding of these systems remains limited. In sum, the choices made by the private developers inherently transform the public sectors that deploy them.

Some put forth that making AI systems less biased is a matter of better tweaking them, or making them more transparent and accessible. Yet, this perspective overlooks the broader infrastructural and economic implications of integrating AI into society. Perhaps it sounds cynical, but in the contexts we are discussing, it's questionable whether integrating public input into the calibration of these systems is a viable or even desirable solution. Such an approach might merely serve as a façade of participation, masking the inherently exclusionary nature of these processes. This "AI washing" could perpetuate harmful systems under the guise of inclusivity, failing to address the underlying extractivist practices.

Caterina, what are your thoughts on this; do you agree that in some cases it may be better to ban, than to try and better the tech?

I think the key issue in our discussion of AI systems, especially in the specific contexts we're dealing with, is that the context of use itself should be contested, even before considering the AI technology. Our advocacy and work on this particular regulation go beyond just the AI system; it's about the context in which these systems are used.

When advocating for a ban on automated risk assessment, we focus less on the technicalities and more on the broader reason of application and implementation, which is inherently problematic. The issue extends beyond the technical aspects of AI systems to include how and where they are applied. There is an existing power imbalance within which these systems are situated. Realistically, merely including those affected in the decision-making process is unlikely to significantly alter or improve the fairness of the system. It's crucial to address the broader context and the inherent power dynamics at play to truly understand and potentially rectify any issues associated with the deployment of AI in these scenarios.

Chapter 5
Mechanics of Expression

What kind of person is the mad bomber? This question buffaloed the New York City Police Department from 1940 to 1957. The mad bomber, otherwise known as George Metesky, planted small bombs around the city: in movie theaters, phone booths, and public libraries. The explosions did not kill anyone but resulted in more than a dozen injuries. Desperate to catch him, the police turned to criminal profiling. Psychiatrist James Brussel generated a remarkably accurate profile; in fact, it paved the way to his eventual arrest. The success established Brussel as a founder of modern criminology. It also prompted a more emphatic integration of psychology in criminal investigations. By the 1970s, the Federal Bureau of Investigation (FBI) created its Behavioral Science Unit. Between 1976 and 1979, agents John Douglas and Robert Ressler pieced together a systemized theory of criminal behavior and created a series of psychological categories in which to place offenders.[1]

Critics of these criminal profiling techniques invariably emerged. Detractors often point to the problem of accuracy. Bryanna Fox, former FBI special agent and now faculty at the University of South Florida, explains that "many experts in the fields of psychology, criminology, and law enforcement have raised serious concerns about the practice, particularly in light of research which suggests criminal profiles are often as accurate as a coin toss." Offender profiling has been deemed ineffective by many experts. One study conducted by Fox found that only 17 percent of the profiles directly assisted in identifying a suspect. Similar studies in the UK and Canada point to equally problematic outcomes, with law enforcement seemingly relying less frequently on criminal profiles to help solve cases than is popularly believed. Another issue is that the methodologies used vary greatly. Some

---

[1] Criminal profiling was practiced as early as the 1880s, when physicians were consulted to construct a personality profile for Jack the Ripper. See Winerman, Lea (2004) "Criminal Profiling: The Reality Behind the Myth," *Monitor on Psychology*, 35/7, 66; and Cannell, Michael (2017) "Unmasking the Mad Bomber," *Smithsonian Magazine*, April, www.smithsonianmag.com/history/unmasking-the-mad-bomber-180962469/.

Political Automation. Eduardo Albrecht, Oxford University Press. © Oxford University Press (2025).
DOI: 10.1093/9780197696989.003.0005

use statistical analysis, while many others rely simply on past experience and intuition.[2]

This leaves the practice open to scrutiny, particularly from those eager to contradict the widespread perception that profiling is a science grounded in incontrovertible facts. Indeed, profiling is often thought to be an exact science—especially by profilers—although much of it is guesswork founded on hunches and anecdotes accumulated through years of experience. According to Norwich University professor of criminology Penny Shtull, it is thus "full of error and misinterpretation."[3] It is interesting to note how these criticisms echo in many ways those reviewed in chapter 3 regarding state efforts to collect data about citizens' physical bodies. Bertillonage, eugenics, and facial recognition have received similar criticism as being susceptible to human error or reliant on faulty science.

Despite the criticism, by the 1980s profiling was taken to the next level. Instead of categorizing a person as belonging to this or that profile as a whole, proponents now asked whether we could identify what particular emotion one is feeling in any given moment. Character is, after all, a mutable thing. To this end, Paul Ekman and colleagues developed the Facial Action Coding System. The system claimed to recognize telltale signs of certain emotions from one's facial expression. Widely successful, derivatives have been used for training "behavior detection officers" working in agencies such as the Transport Security Administration (TSA) and Custom and Border Protection. Officers are taught to categorize people based upon visible signs linked to the six universal emotions—anger, disgust, fear, happiness, sadness, and surprise. These emotions are apparently hardwired into us and common to all cultures, and can be detected by analyzing muscle movements in the face.[4]

Theories connecting facial expressions to specific emotions date back to the nineteenth century. In 1872, Charles Darwin's *The Expression of the Emotions in Man and Animals* used evolutionary biology to argue that facial

---

[2] Fox, Bryanna (2019) "Is Criminal Profiling Dead? Should It Be?" *Psychology Today*, April 4, www.psychologytoday.com/us/blog/real-criminal-minds/201904/is-criminal-profiling-dead-should-it-be.

[3] Shtull, Penny R. (2011), "Criminal Behavioral Profiling—A Critical Perspective," in *Profiling and Criminal Justice in America: a Reference Handbook*, 2nd ed., Bloomsbury, p 114.

[4] See Ekman, Paul (1989) "The Argument and Evidence about Universals in Facial Expressions of Emotion," in *Handbook of Social Psychophysiology*, Hugh Wagner and Antony Manstead, eds., John Wiley & Sons; and Schwartz, Oscar (2019) "Don't Look Now: Why You Should Be Worried About Machines Reading Your Emotions," *The Guardian*, March 6, www.theguardian.com/technology/2019/mar/06/facial-recognition-software-emotional-science.

expressions were not random occurrences disconnected from meaning.[5] Darwin's work borrowed from French neurologist Guillaume-Benjamin Duchenne. Duchenne's 1862 *The Mechanism of Human Facial Expression* explored the ways facial muscles signal emotion. Darwin corresponded with Duchenne, and while their methodologies differ in crucial ways, both texts ultimately suggest a biological basis for emotion.

These early works introduced the idea that emotions may be understood as reflex behaviors that serve adaptive functions. While the theory did not gain much traction at the time, 100 years later psychologists in the US began positing that emotions do, in fact, have distinct neural substrates and muscular configurations.[6] Furthermore, if these are the result of evolution, could it be that all people express emotion with their faces the same way? This is what Ekman and colleagues set out to demonstrate.[7] They showed people from different populations pictures of the same faces and asked them to select what emotion they saw. They found a high degree of correlation between specific expressions and emotions identified, even across different cultures.

Lisa Feldman Barrett, professor of psychology at Northwestern University, was not convinced. She attempted to reproduce these findings, but without offering participants preselected emotional labels to categorize the photographs—as was done in the original experiment. The results were decidedly different. Correlations between expressions and emotions plummeted. In simple terms, Ekman and company were priming subjects by providing the preselected labels.[8] Barrett posits instead that emotions are never objectively real and therefore cannot readily be connected to anyone's expression. Emotions, she argues, "emerge as a combination of the physical properties of your body, a flexible brain that wires itself to whatever environment it develops in, and your culture and upbringing."[9] This innate malleability, and deep subjective origin, disqualifies emotion from

---

[5] Jabr, Ferris (2010) "The Evolution of Emotion: Charles Darwin's Little-Known Psychology Experiment," *Scientific American*, May 24, https://www.scientificamerican.com/blog/observations/the-evolution-of-emotion-charles-darwins-little-known-psychology-experiment/.

[6] Sheaffer, Beverly et al. (2009) "Facial Expression Recognition Deficits and Faulty Learning: Implications for Theoretical Models and Clinical Applications," *International Journal of Behavioral Consultation and Therapy*, 5/1, 31–55, p 31.

[7] Ekman, "The Argument and Evidence," p 143.

[8] Schwartz, "Don't Look Now."

[9] Barrett, Lisa Feldman (2018) *How Emotions are Made: The Secret Life of the Brain*, MacMillan; quote from Barrett, Lisa Feldman (2017) "Why Our Emotions Are Cultural—Not Built-in at Birth," *The Guardian*, March 26, www.theguardian.com/lifeandstyle/2017/mar/26/why-our-emotions-are-cultural-not-hardwired-at-birth.

any attempt at classification. Emotions cannot be attributed under a system, however advanced that system is.

Furthermore, Annie Murphy Paul, a fellow in New America's Learning Sciences Exchange, points to research in cognition that demonstrates how thinking and emotions do not occur solely in the mind.

> A host of "extra-neural" resources—the feelings and movements of our bodies, the physical spaces in which we learn and work, and the minds of those around us—help us focus more intently, comprehend more deeply, and create more imaginatively ... Bodies and spaces and relationships [are] in the service of intelligent thought ... Our culture insists that the brain i s the sole locus of thinking, a cordoned-off space where cognition happens, much like the workings of my laptop are sealed inside its aluminum case. [But] the mind is something more like the nest-building bird I spotted on my walk, plucking a bit of string here, a twig there, constructing a whole out of available parts. For humans these parts include, most notably, the feelings and movements of our bodies; the physical spaces in which we learn and work; and the other minds with which we interact—our classmates, colleagues, teachers, supervisors, friends.[10]

These findings on cognition did not stop the TSA in 2003 from embarking on a new program called the Screening of Passengers by Observation Techniques, or SPOT for short. Ekman's methodology was central to the program. Officers would scan faces for signs of emotion that may betray criminal intent. It was a complete debacle. Passengers were referred for interrogation more or less at random, there were no terrorism-related arrests (the ostensible impetus behind the initiative), and the program itself justified aspects of racial profiling. Proponents of the approach were not dismayed, so they doubled down. The problem with SPOT, they said, was that TSA officers are human and thus liable to error: automation will fix the problem. Indeed, affective computing aficionados now "claim that automatic emotion detection systems will not only be better than humans at discovering true emotions by analyzing the face, but that these algorithms will become attuned to our innermost feelings."[11]

Companies providing facial emotion recognition (FER) software products, often based on Ekman's system or derivatives, have proliferated globally

---

[10] Paul, Annie Murphy (2021) *The Extended Mind: The Power of Thinking Outside the Brain*, Mariner Books, p 8–9, 13.
[11] Schwartz, "Don't Look Now."

in recent years. Once again, governments and large corporations are the main clients. Predictably, China has been testing FER software in police stations across Xinjiang province. The software, used during interrogations, detects even the smallest changes in facial expressions and pore diameters to create a pie chart with a red segment representing negativity and anxiety. High negative scores invite increased suspicion. Sophie Richardson, then the China director at Human Rights Watch, says, "it's not just that people are being reduced to a pie chart, it's people who are in highly coercive circumstances, under enormous pressure, being understandably nervous and that's taken as an indication of guilt, and I think that's deeply problematic."[12]

As seen in chapter 3, there are concerns about the use of biometric surveillance technology in China, primarily as used against Uyghurs. The Chinese government uses advanced systems to target people they believe threaten the rule of the Communist Party.[13] The conduct of Chinese authorities in Xinjiang echoes in some ways that of the Japanese in Manchuria—where the Japanese introduced mass fingerprinting (then a novel technology) for Chinese miners. Another interesting similarity is how, just as fingerprinting was soon adopted as a method of labor management across other industries in mainland Japan, emotion detection software is quickly being embraced to surveil the productivity of office workers in other areas of China.

A system developed by Chinese company Taigusys can monitor employee facial expressions and keep detailed records of how each individual is feeling. The company claims that its system can help address challenges and minimize conflicts connected to certain types of emotions. It does this by assessing facial muscle movements by scanning for positive, neutral, and negative expressions. Positive expressions are happiness and feeling moved, negative ones are disgust, sorrow, confusion, scorn, and anger, and neutral emotions can include how focused one is on a task. The product description reads: "Based on the analysis of one's facial features, the system can calculate how confrontational, stressed, or nervous an individual is ... analyze the person's emotional response and figure out if they are up to anything suspicious ... [and] recommend them for emotional support."[14]

---

[12] Wakefield, Jane (2021) "AI Emotion-Detection Software Tested on Uyghurs," *BBC News*, May 26, www.bbc.com/news/technology-57101248.

[13] Wang, Maya (2020) "Eradicating Ideological Viruses," *Human Rights Watch*, September 9, www.hrw.org/report/2018/09/09/eradicating-ideological-viruses/chinas-campaign-repression-against-xinjiangs#.

[14] Teh, Cheryl (2021) "'Every Smile You Fake': An AI Emotion-Recognition System Can Assess How 'Happy' China's Workers Are in the Office" *Insider*, June 16, www.insider.com/ai-emotion-recognition-system-tracks-how-happy-chinas-workers-are-2021-6.

Governments and companies often complement the automated analysis of facial expression as indicative of emotion with automatic sentiment analysis methods for written and spoken language. Today, natural language processing (NLP), a subset of AI, can ascribe meaning and emotion to written phrases or spoken ones transcribed into text. NLP machines can also perform tasks like translation, summarization, and topic identification. Recent years have seen an explosion in the scope of NLP sentiment analytics. Software is routinely used to attribute an extensive array of negative and positive emotions, but also stance, intent, opinion, and levels of radicalization/extremism in language ranging from social media posts to voice-controlled virtual assistant commands.

The European Union's RED-Alert (Real-time Early Detection) system, launched in 2020, is a good example of NLP in action. The system is built around a toolkit that enables governments to monitor conversations occurring in numerous channels across the internet. Monica Florea, the project's coordinator, explains that "RED-Alert involves a lot more than a computer recognizing certain words ... the technology we are building will process massive amounts of unstructured data, such as social media posts, to identify meaningful relationships and spot potential threats." The toolkit, which includes semantic analysis, network analysis, and complex event processing, is expected to help law enforcement agencies "keep up with the abundance of information within the terrorist domain and the widespread dissemination of disinformation."[15]

Similar initiatives, albeit targeting different types of threats, are being taken elsewhere in the world. In Kazakhstan, for example, the government recently acquired an automated social media monitoring program to track illegal content online. According to research by Freedom House, the tool was acquired from a business with ties to Russia's Federal Security Service. The new capacity, part of the Automated System of Monitoring the National Information Space, significantly broadens government capabilities. Instead of human officials reading specific individuals' posts, NLP software using machine learning methods based on artificial neural networks continuously reviews large portions of the population's social media activity and quickly detects anything deemed problematic. This has concerned rights activists,

---

[15] European Commission (2019) "Advanced Technology Helps Law Enforcement Automatically Detect Online Terrorist Activity," *Cordis EU Research Results*, 87.

as Kazakhstanis have received prison sentences in the past for social media posts critical of the government.[16]

Social media surveillance programs are also being planned throughout Africa. In Nigeria, the government recently allotted budget funds to acquire a software package that will enhance its capacity to monitor online conversations. The acquisition of this "social media mining suite" occurs alongside the country's "Stravinsky Project" and "All Eye Project," which experts believe commit the government to a host of new surveillance technologies, including surveillance drones and mobile phone eavesdropping equipment that can intercept conversations and track location data. The government asserts the technology is necessary to fight the Boko Haram terrorist threat, but observers are concerned it may be used to stifle dissent as there has been a recent rise in arrests related to social media activity.[17]

The technology derives, in part, from the structural approaches to language developed by modern linguists like Leonard Bloomfield in *Language* (1933) and Noam Chomsky in *Syntactic Structures* (1957). The key theme in these works, despite theoretical differences, is that language is a system that can be approached formally and logically. This idea, in turn, informed the efforts of early computational linguists. Conceived as a system, language is susceptible to mechanization, making things like machine translation possible. Something expressed in German, for example, could be accurately translated into English using computers alone. Initial attempts to automate translation were severely limited by a lack of data and processing power. By the turn of the century, however, advances in machine learning methods and the availability of massive amounts of text data in digital format produced significant advances.[18]

There are similar challenges that both FER and NLP technologies face. One challenge an observer may note is that, the technology often being proprietary, not all companies file mental states in the same way. A study at

[16] Shahbaz, Adrian and Allie Funk (2019) "Freedom on the Net 2019: The Crisis of Social Media," *Freedom House*, p 17; Freedom House, "Kazakhstan," accessed December 11, 2023, https://freedomhouse.org/country/kazakhstan/freedom-net/2021; and Woodhams, Samuel (2019) "Social Media in Asia: A New Frontier for Mass Surveillance and Political Manipulation," *The Diplomat*, November 15, https://thediplomat.com/2019/11/social-media-in-asia-a-new-frontier-for-mass-surveillance-and-political-manipulation/.

[17] Shahbaz and Funk, "Freedom on the Net 2019," p 17; and Freedom House, "Nigeria," accessed December 11, 2023, https://freedomhouse.org/country/nigeria/freedom-net/2020.

[18] See Puschmann, Cornelius, and Alison Powell (2018) "Turning Words Into Consumer Preferences: How Sentiment Analysis Is Framed in Research and the News Media," *Social Media + Society*, 4/3, 1–12; and Kaur, Jagreet (2023) "Natural Language Processing with Generative AI and LLM," *XenonStack*, November 22, https://www.xenonstack.com/blog/evolution-of-nlp.

Queen's University Belfast compared three FER systems and found that the same expression on the same face could be interpreted differently depending on the system used and overall context.[19] The same limitation occurs with NLP. Different providers ascribe different sentiments to the same piece of text, particularly regarding the four major pitfalls for NLP accuracy: irony, negation, word ambiguity, and multipolarity (when several entities/aspects are referred to in the same text). Furthermore, just as FER accuracy is impacted by gender and race, so too NLP has been found to reflect and propagate gender and racial biases.[20]

These similarities in limitations are due to the fact that meaning in both facial and language expression depends largely on cultural context. The amount of information from a specific cultural context that makes it into the programming is directly correlated with the system's accuracy in that context. Also, a system cannot ingest context as it is in lived reality, but only context as it is brokered by those involved in the programming. These programmers may or may not have direct experience in that culture, and if they do, it will necessarily be subjective.[21] This means that it is nearly impossible to develop a universal system with the same accuracy across all cultures.

Nevertheless, the drive to create automated emotion and sentiment detection systems that are applicable as widely as possible continues unabated. This drive is at least partially informed by what can be achieved with the harvested data. One advantage in automatically diagnosing an individual's emotions lies in identifying what that individual is likely *to do* in the future because of that emotion. At the individual level, emotion and sentiment detection is key to unearthing psychological patterns. It can, for example, predict future ailments like depression. At the aggregate level, in large groups

---

[19] Dupré, Damian et al. (2018) "Accuracy of Three Commercial Automatic Emotion Recognition Systems Across Different Individuals and their Facial Expressions" *2018 IEEE International Conference on Pervasive Computing and Communications: Proceedings*, August 6, https://core.ac.uk/download/pdf/160107352.pdf.

[20] See Eremyan, Rudolf, "Four Pitfalls of Sentiment Analysis Accuracy," *Toptal Engineering Blog*, accessed December 11, 2023, www.toptal.com/deep-learning/4-sentiment-analysis-accuracy-traps; Yao, Li et al. (2021) "Action Unit Classification for Facial Expression Recognition Using Active Learning and SVM," *Multimedia Tools and Applications*, 80, 24, 287–24, 301; Rhue, Lauren (2019) "Emotion-Reading Tech Fails the Racial Bias Test," *The Conversation*, January 3, https://theconversation.com/emotion-reading-tech-fails-the-racial-bias-test-108404; and Caliskan, Aylin (2021) "Detecting and Mitigating Bias in Natural Language Processing," *Brookings Institution*, May 10, www.brookings.edu https://www.brookings.edu/research/detecting-and-mitigating-bias-in-natural-language-processing/.

[21] One way to obviate this problem is to not include any human knowledge in the programming and simply allow the AI to program itself based on large amounts of data to reduce bias. However, this does not solve the fact that the many datasets fed into the system are generated using human knowledge.

of humans, it has implications for predicting mass behavior like election results or political protest. As discussed in chapter 3, detecting these patterns gives the power to nudge future behavior—whether at the individual or aggregate level.

This takes us to the thorny issue of cognitive security. The argument is as follows: The technologies described above create a degree of vulnerability in people's thought processes that was not there before. People may find themselves thinking things that were "planted" in their mind without them knowing. These may have been planted by nefarious actors intent on creating real-world outcomes that are to their advantage. This is known as cognitive hacking. The state must protect its citizens, and of course itself, by monitoring and countering this type of influence. To protect citizens, the argument continues, the state must fight fire with fire. It must deploy its own human emotion and sentiment detection technologies to uncover threats and protect its digital and physical infrastructure. To this end, cognitive security systems identify the origin and expression of dangerous information and take steps to prevent its dissemination.[22]

The argument has some practical merit. In a digital age, countries must seek to protect not only their physical borders but also their cyber and discursive ones. The North Atlantic Treaty Organization (NATO) now identifies the human domain as the new sixth level of international warfare. Crucially, it is not simply an issue of countering propaganda but a matter of countering the imposition of certain emotional states on large swaths of the nation (as any user of modern information technology is a targeted individual). This has led to the weaponization of the emotion/sentiment detection sciences, for it is now possible, according to the *NATO Review*, to "fracture and fragment an entire society so that it no longer has the collective will to resist an adversary's intentions."[23]

---

[22] See Waltzman, Rand (2017) "The Weaponization of Information: The Need for Cognitive Security," *RAND Corporation*. The term psychological defense is also sometimes used, and includes responses to disinformation campaigns as well as more proactive measures to boost national resilience. See Rossbach, Niklas (2017) "Psychological Defence: Vital for Sweden's Defence Capability," *FOI—Swedish Defence Research Agency*, Strategic Outlook 7.

[23] "Countering Cognitive Warfare: Awareness and Resilience" (2021) *NATO Review*, May 20, www.nato.int/docu/review/articles/2021/05/20/countering-cognitive-warfare-awareness-and-resilience/index.html; Norton, Ben (2021) "Behind NATO's 'Cognitive Warfare': 'Battle for Your Brain' Waged by Western Militaries," *The Grayzone*, October 8, thegrayzone.com/2021/10/08/nato-cognitive-warfare-brain/; and Pierce, Brian (2021) "Protecting People from Disinformation Requires a Cognitive Security Proving Ground," *DefenseNews*, February 11, www.defensenews.com/opinion/2021/02/10/protecting-people-from-disinformation-requires-a-cognitive-security-proving-ground/.

From a practical standpoint, cognitive security programs are very likely to become a significant function of the future state. However, the theoretical case for it is yet evolving. Data scientist and author Kris Shaffer makes this theoretical case in his book *Data Versus Democracy*. "The limits of human cognition," he says, "along with the affordances of social platforms and content recommendation algorithms, make it easy for half-truths and outright lies to spread, for biases to amplify, and for ideologically motivated groups to drift further away from each other." In sum, caps on our intellect make it hard for us to discern fact from fiction online. Online disinformation consequently poses "a threat to free speech and the free flow of information, both of which are vital for a democracy to thrive."[24] This makes us vulnerable to foreign and nefarious actors.

A perhaps more insidious threat to democracy, more so than false information and a fractured political arena (in substance not a historical first), is the fact that to achieve cognitive security we are in some ways forced to fight fire with fire, or rather, fight bots with bots. As described above, foreign actors routinely utilize sentiment detection technologies to influence the domestic conversation to their advantage, the effects of which may even be seen in electoral outcomes. States therefore must deploy their own technologies to prod citizens back on to more favorable paths. This leads to a scenario where foreign actors seek to nudge citizens' emotions one way and state actors the other.

There are a number of risks implicit in this scenario. First, the distinction between foreign and domestic actors is not always clear cut. It may be the case that foreign actors are amplifying existing national voices, making it hard to distinguish the source. In that case defense agencies' mandates to protect against foreign threats do not so neatly apply. Second, as Niklas Rossbach, senior researcher at the Swedish Defence Research Agency points out, "there is a risk that a government agency, unintentionally or otherwise, might lapse into some form of domestic propaganda, which could do much more harm than good."[25] Third, how autonomous can we expect our political decisions in a democracy to be (e.g., voting) if we are being nudged

---

[24] Shaffer, Kris (2019) *Data Versus Democracy: How Big Data Algorithms Shape Opinions and Alter the Course of History*, Apress, pp xii, 17, 44, 88–89.

[25] Rossbach, "Psychological Defence," p 2. We may also reflect on the fact that nudging conducted by a political institution, like a government ministry, is not the same as nudging conducted by political parties or private entities—that clearly have an inherent interest in swaying citizen opinion. When institutions nudge on behalf of parties or private entities, or indeed competing foreign actors, it can be problematic for a democracy.

unaware this way and that? Finally, will cognitive hacking/security models become so complex that officials do not fully understand how they arrive at their many micro decisions (which impact what we see and say online, for example); and if so, will humans lose control over certain aspects of governance itself?[26]

Another missing link in the theoretical case, often glossed over in conversations on the topic, is how to arbitrate between online disinformation and just information. Some suggest that the accuracy of the information itself be the discriminant between these two categories. However, by this criterion, we would lose a good portion of all information on the internet, including a substantial number of the world's scientific classics. It is more likely that the characteristic that enables distinction will be how much harm is potentially caused by the expression of this information (factual or unfactual), by and to whom, and with what intent.

Proponents of political automation argue that this distinction can be achieved on a mass scale using NLP sentiment analytics and machine learning.[27] Combined, these technologies allow for monitoring expression in the population at large and gauging the relationship of such expression to real-world events. They can connect a subjective online expression, for example, to possible objective harm. The way we calibrate these technologies is, therefore, critical. Not only does it have the potential to stop harm from occurring, but it has implications for citizen participation in, or exclusion from, contemporary and future public debates. If the expression of X is statistically correlated to the occurrence of Y, which is connected to the possible harm of Z, then the expression of X might be singled out for disincentivizing.

A concerned citizen may ask several questions about this process: How can we be sure that expression of X is causal to occurrences of Y and Z? How do we know that the correlation is not a function of an error in the statistical modeling or of unconnected hidden variables? Do the benefits of an open society mitigate the risks posed by the unregulated expression of X? Given the immense amount of data to be parsed, such systems will

---

[26] See Benasayag, Miguel (2021) *The Tyranny of Algorithms*, Europa Editions. The author argues that as modernity displaced God, human rationality was placed at the center of collective action. But the rational and bureaucratic nation-state ultimately failed humanity as it brought to the horrors of WWI and WWII. Traumatized by the twentieth century, we now tacitly decided to outsource to AI our yet more rational extension, the task of calculating the greater good.

[27] FER emotion detection will increasingly be used too as more and more online expression occurs via video.

necessarily operate with little to no human supervision; what, therefore, is the appropriate degree of human supervision?

One question that stands out is how sure are we that the expression of X is, in fact, an expression of X. Emotion and sentiment detection technologies rely on creating categories and logical syllogisms—especially deductive ones with a main premise, a minor premise, and a conclusion. For example, these relations between facial features express happiness; Meiling's face has these relations; Meiling is happy. Similarly, these combinations of words express anger; Mohamed uses these combinations of words; Mohamed is angry.

In chapter 3 we discussed how biometric technologies are often calibrated using deductive reasoning. Here, we find that psychometric technologies are also created using this type of reasoning. Indeed, deductive reasoning is engrained in all kinds of algorithmic technologies, which operate through long strings of if-then statements: *If* minor premise matches main premise, *then* conclusion is A and not B. In the edited volume *Life by Algorithms*, anthropologist Hugh Gusterson describes how if-then logics have come to play an important role in our lives.[28]

The advantage, we saw, is that one can form an idea and then select facts to affirm that idea. The idea itself remains unassailable. This is how Ekman was able to provide experiment participants with a series of preselected emotional labels and then claim that those emotions were universal. By impressing prepackaged categories onto a far more complex phenomenon, distinctions based upon such categories can eschew the nuances of the human experience. While not very useful in understanding the natural world, this approach is very helpful in categorizing it.[29] This opens the door

---

[28] Gusterson calls these roboprocesses. "Roboprocesses are everywhere in our society. Many are mundane, and they have become so routinized that we hardly notice them: calling a business and being told to press one for this and two for that; or being forced by an automated system to change a strong password we can easily recall for an obscure password with bizarre characters we cannot remember. Applicants to universities who are defined by their SAT scores and applicants for mortgages who are defined by their FICO scores are inside roboprocesses, as is the criminal defendant whose sentence is predetermined by the precise weight of the amount of cocaine found in his car which, under sentencing guidelines, counts for more than his personal history and circumstances. So also is the medical patient whose treatment is, whether she knows it or not, driven by algorithms that regulate diagnoses and the reimbursement relationship between doctors and insurance companies." Gusterson, Hugh (2019) "Introduction: Robohumans," in Besteman, Catherine and Hugh Gusterson, eds., *Life by Algorithms: How Roboprocesses Are Remaking Our World*, University of Chicago Press, p 3.

[29] The present-day focus on categories derives from Aristotelian natural philosophy, and, as Bertrand Russell famously claimed, "practically every advance in science, in logic, or in philosophy has had to be made in the teeth of opposition from Aristotle's disciples." Russell, Bertrand (1945) *A History of Western Philosophy*, Simon and Schuster, p 202.

to increasingly creative, and at times increasingly invasive, ways of measuring human emotion. It may be useful to review those that loom on our more immediate horizon.

A naturally complementary technology to FER and NLP is speech emotion recognition (SER). Humans convey meaning not only through expression and semantics but also through acoustic attributes such as tone, pitch, and volume. SER automatically recognizes these emotional aspects of speech irrespective of, or in conjunction with, the content.[30] The technology can help machines better understand humans. By detecting users' emotions in real time while they are using mobile phones, speaking with customer service, or driving cars, it is possible to help software provide appropriate emotional responses and to display emotional personalities.[31] It can also play a large number of other roles.

In healthcare, for example, SER systems are expected to pick up signs of underlying health issues. Sonde Health is one company developing a vocal biomarker device that would give healthcare providers deeper insights into a person's physical and mental health. Sonde Health uses everyday consumer devices, such as smartphones and smart speakers, to identify vocal cues indicating a physiological or mental health concern. Likening it to a regular thermometer, the company says its "vocometer" will increase diagnostic precision and allow for more effective preventive intervention. The algorithm underpinning the technology, initially developed by researchers at the Massachusetts Institute of Technology, can detect mental health conditions by analyzing patterns of speech such as harmonics, pitch, and articulation timing.[32] One study found that vocal biomarker tools can accurately detect depression.[33]

---

[30] This technique is considered in some ways to be more promising than FER or NLP. For example, speech characteristics like tone are thought to be more independent of cultural influences, addressing issues like bias. See Hudlicka, Eva (2003) "To Feel or Not to Feel: The Role of Affect in Human-Computer Interaction," *International Journal of Human-Computer Studies*, 59/1–2, 1–32.

[31] Lech, Margaret et al. (2020) "Real-Time Speech Emotion Recognition Using a Pre-trained Image Classification Network: Effects of Bandwidth Reduction and Companding," *Frontiers in Computer Science*, 2/14, 1–14, p 1.

[32] Pennic, Fred (2019) "Sonde Health Nabs $16M to Commercialize Vocal Biomarker Device to Diagnose Diseases," *Hit Consultant*, April 12, https://hitconsultant.net/2019/04/12/sonde-health-vocal-biomarker-funding/#.YYB-HEbMLOQ; and Taylor, Phil (2021) "Sonde Health Partners with Qualcomm on Vocal Biomarker Tech," *Pharmaphorum*, July 9, https://pharmaphorum.com/news/sonde-health-partners-with-qualcomm-on-vocal-biomarker-tech/.

[33] Sverdlov, Oleksandr (2021) "A Study of Novel Exploratory Tools, Digital Technologies, and Central Nervous System Biomarkers to Characterize Unipolar Depression," *Frontiers in Psychiatry*, 12/640, 741.

VibraImage is another company pioneering creative approaches to human behavior. Video footage is analyzed to identify tiny movements of the head caused by muscles and the circulatory system. These vibrations indicate one's emotional state. The key theory at work here is that the body's balance and spatial orientation systems, and muscle energy expenditure patterns, are linked to certain psychological conditions. VibraImage connects the dots on these and offers insights to security and corporate clients. The system has been used at two Olympic Games, a FIFA World Cup, and a G7 Summit, among many other applications.[34] According to its website:

> VibraImage technology measures micromovement (micromotion, locomotion, vibration) of a person by a standard digital, web or television cameras [sic] and image processing. Human head microvibration is linked with the vestibular-emotional reflex and depends on emotion status. VibraImage system detects human emotions by the control of 3D head-neck movements accumulated in several frames of video processing. VibraImage is a system that detects all human emotions![35]

James Wright from the Alan Turing Institute is not convinced. His research into the tool finds that many of its claims are not supported. Research underpinning the technology, he finds, is often conducted by persons with an interest in its success and relies on experiments that assume its effectiveness. Most worryingly, there is no explanation for how exactly specific head movements correspond to specific emotional-mental states. One independent study by Kagawa University in Japan found almost no connection between the emotions identified by VibraImage and the results of existing psychological tests on the same persons. This can be problematic since not only are one's general personality and real-time emotions diagnosed through the use of the system, but also their *intentions*. Supporters of the technology believe it can be used to determine, for example, how *likely* persons are to commit a crime, or levels of "loyalty to the values of a company or nation, based on how someone's head vibrations change in response to statements."[36]

The head is not the only part of the body that can tellingly quaver. The rest of the body can also move in a way that unveils psychological information. Researchers in South Korea have developed initial studies for the

---

[34] Wright, James (2021) "Suspect AI: Vibraimage, Emotion Recognition Technology and Algorithmic Opacity," *Science, Technology and Society*, April 22, pp 1–20; and Wright, James (2021) "AI is Being Used to Profile People from their Head Vibrations," *Fast Company*, June 25.
[35] VibraImage, "Homepage," accessed December 11, 2023, http://psymaker.com/.
[36] Wright, "Suspect AI," and Wright, "AI is Being Used to Profile People."

5G-I-VEmoSYS, an emotion detection system that can recognize five kinds of emotion—joy, pleasure, sadness, neutrality, and anger—through body movements. It works by relying on 5G networks and devices, and "the reflection of wireless signals from a human subject to detect emotions."[37] While mindful of the challenges, the ideators envision a comprehensive emotional detection system that will enable citizens to lead safer lives in smarter cities. They claim:

> Some emotions can disrupt the normal functioning of a society and put people's lives in danger, such as those of an unstable driver. Emotion detection technology thus has great potential for recognizing any disruptive emotion and, in tandem with 5G and beyond-5G communication, warn others of potential dangers . . . In the case of the unstable driver, the AI-enabled driver system of the car can inform the nearest network towers, from where nearby pedestrians can be informed via their personal smart devices . . . Furthermore, when a serious emotion, such as anger or fear, is detected in a public area, the information is rapidly conveyed to the nearest police department or relevant entities, who can then take steps to prevent any potential crime or terrorism threats.[38]

Brainwaves are another recent target for psychometric enthusiasts. A program developed by government-funded project Neuro Cap, in China's Ningbo University, places wireless sensors in the hats or caps of workers to discern employees' levels of rage, anxiety, or sadness. Employers can use these brain-computer interface (BCI) technologies for optimizing workflows and improving productivity and profitability. Workers, for example, can be preemptively moved to different places, or given strategically timed breaks. Similar programs are used in the Chinese military and in large public transportation systems.[39]

It is worth noting how the emergence of generative AI, like large language models (LLMs) and other generative tools, connects with advancements in BCI technologies. For example, it can be used to augment the information

---

[37] Hyeong-woo, Kan (2021) "Scientists Develop AI System Capable of Reading Human Emotions," *The Korean Herald*, February 16, www.koreaherald.com/view.php?ud=20210216000775; and "Artificial Emotional Intelligence: A Safer, Smarter Future with 5G and Emotion Recognition," (2021) *Science Daily*, February 11, www.sciencedaily.com/releases/2021/02/210211113917.htm.

[38] "Artificial Emotional Intelligence," *Science Daily*; see also Kim, Hyunbum et al. (2020) "Research Challenges and Security Threats to AI-Driven 5G Virtual Emotion Applications Using Autonomous Vehicles, Drones, and Smart Devices," *IEEE Network*, 34/6, 288–294.

[39] Chan, Tara Francis (2018) "China is Monitoring Employees' Brain Waves and Emotions—and the Technology Boosted One Company's Profits by $315 Million," *Business Insider*, May 1, www.businessinsider.com/china-emotional-surveillance-technology-2018-4.

that comes from our brains by amplifying the limited electroencephalographic (EEG) data typically harnessed by BCI systems, enabling the conversion of EEG recordings into text, audio, and visual modalities that are easier to interact with or extract commands from.[40] This technique is likely to boost the burgeoning ecosystem of emerging startups that use BCI to serve individuals with physical disabilities.

During the 2024 Olympic torch relay in France a torch bearer with a motor disability was able to move an exoskeleton-augmented arm to carry the torch by using an AI-enhanced BCI called Prometheus. The tool, created by French startup Inclusive Brains, was conceived with the express goal of harnessing the synergistic capabilities of generative AI and BCI systems. The company aspires to accelerate progress by capturing a range of neurophysiological data, including eye movements, heart activity, facial expressions, and brainwaves and translate it into specific commands—thereby enabling increased agency for disabled persons. Beyond sports, these systems have the potential to facilitate access to the workforce. People with disabilities could "operate workstations and navigate digital environments without the need to type on a keyboard, to touch a screen, or to use vocal commands."[41]

Inclusive Brains' founder, Olivier Oullier, professor of behavioral and brain sciences at Aix-Marseille University, is open about his ambition to extend use of these technologies from people with disabilities to the rest of the population. He notes that "today there is not a single business in the world, or public organization, that wouldn't benefit from improving the way people interact with machines." To do this, he says, we will need to better "integrate signals from our brain and body." The idea is that the productivity of corporate employees, medical personnel, or public administration staff could be monitored and optimized using generative AI-enhanced information gathered from measuring "things like attention, cognitive load, stress, and fatigue." Inclusive Brain's technology is noninvasive, reminds Oullier, and can be used with "off-the-shelf wearable neurophysiological sensors (a kind of electronic headband)."[42]

---

[40] Eldawlatly, Seif (2024) "On the Role of Generative Artificial Intelligence in the Development of Brain-Computer Interfaces," *BMC Biomedical Engineering*, 6, May 2, https://bmcbiomedeng.biomedcentral.com/articles/10.1186/s42490-024-00080-2.

[41] Schenker, Jennifer (2024) "How Brain Computer Interface Technology Could Transform The Workplace," *The Innovator*, June 20, https://theinnovator.news/how-ai-powered-mind-reading-could-make-work-more-inclusive-and-productive.

[42] Ibid.

Imagine a citizen going to a public administration office and interacting with a civil servant. Imagine that civil servant wearing a headband that monitors their productivity and suggests when to take breaks, when to plow on, and perhaps what kind of optimal decisions to make. Once we have imagined that, it is not too big a step to realize that the citizen, too, may be asked to wear the headband. The nature of the interaction between the civil servant and the citizen will be very different from anything we have seen before. Quite literally, a portion of the interaction will flow from civil servant to headband, from headband to headband, from headband to citizen. It will be unlikely either will even have to leave their home. Very convenient, of course, but the question remains: What else is the headband monitoring?

How certain are we that it will never be used to monitor the productivity of citizens—*as citizens*. If so, how will that be defined? How is one a productive citizen? It is not unthinkable for technologies that broker employer–employee relations to expand and be used to broker state–citizen relations as well. This is particularly the case when cultural circumstances favor corporatist political systems. At the moment, it seems to be societally acceptable to promote the use of BCI tools to monitor the productivity of workers. Going forward, governments too may seek ways to use these tools to optimize citizen performance, raising serious ethical concerns that we are not equipped to deal with.[43] Of note, however, is the fact that, similarly to the rise of eugenics in the 1930s, this type of trend always seems to start in dealing with the disabled and then roots itself in narratives for the common good.

One main difference between the 1930s and today is just how powerful our augmented minds are set to become. John Nosta, founder of NostaLab, an innovation think tank, believes that the convergence of generative AI and BCI "could revolutionize how we interact with information, experience storytelling, and even perceive reality." He envisions individuals creating rich multimedia content simply by "imagining" it. In other words, by just thinking of something we would set off a certain set of prompts that drive the multimodal generative AI tools to produce text, audio, images, and video. Imagine thinking of a book storyline in your mind, and then see it appear

---

[43] Law enforcement, border control, and judicial authorities are just some examples of public entities that could introduce the use of BCIs. During interrogations, asylum interviews, or witness examinations, BCIs could automatically monitor stress levels or detect deception. However, these are entry level examples. More problematic would be using BCI data to mine for predictive signals in the general population: likelihood of developing maladaptive or hateful behavior, committing a crime, and so forth.

in full text form a few minutes later on your laptop. Same with a movie, an epic poem, a progressive rock album, a scientific treatise, and so forth.[44]

Nosta acknowledges the unprecedented philosophical quandaries that must be navigated pertaining to notions of creativity, authenticity, and authorship. He notes that the central question is a matter of identity. When "our thoughts can directly interact with and control external devices, [and when] this fusion of mind and machine blurs the lines between the biological and the artificial, [we are] challenging the Cartesian dualism that has long defined our understanding of the self as distinct from the physical world."[45]

This will be especially the case for implantable BCIs. California-based Neuralink is one of several companies developing subcranial BCI technology. As in chapter 3, where we considered future developments of biological data collection technologies, the trend here too points to data collection ultimately penetrating the human body. Flexible thread-like electrodes wrap around blood vessels in the brain and transmit to a wireless device worn behind the ear and controlled by a smartphone. Each thread can read from, and stimulate, up to a thousand different locations in the brain.[46] The chief advantage of this approach is that a person would be able to push out far more information to a computer interface than they currently can using noninvasive sensors.

It is important to temper excitement about BCIs with the fact that, potentially, they are a two-way highway. Just as information can flow out of the brain, it can also flow in to the brain. As the technology progresses, it could become feasible to "edit" our emotions with BCIs. For example, we could "remove or adjust" unwanted feelings. Understanding the neural mechanisms involved in how our emotions are formed opens the way for modifying those emotional states, or creating altogether new ones.[47]

---

[44] Nosta, John (2024) "The Brain-Computer Interface Is Only the Beginning," *Psychology Today*, February 20, www.psychologytoday.com/us/blog/the-digital-self/202402/the-brain-computer-interface-is-only-the-beginning.
[45] Ibid.
[46] Smith, Thomas (2020) "How Elon Musk's Neuralink Will Read Your Mind," *Medium*, March 10, https://onezero.medium.com/how-elon-musks-neuralink-will-read-your-mind-bc06b09a0550; Lopatto, Elizabeth (2019) "Elon Musk Unveils Neuralink's Plans for Brain-Reading 'Threads' and a Robot to Insert Them," *The Verge*, July 17, www.theverge.com/2019/7/16/20697123/elon-musk-neuralink-brain-reading-thread-robot; and "Neuralink: Elon Musk Unveils Pig with Chip in Its Brain" (2020) *BBC News*, August 29, www.bbc.com/news/world-us-canada-53956683.
[47] Sandal, Gökce (2023) "Can We Edit Our Emotions with a Brain-Computer Interface?" *Futures Platform*, June 23, www.futuresplatform.com/blog/can-we-edit-our-emotions-brain-computer-interface.

Developments reviewed thus far, collectively, have fueled mounting preoccupation in the public and academic debate around ethical aspects. Andrew McStay, professor of digital life at Bangor University, notes that while there is "keen interest in using these technologies to regulate and optimize the emotional experiences of spaces, such as workplaces, hospitals, prisons, classrooms, travel infrastructures, restaurants, retail and chain stores . . . there exists a limited window of opportunity to societally agree on principles of practice regarding privacy and the use of data about emotions."[48] Policymakers concede that the technology can help, for example, identify terrorist threats, track migration, and detect certain illnesses, but caution that issues of privacy and data storage could quickly erode public trust in these new systems.[49] There are also questions of access. What actors get to see the information collected? Upon whose consent? Can data be used for purposes other than those initially intended? The Indiana University research ethics scholar Kenneth Pimple, using an anticipatory ethics approach, notes that in practice:

> The data collected can go anywhere. While it is useful for my physician to have easy access to my hospital records and vice versa, by the nature of the beast many other people have legitimate access to the same data streams; furthermore, the data is transmitted by the Internet and resides on a number of servers in different locations, setting the stage for illegitimate and malicious access. My health data could be pooled with other data sets to create a huge data set that reveals otherwise unknown facts about my life, behavior, preferences, and predilections.[50]

There is a promiscuity problem built into the very nature of the beast. The incentive to share data across entities, private and public, is larger than is commonly realized. There is, and will increasingly be, strong and constant pressure for information about our emotions to be distributed across actors. It will be done in legal, semi-legal (i.e., yet-to-be regulated), and in some

---

[48] McStay, Andrew (2020) "Emotional AI, Soft Biometrics And The Surveillance Of Emotional Life: An Unusual Consensus On Privacy," *Big Data & Society*, 7/1, 1–12, p 1.

[49] Van Woensel, Lieve and Nissy Nevil (2019) "What If Your Emotions Were Tracked To Spy On You?," *European Parliamentary Research Service*, March, www.europarl.europa.eu/RegData/etudes/ATAG/2019/634415/EPRS_ATA(2019)634415_EN.pdf.

[50] Pimple, Kenneth (2014) "Introduction: The Impact, Benefits, and Hazards of PICT," in *Emerging Pervasive Information and Communication Technologies (PICT): Ethical Challenges, Opportunities and Safeguards*, Kenneth Pimple, ed., Springer, p 2.

instances blatantly illegal ways—particularly where governments enjoy public support for their interpretation of the greater good, or in authoritarian contexts. It is useful to think of data in the same terms as territory in colonial circumstances. If it is there for the taking, technologically and ideologically enabled outfits will vie for it. The twenty-first century may well be characterized, in part, by this competition as data streams converge and flow into everchanging hands.

Given this concern, this book argues that it is necessary to understand: 1) the additional power granted to state entities through psychometric data collection technologies, and 2) how the deductive frameworks that inform the design of these technologies contribute to this power. These two points are interrelated and must be interrogated together. In *If . . . Then: Algorithmic Power and Politics*, Taina Bucher at the University of Oslo explains that we cannot properly know the impact of algorithmic technologies without understanding how they are based on material relations of power and embedded within social systems.

> Increasingly, we have come to rely on algorithms as programmable decision-makers to manage, curate, and organize the massive amounts of information and data available on the Web and to do so in a meaningful way. Yet, the nature and implications of such arrangements are far from clear . . . [T]he power and politics of algorithms stems from how algorithmic systems shape peoples encounters and orientations in the world. At the same time . . . this shaping power cannot be reduced to code . . . Examining algorithmic media and the ways in which life is increasingly affected by algorithmic processing, means acknowledging how algorithms are not static things but, rather, evolving, dynamic, and relational processes hinging on a complex set of actors, both humans and nonhumans . . . [This requires] a conceptual repertoire that goes beyond the textbook definition of algorithms as step-by-step instructions for solving a computational problem . . . to better account for the fundamental interlinking or entanglement of the social and material implicated by algorithms.[51]

Bucher is correct. The social and the material are "entangled" when coding, for example, how many categories there are, what they mean, and how they are hierarchized. Algorithms, in this sense, do much more than deliberate

---

[51] Bucher, Taina (2018) *If . . . Then: Algorithmic Power and Politics*, Oxford University Press, pp 4, 13–16.

the fate of humans, they are fundamentally constitutive of a new way of organizing the world. Are faulty premises used to categorize real-world phenomena in such a way that increases certain entities' power, and does this power accrue to the further exclusion of those, or some, in their charge? The literature reviewed thus far suggests that systems based on inadequately calibrated data collection can be dangerous to citizens (particularly those already on the margins of society) but can also be potent tools in the hands of public and private organizations. The interplay between these two factors (poor calibration and accrued power) needs to be better understood.

Francis Bacon long ago said that if successful, a scientist would become like a bee and not a spider. Bees, he said, collect natural matter (facts) and then work on it to produce honey (laws). Spiders, on the other hand, spin arguments out of their reason alone and believe only those. The Baconian method starts from facts and, from these, arrives at the laws that govern nature. Along the path, one must guard against the four idols produced by the "uneven mirror" of the human mind: trusting one's physical senses, personal prejudice, following received authority, and relying on the semantic limits of language.[52]

In this book it is hypothesized that there is a higher proportion of spiders in the field of political automation and this has contributed to a resurgence of the four idols at the intersection of science and policymaking. Technological prosthetics (cameras, sensors) have dispelled distrust in the senses, political exigencies regularly trump scientific rigor, received authority calibrates analysis (e.g., the "universal" emotions), and language is considered exhaustively indicative of meaning. The reason for this resurgence of the four idols is that significant shifts in existing power balances are at stake, and "idolaters" have an advantage. Interviews in chapter 4 and throughout the book will try to probe this dynamic.

---

[52] Bacon, Francis ([1620] 2019) *Novum Organum*, Anados; and Bacon, Francis ([1626] 2019) *New Atlantis*, Compass Circle.

PHOTO SECTION
EMOTIONS

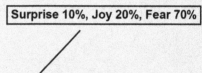

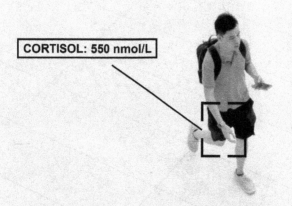

Chapter 6
Africa

In this chapter we take a look at the impact of surveillance technologies in Africa and the implications for citizens there through two interviews. The first is with Patricia Boshe of The African Law and Technology Institute (AFRILTI). This institute promotes innovative research on the interaction between technology, law, and society in Africa. Based in Tanzania, AFRILTI provides research, training, and consultancy services on various topics including legal informatics, data protection, eGovernment, and cyberlaw to policy makers, nonprofits, regulators, and industry professionals. Boshe also teaches law at the University of Passau in Germany. Her research interests include human rights and data protection, a subject that she has published on extensively, including in her book *Data Protection in the Global Contexts: Africa, EU, and the US*.[1]

The second interview is with the director of Penplusbytes, a nonprofit based in Ghana. Penplusbytes strives to promote good governance in Africa by empowering the media, civil society, and different stakeholders to use innovative digital technologies. Their work includes projects related to elections in Africa, media and information literacy, enhancing journalism through new digital technologies, and improving civic participation using digital tools.[2] The director, Kwami Ahiabenu II, is one of Ghana's foremost experts on democracy and new communication technologies and previously founded the International Institute for ICT Journalism.

In the interview with Patricia Boshe, she discusses the surveillance and data collection technologies that are being used by various governments in Africa, and laments the lack of transparency in their activities. She notes that the law in these nations often allows for surveillance activities, and describes the Tanzanian government's monitoring of citizens' social media activity. She explains that, ordinarily, local social media platforms do not have the resources or support to resist government pressure, and gives the

---

[1] Boshe, Patricia (2018) *Data Protection in the Global Contexts: Africa, EU, and the US*, SVH-Verlag.
[2] Penplusbytes, "Homepage," accessed November 9, 2023, https://penplusbytes.org/.

example of the retaliation faced by social media company Jumuiya Forums for refusing to cooperate. She expressed concern about the ability of governments to employ technology to surveil citizens with little oversight, and the consequences for democracy.

In Kwami Ahiabenu II's interview, he describes the impact of surveillance tools, predictive technologies, and digital currencies on civil liberties in Africa. He raises concerns about governments in Africa using surveillance tools like Pegasus to monitor citizens, and clarifies how the introduction of central bank digital currencies, like eNaira in Nigeria and E-Cedi in Ghana, could potentially restrict citizens' financial freedom. He explains that there is little opposition from the public to the deployment of digital currencies in Ghana due to a general lack of awareness. Ahiabenu highlights the need for data ownership by individuals, rather than national governments or multilateral organizations, and notes the potential for modifying freedom of information laws to realize this. Below follow more detailed replies to specific questions posed during the interviews.[3]

Patricia, what motivated you to co-found the African Law and Technology Institute, and what are the institute's primary objectives in relation to the interplay between law, technology, and society in Africa?

The institute was an idea I had with one of my colleagues, Professor Alex Makulilo, a notable scholar in data protection and privacy in Africa. At that time, there weren't many scholars in the field of data protection across the continent. Recognizing this gap, we envisioned creating a platform that could lay the groundwork for this profession in Africa. Our aim was to facilitate discussion and collaboration on topics specifically relevant to Africa, such as data protection, privacy, digital economy, and technological innovations—subjects widely discussed globally but less so in Africa.

Traditionally, most universities have taught courses related to policy, law, data protection, privacy, and so forth separately from courses in technology. We identified a crucial need to merge these domains. The intersection

---

[3] Interviews held via videoconferencing technology on June 8 (Boshe) and October 4 (Ahiabenu), 2023; replies paraphrased by author.

of policy and technology is integral to understanding the contemporary landscape; one cannot be comprehensively addressed without considering the other.

Our belief is that these domains are interrelated and need to be approached as such to fully grasp their dynamics. This perspective led to the establishment of an institute that treats these subjects as interconnected parts of a whole, rather than isolated entities. By bringing them together on a common platform we aim to foster a more holistic understanding and approach to these crucial areas, especially in the context of Africa's growing engagement with digital and technological advancements.

What are some of the most prevalent surveillance and data collection technologies currently being deployed by governments in Africa, and what are their intended purposes?

The issue of surveillance technology deployment in Africa poses a complex and somewhat elusive challenge. Governments across the continent are known to engage in surveillance activities, yet no government openly acknowledges the use of spyware, Trojans, or similar technologies. This secrecy makes it difficult to specify what types of surveillance technology are being deployed, as such information is not publicly disclosed.

However, it is evident that many African countries are forming partnerships with Western and Asian nations for technological capacity development. These partnerships often involve technology transfers that could potentially include surveillance technology, including for foreign nations. For instance, there has been speculation, which one can find online, about the African Union receiving technology support from China, including computers and printers for their offices in Addis Ababa, Ethiopia. There were rumors that these computers would switch on automatically after midnight, leading to suspicions of surveillance mechanisms being embedded in them. While the veracity of these claims is uncertain, it led to the African Union reportedly discontinuing the use of these devices.

While the direct importation and use of surveillance technologies in African countries are not openly discussed, it is clear that many policies and laws in Africa create an environment conducive to surveillance. Often, these laws do not explicitly authorize surveillance but lack proper oversight mechanisms. This lack of regulation and oversight enables government and law enforcement agencies to conduct surveillance activities, often without the awareness or consent of the citizens being monitored. Consequently, while the specific technologies and methods may remain obscured, the broader context indicates a trend toward increasing, yet unregulated, surveillance across the continent.

Can you describe any data collection technologies in Africa that specifically target a person's expression on social media, and any regulatory or legal issues around that?

The dynamics of government surveillance over social networks in Africa offer a telling example of the intersection between technology, media, and state authority. Governments have increasingly utilized social media platforms to monitor and target specific individuals. This surveillance is not just about technology but also about leveraging media platforms to identify dissenting voices.

In a white paper I recently authored, I explore this phenomenon, particularly focusing on a platform in Tanzania. Historically, people would express dissent or discontent with government actions in public, physical spaces. However, the risk of police brutality or unfair imprisonment has pushed many to migrate these expressions to online platforms. Recognizing this shift, African governments have moved to monitor digital spaces. However, the challenge for governments lies in identifying the individuals behind specific digital posts, without possessing adequate technological tools to do that. This leads them to employ intimidation tactics.

For instance, government authorities have intimidated platform owners to make them reveal user information, especially when content posted online is perceived as threatening. The story of a Tanzanian platform is particularly instructive. The government, having observed dissenting voices on the platform, tried to coerce the platform's owner into revealing user information. Despite the lack of data protection laws in Tanzania at the time, the owner resisted, citing constitutional privacy guarantees. The government's attempt to bypass this resistance by invoking national security did not succeed. Interestingly, the platform owner had preemptively secured the data outside Tanzania, thwarting government attempts to access it. Subsequently, the government resorted to legal intimidation, indicting the owner on multiple, seemingly related charges across different courts.

This case exemplifies the lengths to which governments can go to suppress civic rights and how they use their authority to intimidate not just citizens but also those providing a platform for free expression. It highlights a broader trend where African governments, lacking the technical expertise to conduct sophisticated digital surveillance, resort to more direct, often coercive methods to control information flow and suppress dissent. This approach poses significant threats to civic rights and the fundamental principles of freedom of expression and privacy.

Is it different when we're talking about global companies? Like say Facebook or WhatsApp? Do local companies face unique challenges?

Explaining the challenges faced by local platforms in Africa is complex, especially in the context of government demands or law enforcement requests. Unlike global platforms like Facebook, which possess ample manpower, skills, and financial resources, local platforms often lack the means to resist government encroachment. Global platforms have a better understanding of their rights regarding personal information protection and the capability to lawfully deny government access. In contrast, local platforms find it exceedingly difficult to resist government authority, which can exert immense pressure and even alter laws to expand its control.

For instance, in Tanzania, the government amended several laws to increase its authority over social networks and other digital platforms. This legislative change enabled the government to legally penetrate and surveil these platforms. Intriguingly, these laws were altered for specific politically motivated surveillance purposes, as evidenced by their reversal following a change of regime. The death of the previous president and the subsequent assumption of power by a new leader led to these laws being reverted to their original form.

This situation highlights the multifaceted tactics governments can employ, extending beyond technology and intimidation. They wield the power to swiftly change laws, thereby legitimizing their surveillance activities and accessing information legally. Such actions demonstrate a significant challenge for local platforms in maintaining autonomy and protecting user privacy. Governments can manipulate legal frameworks to facilitate surveillance, exerting control over digital spaces and curtailing the freedom and rights of both platforms and their users.

What was the name of the social media platform in Tanzania? How did the case end?

The platform in question was Jumuiya Forums, with "Jumuiya" being a Swahili word meaning "community." As the name suggests, it was a community forum designed to provide a space for open and anonymous discussion. This feature enabled users to freely express their views and share evidence of governmental malpractice, which led to the forum becoming a target for government scrutiny.

The founder faced three separate legal challenges. In the first case, he was acquitted as the magistrate found no basis for the indictment. In the second, he was given the option of either a three-year prison sentence or a fine of five million Tanzanian shillings (approximately $2,000). The third charge, related to obstruction of justice for denying law enforcement access to user data, resulted in a guilty verdict. However, the magistrate refrained from imposing any punishment, citing the penalty already levied in the previous case.

In the first case, where the magistrate acquitted him, that magistrate was transferred to a remote location within the same week and tragically passed away within two months. While one might speculate about the circumstances, these events underline the high level of intimidation associated with surveillance in Africa.

Surveillance in the African context involves more than just technology. It encompasses law enforcement, legal manipulation, and, significantly, intimidation. In many instances, the threat and implementation of intimidation tactics overshadow the technological aspects of surveillance. This multifaceted approach to surveillance in Africa highlights the complex challenges faced by those who seek to provide platforms for free speech and stand against government overreach.

How does this impact African social, cultural, and civic life?

The impact of technology in Africa can be seen from both positive and negative perspectives. On the positive side, technology provides platforms for civic engagement, where individuals can express their grievances, socialize, and share their experiences online. This aspect of technology fosters a sense of community and enables people to connect with each other, even beyond their immediate geographical boundaries.

However, the negative impacts stem from a general lack of awareness about privacy issues among the African population. Many people, in the interest of socializing, tend to share too much personal information online without fully understanding the potential risks. This behavior opens the door to government surveillance, where authorities can monitor online activities to identify and potentially blackmail dissenters. Additionally, this lack of awareness can also make individuals vulnerable to fraudsters who might exploit their personal data.

Contrasting this with experiences in countries like Germany, where children are educated from a young age about online privacy and the importance of not sharing personal information, it becomes evident that there's a significant gap in digital literacy and privacy education in many African countries. People often don't realize the implications of seemingly simple actions like posting a birthday celebration online.

Therefore, the need for training and education about the pros and cons of technology is paramount. Awareness about how technology can potentially infringe upon one's privacy or be used against them is crucial. On the flip side, technology also opens up a world of opportunities, allowing people to explore and learn about different cultures and lifestyles beyond Africa, expanding their horizons and understanding of the global community.

Technology's impact on privacy in Africa is a double-edged sword. It can be a powerful tool for promoting civic rights and global connectivity, but it also poses risks to personal privacy and security. The key lies in how it is used and the level of awareness and education about its potential impacts. Enhancing digital literacy and understanding of privacy issues can help harness the positive aspects of technology while mitigating its negative effects.

What are the key ethical considerations that should be taken into account when assessing the deployment of new surveillance and data collection technologies in Africa?

When discussing capacity-building, it's crucial to consider the wide spectrum of technology's impact—both its potential benefits and the risks it poses to individuals and communities. This includes understanding and navigating challenges like surveillance and cyberbullying. An essential aspect of deploying technology, especially in the African context, is ensuring that users are not only equipped with the tools but also with comprehensive knowledge about their use, including the potential for misuse.

There's a significant gap in this area within many African communities. While there is an influx of technology and people are increasingly buying and using these tools, there is a lack of formal training on effective and safe usage. Self-learning is common, but it often neglects the darker aspects of technology. Aside from the more visible issues like cyberbullying, other negative aspects of technology use are not widely discussed. This lack of discourse leaves many people vulnerable, finding themselves overwhelmed by the adverse effects of technology without knowing how to navigate back to safer, more positive use.

It's important that technology deployment be accompanied by thorough education on its pros and cons. Users should be informed not only about how technology can aid them but also about the potential dangers it poses. Moreover, they should be equipped with strategies for dealing with problems, including knowing the appropriate steps to take and authorities to contact in such situations.

Governments and technology providers should prioritize this educational aspect, ensuring that with every technological advancement introduced, there is an accompanying framework for education and support. This approach will empower users to leverage technology effectively and safely, enhancing its benefits while reducing its risks. Essentially, this holistic approach to technology deployment, which balances the provision of digital products and services with essential citizen education, is vital for fostering a more informed, resilient, and responsible community.

Can you describe specific cases where the use of surveillance and data collection technologies in Africa have raised legal controversies?

I think that's a problem that's cutting across every continent, not only Africa. It's something that you find everywhere. You find it in China, Japan, Europe, it is everywhere. Many African governments lack fully democratic structures, and this lack of democracy grants governments more authority to exercise control over technology, including surveillance practices, which can differ significantly from those in more democratic regions.

In Africa, openly speaking out against government or expressing dissent in public can lead to intimidation and severe consequences, a reality less common in more democratic societies. This oppressive atmosphere fosters an environment conducive to pervasive surveillance.

The legal framework in many African countries often supports this. For example, in Uganda, intelligence agencies are permitted by law to tap into communication networks without obtaining a court warrant for reasons such as national security or intelligence gathering. This approach raises questions about the indiscriminate nature of surveillance. Tapping into a network affects all users, making it challenging to segregate targeted individuals from the general population. Often, these activities can continue for extended periods without judicial oversight, leading to potential civil rights infringements.

A similar situation was observed in South Africa, where a journalist's suspicions about mass surveillance were initially dismissed by authorities. However, in 2021, the Constitutional Court ruled against the National Intelligence Act on the grounds that it allowed for bulk collection of citizens' data, confirming the journalist's suspicions. This ruling highlighted the tension between national security needs and individual privacy rights, prompting a reevaluation of the law to balance intelligence gathering with civil liberties.

These examples from Uganda and South Africa reflect a broader trend across many African countries, where surveillance laws are often utilized to prioritize criminal justice enforcement and national security at the expense of individual citizen rights. The lack of transparency and oversight in these processes exacerbates the issue. The cases cited illustrate the common approach to surveillance across the continent, highlighting the need for reforms that protect citizens' rights while catering to national security concerns.

Can you further explain how certain governments collect private information without a warrant?

The laws in many African countries allow for defense or intelligence agencies to tap into communication networks for surveillance and intelligence collection. Some nations mandate these agencies to first obtain a warrant from a judge or court. However, others allow government agencies to conduct surveillance without this requirement, either permitting them to seek a warrant retroactively, or bypassing the need for a warrant altogether. Often, even those nations mandating warrants lack provisions for proper judicial supervision of government surveillance activities. While requiring warrants, the laws don't explicitly grant supervisory authority to the judges or courts to oversee the surveillance process. This variance in legal requirements reflects differing approaches to the balance between state needs and citizen rights.

We know that digital technologies create large amounts of data that can be difficult for human teams of intelligence officers to properly monitor. What tools have you seen being used by government agencies in Africa to automate the monitoring process?

I haven't physically observed the specific surveillance tools in use, but my understanding is that they are rooted in common methods like geolocation tracking and social network monitoring. In African nations, SIM card registration is obligatory, linking personal data to national IDs. This integration of personal information enables comprehensive government surveillance across financial, social, and various other domains. With the national ID tied to the SIM card, authorities possess extensive data triangulating ones' communications record, bank account transaction history, and travel information. This amalgamation of data forms a holistic 360-degree surveillance framework, granting the government unparalleled access to mine citizen data across multiple aspects of their lives.

How, in your opinion, does that modify the relationship between the state and the citizen?

In my view, this governmental oversight yields extensive control over individuals. Possessing data on one's whereabouts, communications, and financial status grants unprecedented power. Designating someone as a "terrorist" based on surveillance data enables the freezing of their accounts and monitoring of associates, restricting their support network. Geolocation tracking provides insights into personal activities, acquaintances, and plans. If an individual is deemed to be oppositional to the government, then these surveillance mechanisms offer an all-encompassing insight into their life, amplifying government control over their actions and networks.

What steps can be taken to strike a balance between the potential benefits of surveillance and data collection technologies and the protection of individual rights and freedoms in Africa?

In terms of legal and policy development, progress has been evident with ongoing steps in law and policy formulation across many African nations. However, as we have seen, the mere existence of laws might not prompt change if enforcement mechanisms lack effectiveness. Presently, over thirty-eight out of fifty-four African countries boast data protection laws, a positive stride. Yet, these data protection laws often allow for exceptions that make it difficult to properly guarantee judicial oversight of law enforcement agencies' activities.

Having scrutinized various intelligence and surveillance laws in Africa, I perceive a need for alignment between these laws and broader data protection values and principles. The legal allowance for intelligence agencies to access and gather banking information, for example, contradicts the minimalist principles enshrined in data protection frameworks. Harmonizing criminal enforcement and intelligence laws with data protection frameworks is imperative to ensure congruence. Such alignment should fortify data protection principles while enabling national security preservation and law enforcement activities.

The objective isn't to hinder national security or impede the functions of criminal justice institutions but rather to ensure adherence to human rights standards and individual privacy protections. Striking a balance between these crucial aspects is essential, establishing a clear guideline where the protection of individual rights aligns with the mandates of maintaining national security and upholding law and order.

What would you say is the connection between power and technology in most African countries?

In my perspective, technology itself doesn't inherently grant power to the government; rather, it's the capacity to utilize technology effectively that confers influence. Across many African countries, technology adoption, particularly within government institutions, remains limited. Technological proficiency among public officials is sparse, constraining their ability to exploit its full potential.

Consider the example of Jumuiya Forums, where individuals utilized technology to bolster their exercise of civic rights. Government then endeavored to leverage their limited technological capabilities to monitor discourse on this platform and possibly penalize those expressing dissenting views. However, their proficiency in manipulating technology is circumscribed, prompting reliance on legal frameworks for control.

Even if a government dispatches a team of experts to manipulate technology for their benefit, a private individual might possess superior skills, potentially nullifying the government's efforts. Consequently, governments revert to leveraging laws, stipulating requirements such as demanding information for national security under the guise of legal authority. These laws pose formidable challenges regardless of an individual's technological acumen, compelling reliance on the involvement of the judiciary for recourse.

Presently, most African governments do not wield technology-related skills as a primary means to exercise authority. Instead, they rely on legislation, policy, and at times the coercive force of law enforcement agencies to intimidate dissidents. The utilization of advanced technologies to command authority is a facet that, at the moment, remains unexplored in these governance structures. Ultimate authority rests in the legal framework delineated by the state. Unless individuals find ways to reinterpret or contest these laws, often necessitating new legal avenues, the use of technology alone—as in the case of Jumuiya Forums—might not suffice to counteract governmental assertions of power.

Kwami, some time ago you founded the International Institute for ICT Journalism. Could you explain why you felt it was needed?

Around twenty years ago, as newsrooms in our region grappled with integrating technology, debates emerged about its impact. Questions arose on whether it would facilitate journalists' work and enhance journalistic standards. Our initiative aimed to aid journalists in navigating this transformative journey, especially considering the groundbreaking nature of technology during that period.

Our organization was established to train journalists in utilizing digital technology within newsrooms. This encompassed various aspects: empowering them in story development through technology, leveraging it for effective storytelling, understanding its application for online publishing, and grappling with ethical concerns in online content creation. Moreover, we aimed to elevate journalism's standards, recognizing its deep-rooted traditional aspects. The adoption of technology introduced novel approaches, particularly in managing fast-paced online breaking news, diverging from the traditional editorial scrutiny prior to publication. These facets prompted our institution's focus on capacity-building and research in this evolving landscape.

There have been reports of some governments in Africa using social media surveillance tools, alongside legal intimidation tactics, to monitor private citizens and quash dissent. Are you aware of any instances of this and do you know what tools are used?

Several surveillance technologies are increasingly prevalent in African countries. For instance, in Ghana, there's the Pegasus system, developed by an Israeli company, known for its capacity to monitor social media extensively. While the legal framework around these technologies remains ambiguous, existing use suggests that civil liberties might be adversely affected by such surveillance.

Apart from digital tools monitoring voice calls and social media, Chinese-made cameras are being installed in major cities across Ghana and other African nations. The concerns raised pertain to the storage location of the surveillance footage. It's unclear whether the videos are stored within the continent or in China. This lack of transparency poses significant challenges in comprehending the extent and implications of the deployed surveillance technologies.

This situation raises pertinent questions about the secrecy surrounding the deployment and its consequences. The absence of information regarding these technologies and their operational impact presents a pressing issue for comprehending the current surveillance landscape in Africa.

We know that AI-based tools are available that can crunch a lot of data generated by citizens and make predictions in terms of what individuals or populations may or may not do. Are you aware of any such predictive technologies in use in Africa?

Government involvement in such technologies lacks concrete evidence, though suspicions persist. For example, healthcare institutions may employ it for public health purposes, forecasting pandemics and related outbreaks. We know commercial entities utilize it for marketing purposes. These applications showcase its utilization in marketing and health sectors, indicating its potential varying uses, but the evidence regarding use by government remains inconclusive in this region. However, indications suggest a potential threat where governments may adopt a "Big Brother" role, amassing extensive information about citizens. This prospect raises concerns among individuals wary of governmental overreach. The use of AI as a tool to curtail civil liberties looms as a genuine possibility.

Consider the emergence of central bank digital currencies (CBDCs) like Nigeria's eNaira and Ghana's eCedi. These digital tools allow governments to control access to funds stored in digital wallets. This signifies a shift from physical cash to digital wallets, granting authorities the power to restrict citizens' access to their own money. Such technological advancements demonstrate how digital tools might impede citizens' freedom by enabling government control over financial assets, portraying a tangible example of the potential limitations posed by digital technology on personal autonomy.

Can you explain more about these digital currencies and provide more detail around the civil liberty issues involved?

The concept of CBDC replaces physical money like dollar bills or coins with a digital equivalent, stored in a digital wallet. Unlike cryptocurrencies that do not have central control, CBDCs are governed by the central bank or government, giving them authority over the digital currency. This control allows them to potentially regulate how citizens spend the digital currency. For instance, authorities could restrict specific expenditures, offering unprecedented control over individuals' financial activities. While this prospect remains somewhat speculative, concerns linger about the possible risks associated with CBDCs. Many oppose this technological advancement due to apprehensions about its adverse effects on citizen rights and autonomy, fearing potential government overreach and control.

Can you describe that pushback? What civil society organizations are involved in pushing back against the deployment of CBDCs in Africa?

Unfortunately, there's no pushback because this issue is only discussed in the realm of a few elites or experts in the area. It has not trickled down to a point that it will create a pushback. So there's a need for advocacy and there's a need for discussion around the issue. So currently there's no pushback and the issue is well under the radar of most civil society organizations for now.

This type of financial information, alongside other data from social media usage and geolocation tracking, could potentially be mined for predicting and perhaps preventing social and political unrest—which is a stated goal of both national governments and multilateral organizations operating in the region. What are your thoughts on that?

Starting in 2012, we've experimented with predictive tools for anticipating civil unrest. While it's an existing technology, managing its impact poses challenges. I advocate for establishing fundamental standards or rules governing its application. Codifying these guidelines can foster better conduct and practices when employing predictive tools to anticipate violence. This foundation could encourage responsible behavior and promote ethical practices in such scenarios.

In my view, many national governments lack the capacity and expertise needed for this task of creating standards. Therefore, the initiative should commence at an international level, led by organizations like the UN, which possess the necessary resources to formulate these best practices. Once developed, these standards should be adapted to suit local contexts through an inclusive and consultative process. By incorporating diverse perspectives, we can tailor these international guidelines to fit specific country scenarios, ensuring relevance and effectiveness in implementation. This approach allows us to leverage international bodies' expertise while ensuring local relevance through a collaborative and inclusive process.

These tools would both rely on, and generate new, data on the behavior of citizens in Africa. Who will own it?

I see the necessity for a nonexclusive data ownership structure. Establishing such a system is an intricate task, albeit crucial. I emphasize the significance of localization. Data gathered about individuals from places like Ghana, Nigeria, Gambia, or Liberia should grant primary ownership to those individuals. In essence, data pertaining to oneself should be one's own possession. Subsequently, an opt-in framework could allow individuals to contribute their data for collective purposes. Presently, social media corporations possess, and base their business models on, the data they accumulate.

Should governments collect data, I advocate for a model where individuals retain ownership of their data and selectively participate in certain data-sharing scenarios. I envision a flexible and evolving approach. While this notion might seem somewhat idealistic, it represents my perspective on the direction we should take.

What institutions and legal mechanisms do you foresee that could potentially guarantee, or manage, that right to data and allow citizens to choose to have their data "opted-in" and used for different purposes by the state or multilateral organizations?

I think this issue is very important. For me, if you look at any legal regime, the constitution sits on top. We have to advocate for some of these provisions to be written into constitutions when there are opportunities for reviews. Beyond the constitution, you may want to look at some freedom of information laws that actually make provisions for this kind of protection.

So a freedom of information law that allows citizens to view what kind of data governments, companies, and international organizations are collecting about them and what they are doing with it?

Yes. Current freedom of information provisions are centered on governments. So if I want information about the Ministry of Defense, for example, I apply for that and under the freedom of information law that information is released to me. Since we already have this law in place, rather than create a new one it can be expanded to make provision for the release of that data and the contents that I just described, data that a government institution or intergovernmental actor has collected.

Chapter 7
Digitized Biographies

How do you know what sort of people your subjects are consorting with? This was the question vexing Russian Tsar Nicholas I in 1826. In response, he created the Third Department with the express task of secretly monitoring key individuals and their social relations. Historian Kees Boterbloem at the University of South Florida writes that the Third Department was especially notable for its monitoring of Russians' cultural lives and intellectual ties. Members of the Russian intelligentsia were singled out and their relations mapped and investigated. Foreign influences connected to the European Revolutions came to be seen as particularly dangerous. Even a young Dostoyevsky was targeted and banished to hard labor in Siberia for a time. Indeed, the tsar knew all too well that it was the intellectuals who could most successfully "ponder a change in Russia's governance and social organization."[1]

According to criminal justice historians Mark Jones and Peter Johnstone, the absolute monarch used the Third Department to "spy on and terrorize people perceived as unfriendly to the monarchy." The department, they note, made Nicholas's control over the people all the more oppressive and "complete."[2] Former British intelligence officer and academic Peter Squire offers more context. He considers that Nicholas created the Third Department in response to the failure of earlier police systems, which were deemed to be corrupt and incompetent by many in government. More importantly, these police systems were also inefficient, as they had not warned the tsar in time of the Decembrist Revolt of 1825.[3] Squire points out that from the tsar's perspective, the revolt had demonstrated an urgent need to re-establish law and order as autocratic rule was being menaced by "changes in social thought

---

[1] Boterbloem, Kees (2013) *A History of Russia and Its Empire: From Mikhail Romanov to Vladimir Putin*, Rowman and Littlefield, p 80.
[2] Jones, Mark and Peter Johnstone (2010) *History of Criminal Justice*, 4th ed., Anderson, p 255.
[3] Squire, Peter (1968) *The Third Department: The Establishment and Practices of the Political Police in the Russia of Nicholas I*, Cambridge University Press.

brought about by the growing success of revolutionary movements abroad and their influence on internal politics at home."[4]

These foreign influences were of course compounded by a number of factors in Russia. Nicolas' succession to the throne was itself marred by uncertainty (and disputed by the Decembrists), and there was widespread social unrest throughout the Empire. This created the perfect conditions for the Third Department to grow in influence and size. Olga Semukhina and K. Michael Reynolds, criminologists at Marquette University and the University of Central Florida, respectively, believe that, while the Third Department's original mission was to protect the monarchy from revolt, it quickly grew to become the most powerful government office in all of Russia. They explain that even though it was structured separately from the Ministry of the Interior (i.e., the police), its influence grew so that it oversaw all the ministry's work. Indeed, the Third Department's *Corps de Gendarmes* were charged with setting a moral example for all branches of the imperial government. Over time, the *Gendarmes* came to think of themselves as above the law, and often outright replaced the role of the regular police. As may be expected, abuse and corruption increased concomitantly with their power. They were also notorious for their wanton use of violence.[5]

The network of Third Department agents was vast and they became a powerful tool in the hands of the tsar, yet the real innovation—and the one that concerns us most here—was in their modus operandi. The main novelty was that they were able to systematically investigate the private lives and social networks of ordinary Russian citizens, as well as individuals working in other branches of the government, to a degree and with a zeal not seen before. It is not difficult to see in the Third Department's practices of methodically filing and organizing relational information on citizens a clear precursor to those of the Soviet Union's Committee for State Security, or KGB. Yet, the tsar and the Russians were by no means the only ones experimenting with novel ways to politically categorize persons based on their relational data.

In Maoist China (1949–1976) the Dang'an, or "archived record," was a file that contained large amounts of information on Chinese citizens in urban

---

[4] Squire, Peter S. (1960) "Nicholas I and the Problem of Internal Security in Russia in 1826," *The Slavonic and East European Review*, 38/91, 431–458, p 431–432.

[5] Semukhina, Olga and K. Michael Reynolds (2013) *Understanding the Modern Russian Police*, Taylor and Francis, p 9.

centers. It grew during elementary school, high school, and with subsequent employers—and was complete only when the eulogy was added. The file contained information on things like education, employment, notable achievements, and criminal convictions, but also on relational factors like family background, club/society memberships, and political group activity. The Dang'an affected the lives of all urban citizens, determining job prospects and promotions as employers typically reviewed an applicant's file before recruiting. Political evaluations took on special importance for those seeking employment as government officials, teachers, or academics, and could affect their career prospects and ability to travel. Jie Yang, anthropology professor at Simon Fraser University, considers the Dang'an to be a central pillar of Maoist power.

> The Dang'an reveals the inner, hidden bureaucratic workings of the state on the individual ... Scrutinizing and entextualizing the attitudes, performances and everyday existence of urban Chinese citizens, the Dang'an was the basic socialist database authorized by the communist party, the only legitimate hermeneutic authority and a central domain for the production and reproduction of state power. It was the site at which life and society were fused in politics. The rule of the Dang'an represents the intimate involvement of the state in people's lives, and constitutes the subjective and psychic dynamics through which power mobilizes and constructs sets of effects within the body and the unconscious of the subject. Such subjective and psychic dynamics sustain the state as a powerful and inescapable social reality.[6]

The Dang'an introduced what Yang describes as a form of "technoscientific administration," through which the governing of people is transformed into a "governing of things," that lasted well beyond the Mao era. The case of Tang Guoji illustrates this well. Tang had graduated with good grades from teachers' college in 1983, but despite high demand, had been unable to find work as a teacher for some twenty years, suffering inexplicable personal hardships and discrimination. Despite being a well-known writer, he worked in a school canteen. Then, in 2002 the local education bureau asked him to deal with some paperwork relating to his "mental disability." Upon investigation

---

[6] Yang, Jie (2011) "The Politics of the Dang'an: Specialization, Spatialization, and Neoliberal Governmentality in China," *Anthropological Quarterly*, 84/2, 507–533, p 508.

he discovered that he was officially labeled as mentally ill for decades. A sympathizer in the bureau anonymously provided him with the documentation that was the source of his difficulties—records in his Dang'an originating from an erroneous assessment by one of his professors at university. Yang notes that in the case of Tang Guoji, and likely many others, "the Dang'an 'became' the person."[7]

A key innovation here, like with the Third Department, is that the state in this way can have a relation with "the file" and not with the person. This makes it easier for the state, as matters can be reduced to simplified categories such as conspirator versus loyal, mentally ill versus sane, but it leaves the actual person out in the cold. One can hardly expect to defend themselves, as Dostoyevsky found when he responded to charges of reading works critical of Russia by saying he only had a literary interest. The file is the evidence. The file can even work against you without you knowing it, as in Tang Guoji's case.

While the state offloads any inefficiencies that come with having to deal with the nuances of actual human experience, citizens on the other hand are burdened with a wide array of additional anxieties. Yang paints a picture of the Dang'an record as "an object of constant speculation, rumor, and fear, both hallucinatory and spectral."[8] Indeed, by "entextualizing" the person, the state can transform a human life narrative into snippets devoid of context. One is lifted out of their real interactional setting, and reduced to a kind of static node in a likewise static network of other people, social groups, and institutions. Furthermore, the nature of the relationship between these nodes is often based upon spurious, biased, and incomplete assessments. This leaves plenty of scope for abuse of power and recording misinformation as fact, and generates fear alongside compliance.

Another example of this process can be found in twentieth-century United States. Following the Russian communist revolution in 1917, the success of leftist ideologies in Europe, and a growing and disgruntled labor force at home, government and business leaders were nervous about the potential rise of Bolshevism in the United States. This apprehension was amplified with the formation of the Communist Party of the United States in 1919. William Walker, professor of history at Chestnut Hill College, describes the political climate of that year as characterized by labor strikes, militant

---

[7] Ibid, p 510.
[8] Ibid, p 512.

bombings, and race riots. Many in the press and Congress saw these as the potential first sparks of a broader socialist revolution, and increased calls to "preserve the nation and the American way of life."[9]

This first "Red Scare" led then Attorney General Alexander Mitchell Palmer to create a General Intelligence Unit within the Department of Justice. He put a young and eager J. Edgar Hoover in charge. The subsequent "Palmer Raids" resulted in the detention and deportation of hundreds of foreign-born radicals without due process. Elected officials that identified as socialists were expelled from office. Palmer also advocated for a peacetime version of the 1918 Sedition Act, citing dangerous foreign influences on American values. During this time, which has been described by historians as "the federalization of political surveillance," overt and covert methods to identify one's social relations were introduced into the state's arsenal. Overt methods included indexing members of unions, clubs, and associations, subscribers to radical newspapers, and owners of cars parked at meetings and speeches. Covert methods included intercepting mail, shadowing people, searching offices without warrants, and bugging conversations.[10]

The scare eventually abated but left a legacy that would rear its head again throughout US history. The second Red Scare from 1947 and 1957 was associated with Senator Joseph McCarthy's crusade against communists in government. This led to the creation of the federal employee loyalty program (formalized in 1947). The program sought to root out communists believed to be manipulating United States policy in favor of the Soviets. Loyalty screenings of over five million employees resulted in approximately 2,700 dismissals and over 12,000 resignations. According to Landon Storrs, political historian at the University of Iowa, the program was not only about targeting communists, but also stemmed from conservatives' unease over progressive political reforms launched since the New Deal in the previous decade. The scare, according to her, served to ultimately stifle political debate and dampen the discussion of social democratic ideas—putting constraints on the development of the American welfare state to this day.[11]

Connected to this second scare, and somewhat less known, was the Internal Security Act of 1950. While its provisions were abolished by the early

---

[9] Walker, William (2011) *McCarthyism and the Red Scare: A Reference Guide*, ABC-CLIO, p 6.

[10] See Schmidt, Regin (2000) *Red Scare: FBI and the Origins of Anticommunism in the United States, 1919–1943*, Museum Tusculanum Press, p 362.

[11] Storrs, Landon (2012) *The Second Red Scare and the Unmaking of the New Deal Left*, Princeton University Press, p 13.

1970s, the act (which was passed despite President Harry Truman's veto), introduced novel abilities for the state to compose political narratives on its citizens. The law made it mandatory for members of communist and other radical organizations to register with the Attorney General's office. A Subversive Activities Control Board was also created with the mandate to investigate those who might be associated with these organizations, or were otherwise suspected of promoting radical ideas, but had neglected to register. Being on this list, alone, was an indication of guilt. The intentions of the individual member were assumed to be the same as the intentions of the association of which they were a part. This made people liable for prosecution based solely on their membership to a group.[12] Again, like for Dostoyevsky in Russia, the file is the evidence. Finally, it gave the federal government authority to arrest a person without a trial if there was reason to believe that this person may engage in *future* acts of treason, legally foreshadowing preventive justice approaches of more recent years.

In each of these three historical cases—the creation of the Third Department in Tsarist Russia, the establishment of the Dang'an in Maoist China, and the Red Scare initiatives of both postwar periods in the United States—we see the same basic development in the history of state–society relations. The key novelty is the introduction of a storytelling ability that the state develops in lieu of its citizens. This story is "composed" by designated and specialized state officials, and codified according to classifications that are generated by yet other officials and policymakers that operate at higher levels. The result is a state-owned political prosopography that describes one's connections to groups, other people, institutions, and ideas.

The term prosopography derives from the Greek *prosopopeia*, which in turn comes from *prósopon* "person" and *poiéin* "to make." In sum, to make a person. In classical rhetoric, prosopopeia was a technique in which one person would impersonate another, either dead or entirely fictional, and speak as if they were that person. It can be argued that the files crafted in nineteenth-century Imperial Russia, in twentieth-century Red Scare United States, or for the Dang'an in Maoist China in the second half of the twentieth century were in fact prosopographies, as they spoke for that person.

The foundations were thus laid for the expansion of this technique in more contemporary times. Three new and interrelated state functions were

---

[12] See Ybarra, Michael (2004) *Washington Gone Crazy: Senator Pat McCarran and the Great American Communist Hunt*, Steerforth Publishing.

introduced that would allow the creation, and automatic updating, of digitized social biographies for all citizens: 1) the use of binary categories (i.e., loyal/disloyal) as exhaustively representative of a person's reality, incidentally paving the way for later rounds of digitalization of the process; 2) the establishment of the association fallacy as a legitimate legal instrument, in which the stated thoughts and actions of the group are considered identical to those of each of its members; and 3) the pioneering of systemized and standardized approaches to the collection of large amounts of sociological data about citizens. Each of these innovations draws upon similar logics to those we saw at work in previous chapters that considered state-sponsored initiatives to collect physiological and psychological data. The ascription of a particular quality by association, for example, was also found to be at the root of modern algorithmic techniques that assign meaning to an utterance or facial expression based on association to a broader category of utterances and expressions.

Similarly to state programs in physiological and psychological data collection, a major leap in scale occurs with the introduction of digital technologies. Automation in data collection revolutionizes the process of creating state-managed prosopographies, or the ever-evolving "files" that describe one's social, political, and ideological relations. In particular, the arrival of modern telecommunications technology and eventually the internet radically increases the amount of information about peoples' relations that can be automatically gathered. Consider the tales told by a person's phone call, texting, and email history, or the stories that can be weaved out of one's browsing activity (i.e., "the websites you visit, social platforms you use, searches you perform, and content you consume").[13] In some ways, we may consider this new type of digital fingerprint to be superseding the previous one reviewed in chapter 3.

One of the earlier attempts to harness this newly available digital data was called ThinThread. Developed by a US National Security Agency (NSA) team in the late 1990s, it had the capacity to collate vast amounts of telecommunications data without violating US privacy laws. This was due to its ability to automatically separate US-related communications from international ones. US data were encrypted via an anonymizing feature to respect citizens' privacy. The program then used advanced automated methods to

---

[13] Kessler, Daniel (2018) "This is Your Digital Fingerprint," *The Mozilla Blog*, July 26, https://blog.mozilla.org/privacy-security/this-is-your-digital-fingerprint/.

sort through these mountains of phone and email communications (including anonymized US ones) and detect any suspicious activity.[14] It could, for example, establish relationships between an individual and others already on criminal watchlists. If a pattern looked suspicious enough the system would indicate that a warrant was justified. Only once a warrant was obtained could the US records be decrypted.[15]

ThinThread was pivotal to the history of automated sociological data collection because it overcame two important engineering challenges. First, at the time, the NSA was accumulating far more data than it could manage. Analysts at the agency were struggling to extract useful leads from the vast amounts of information resulting from the rapid rise in digital communications, in particular voice and text communication conducted over the internet and by cell phones. Second, many international criminal actors were increasingly in contact with US citizens, which prohibited the NSA from monitoring those calls. ThinThread leaped over both these hurdles at once by taking humans out of the loop and reducing data to metadata. Metadata is essentially data *about* data; it includes, for example, all the records of a phone conversation (who called whom, from and to where geographically, at what time, and for how long), but not what is said. By having a machine map out the social networks in the metadata, there was no need for a government official—doubly bound by law and human cognition—to listen in on actual conversations.[16]

By mid 2001, ThinThread was shut down in favor of another, far larger, NSA initiative with similar objectives called Trailblazer. Then, in 2005, Trailblazer was replaced by yet another program called Turbulence. By now there were over one billion people using the internet daily, and communications traffic was becoming harder to keep up with. Turbulence was designed to address this challenge in steps, and comprised a suite of subprograms. The goals of these were to map "social networks based on intercepted

---

[14] In addition to communication data, the program could also analyze other sources of information like financial transactions and travel records.

[15] In his memoir, General Michael Hayden, then NSA director, says that despite the use of encryption the program was discontinued because it was deemed illegal under US law at the time. See Hayden, Michael (2017) *Playing to the Edge: American Intelligence in the Age of Terror*, Penguin. For more context, see Whittaker, Zack (2015) "Drowned in Data: Whistle-Blowers Speak of NSA's 'Largest Failure,'" *ZDNet*, November 20; and Gorman, Siobhan (2006) "NSA Rejected System that Sifted Phone Data Legally," *The Baltimore Sun*, May 18.

[16] See chapter 7, "Ministries of Truth," in Mueller, Tom (2020) *Crisis of Conscience: Whistleblowing in an Age of Fraud*, Atlantic Books.

communications," embed "technology on networks to collect data," and search for "patterns across hundreds of NSA databases."[17]

One element that remained constant throughout various iterations was the use of communications metadata for social network analysis. The innovative metadata database introduced with ThinThread was, in fact, continually scaled up to contain larger and larger amounts of phone call and related telecommunication records, both domestic and international.[18] This database, still in use, eventually became known as MAINWAY. It is incredibly valuable. Mathematician and cybersecurity expert at Tufts University, Susan Landau, puts it quite succinctly: "Who you call, and who they call. If you can track that, you know exactly what is happening—you don't need the content."[19]

Landau is correct. Metadata is perhaps even more valuable than content because it is structured. It is clear cut, and therefore ideal for software to sort through. A call is either made or not made, just like a doorbell is either rung or not rung. You cannot plausibly deny ringing it. Transcripts of telephone or email conversations are unstructured data: emotional, imprecise, and vague. Unstructured data can only be transformed into structured data via tools like natural language processing (NLP) software. In chapter 5 we saw how these can be inaccurate in myriad ways. Digitalization will always approximate semantic meaning. Focusing on solid, structured metadata was the ThinThread team's main insight. Metadata is what made ThinThread work so well.

Yet that team also had a second insight. It was understood that metadata can reveal a lot of private information, and that the state only has the right to investigate this if there is evidence of criminal activity. Chris Berg, associate professor at RMIT University, would agree. In his book *The Classical Liberal Case for Privacy in a World of Surveillance and Technological Change*, he reminds us that governmental breaches of our privacy are only justified when wrongdoing is involved.[20] Indeed, this is the logic behind the legal practice of establishing "probable cause" before issuing a search warrant in

---

[17] Gorman, Siobhan (2007) "Costly NSA Initiative Has a Shaky Takeoff," *The Baltimore Sun*, February 11.

[18] For narratives on the evolution of this type of intelligence gathering, see Risen, James (2014) *Pay Any Price: Greed, Power, and Endless War*, Houghton Mifflin Harcourt; and Jeffreys-Jones, Rhodri (2017) *We Know All About You: The Story of Surveillance in Britain and America*, Oxford University Press.

[19] Mayer, Jane (2013) "What's the Matter with Metadata?" *The New Yorker*, June 6.

[20] Berg, Chris (2018) *The Classical Liberal Case for Privacy in a World of Surveillance and Technological Change*, Springer.

the US. This is also the logic that the NSA followed when they devised a way for the government to gain actionable knowledge from citizens' metadata, without actually knowing it. It could be known only after probable cause was established and judicial approval obtained.

What the NSA at the time did not foresee was that this would turn out to be an unnecessary precaution. The privacy protection feature installed for US citizens would soon be taken out of newer versions of the database.[21] In MAINWAY, US-related communications are no longer encrypted (names of individuals are not included, but telephone numbers are, which can be easily linked to a name). Fueled by the security perturbations that gripped the nation in the wake of the Twin Towers' collapse, a portion of the political and legal establishment, and to a degree society at large, simply began to depart from the principle of probable cause in the case of metadata. The argument was made that this information was to be considered public and not personal. It was the equivalent of looking at what is written on the outside of an envelope containing a letter—just functional, transactional, businesslike information. Dianne Feinstein, chair of the Senate Select Committee on Intelligence from 2009 to 2015, would clarify that the "courts have consistently recognized that there is no reasonable expectation of privacy in this type of metadata information."[22]

Evidence of wrongdoing would no longer be needed for the government to know whom citizens are calling, from where, how long, and with what frequency. With that ship sailed, and the technology in place, the state could now begin composing individualized social biographies on US citizens (or rather, on their phone numbers) using metadata.[23] This represents

---

[21] Mayer, Jane (2011) "The Secret Sharer: Is Thomas Drake an Enemy of the State?" *The New Yorker*, May 23.

[22] Mayer, "What's the Matter with Metadata?"

[23] In some cases, US citizens' content data—what is written in text messages and emails, for example—is analyzed alongside the metadata. Starting in 2007 a new generation of programs emerged with the ability to automatically collect and store the content of Americans' written cross-border electronic communications (into and out of the US), so long as this content contains any of a number of keywords, or "selectors," about a target. A target is a foreign suspect citizen. Apparently, as a large portion of electronic communications do cross international borders, and as the US monitors a high number of foreign targets, this creates a wider net for gathering US-related content than commonly imagined. For details on content data collection processes see Savage, Charlie (2013) "NSA Said to Search Content of Messages to and from US," *The New York Times*, August 8; Gellman, Barton and Ashkan Soltani (2013) "NSA Collects Millions of E-mail Address Books Globally," *Washington Post*, October 14; Savage, Charlie et al. (2013) "NSA Said to Tap Google and Yahoo Abroad," *The New York Times*, October 30; MacAskill, Ewan et al. (2013) "GCHQ Taps Fiber-optic Cables for Secret Access to World's Communications," *The Guardian*, June 21; and Gellman, Barton and Ashkan Soltani (2013) "NSA Infiltrates Links to Yahoo, Google Data Centers Worldwide, Snowden Documents Say," *The Washington Post*, October 30.

a massive step forward in the development of political automation since these prosopographic files, which contain detailed descriptions of a person's social, professional, religious, and political relations, are put together with little to no human supervision. Indeed, NSA software technologies automatically sort and classify data for social network and risk analysis. George Lucas, research professor at the University of Notre Dame's Reilly Center for Science, Technology, and Values and author of *Ethics and Cyber Warfare*, notes how one program called Treasure Map "displays the data in patterns resembling a constellation or mandala of intricate communication nodes," and can "review the connections and attempt to discern meaningful patterns within them."[24]

Should the American public have been informed of these developments? Could they have? Lucas offers an intriguing and balanced reflection on this question. He asks whether it was even a reasonable expectation for the US government to have sought "collective informed consent to a policy of cyber surveillance whose technological sophistication and scope stagger the imagination, and whose implications neither we nor those implementing the policy can possibly foresee?" As a matter of fact:

> Not only do we (that is, the collective body politic) lack the technological sophistication to fully appreciate all the dimensions involved in the workings of this policy, but ... we may need to be deliberately blind to some of the features of our own surveillance, lest we (the protected) and those seeking to harm us (criminals, terrorists, agents of adversarial nations) begin to alter our respective behaviors in response.

Lucas argues that full public consent is essentially out of reach, since the people being surveilled are technically too ill-equipped to correctly weigh in on the matter—much like patients can't be expected to understand all the details of a medical treatment path prescribed by a medical professional. Knowing too much may even be counterproductive to the patient's health, as it may alter behavior in dangerous ways. Therefore, Lucas proposes a midway solution. Government surveillance programs, he says, should still

---

[24] Lucas, George (2016) *Ethics and Cyber Warfare: The Quest for Responsible Security in the Age of Digital Warfare*, Oxford University Press, p 146. It is useful to note that these programs are often managed in cooperation with intelligence agencies in other countries, in particular the UK Government Communications Headquarters (GCHQ) and others in the Five Eye intelligence alliance (US, UK, Canada, Australia, and New Zealand). For a review of the evolution of this international collaboration see Lemieux, Frédéric (2018) *Intelligence and State Surveillance in Modern Societies: An International Perspective*, Emerald Publishing.

seek to inform, and to obtain voluntary consent from the subjects of security surveillance, [but simultaneously] *making it clear that they must be willing to remain ignorant of certain features of the program for the sake of its effectiveness.* That is, certain procedural details . . . will remain secret, but the general operations (undercover police work, big-data surveillance, and so on) should be disclosed, and the nature of the risks to privacy and other basic rights generally entailed should be fully divulged to the affected parties, or to those on whose behalf the policies are being carried out.[25]

It is a good argument. So why wasn't the public informed even of the general risks/benefits involved? It is a fact that very little if any level of detail was divulged. Typically, investigative journalists—often working with material provided by whistleblowers—did that. One explanation may be that there is a deeper cultural shift occurring below the surface of public discourse that has enabled the introduction of these capacities without the need to gain consent. We are witnessing an altogether new collective attitude toward the very notion of privacy. Citizens by and large seem to find surveillance agreeable. Randolph Lewis, associate professor of American studies at the University of Texas, conjures the image of a "Funopticon" (as opposed to Jeremy Bentham's grimmer panopticon) to describe the "increasingly playful surveillance culture of the twenty-first century." Our everyday media is infused with surveillance tools that people are encouraged to "play" with, relentlessly "monitoring, sorting, and archiving" behavior in the guise of entertainment.[26] It should come as no surprise, then, that if the government engages in a measure of its own monitoring, sorting, and archiving, it is seen as altogether acceptable by much of the population.

The fact is that many have become so accustomed to sharing intimate details of their lives (on social media for example) that a kind of privacy fatigue has set in. It is hard to keep things private in an era of cheap and quick self-documenting. It becomes hard even to *imagine* things can or should be private. Within this general culture of oversharing, government surveillance can come to be seen as relatively trivial. Furthermore, just as citizens are passive consumers of the tech companies' surveillance, so too there is no real expectation of shared governance for the political kind. In the Funopticon, Lewis points out, we have created a culture where surveillance systems feel

---

[25] Lucas, *Ethics and Cyber Warfare*, p 149–151, emphasis added.
[26] Lewis, Randolph (2017) *Under Surveillance: Being Watched in Modern America*, University of Texas Press, p 54, 65.

"nurturing and joyful," forming a "beautiful connective tissue that brings us together in new and exciting ways." We have become more accepting of the surveillance bubble; whether in "the form of a CCTV camera, a Facebook page, or a Visa statement, surveillance is the one place where we know that our lives will register and resonate." Being under surveillance allows people to say with certainty: "We made a mark. We were here. We mattered. Just check the file."[27]

The complication is that this is not solely a matter of privacy. As discussed at the beginning of this chapter when reviewing historical approaches to sociological data collection like the Russian Third Department or the Chinese Dang'an, the danger is that the state-generated file can come to replace the actual person in ways that are consequential to that person's political life. Elliot Cohen, professor of philosophy at Indian River State College and author of two books on mass surveillance, is correct to note that "the danger goes beyond the obvious abridgment of privacy," the real danger is in "opening up the possibility of creating false or misleading associations with persons with whom one may not have had any substantive relationship, for example, a Facebook 'friend' whom one does not really know."[28]

How this danger will be managed, or at least mitigated, by citizens eager to contribute to the political life of their polity will be a main issue for democracies going forward—particularly as more and more public decision-making functions are taken over by algorithmic technologies that rely on data contained in the digitized social biographic files. Without having to know too much about the technology itself (which would, as Lucas correctly points out, compromise the integrity of the system by allowing criminals and adversarial nations to game it), citizens may have legitimate transparency and accountability questions. For example: How are my social relations being defined? What parameters govern definitions of risk? What are the public deliberation processes that we, or our representatives with security clearances, may participate in to define these things? While it will not be easy to find a balance between what can be debated publicly and what cannot (for security reasons), these are some examples of the types of questions that may need to be addressed for the public to authentically grant informed consent to a policy.

---

[27] Ibid, p 77.
[28] Cohen, Elliot (2014) *Technology of Oppression: Preserving Freedom and Dignity in an Age of Mass, Warrantless Surveillance*, Palgrave, p 25; see also Cohen, Elliot (2010) *Mass Surveillance and State Control: The Total Information Awareness Project*, Palgrave.

While in the US surveillance programs tend to come to the attention of the public via whistleblowers, in China surveillance programs are widely promoted by the government itself. The best known of these is the Social Credit System (SCS). Min Jiang, professor of communication studies at the University of North Carolina at Charlotte, provides us with a brief review of the system's genesis. Perhaps unsurprisingly, she identifies its roots in the previously discussed Dang'an—which is still in operation to this day, running parallel to the SCS. She recalls that the first official use of the term "social credit system" was in 2002 by then-President Jiang Zemin in his annual report to the Party Congress. This initial version sought to largely replicate the financial credit score systems that were being used in the West. It was not until 2014 that the State Council, the chief administrative authority in China, extended the concept to embrace non-financial activities too, like civil court judgments. Then, in 2019, China's highest internet regulatory body, the Cyberspace Administration of China, expanded the concept once more to include anything one buys or says online.[29]

Today, the SCS keeps tabs on a wide variety of aspects of citizens' social life, including their finances, purchases, grades at school, performance at work, forms of leisure, health records, and so on. In sum, anything that leaves a physical or digital footprint that can be traced and siphoned off. Amy Dobson and Karen Li Xan Wong at Curtin University in Australia explain that from the perspective of the Chinese government, the primary purpose of the SCS is to enhance the levels of "trust" in society. Trustworthiness, they explain, is considered one of the highest virtues in Chinese society, while dishonesty is viewed as the root cause of many societal ills. From this point of view, utilizing digital technology to reward honest, trustworthy, and virtuous citizens (while punishing dishonest, corrupt, and deceptive ones) seems like an obvious solution to the public moral decay many government authorities perceive as occurring in modern Chinese society. Digital tools are just one more way to help create a "virtuous state of social harmony in China."[30]

The trouble is that this solution may come with hidden complications, as easy fixes often do. For some scholars, like Liav Orgad and Wessel Reijers,

---

[29] Jiang, Min (2020) "A Brief Prehistory of China's Social Credit System," *Communication & the Public*, 5/3–4, 93–98, p 93.

[30] Dobson, Amy and Karen Li Xan Wong (2019) "We're Just Data: Exploring China's Social Credit System in Relation to Digital Platform Ratings Cultures in Westernised Democracies," *Global Media and China*, 4/2, 220–232, p 221.

both with the European University Institute, the social harmony achieved comes at a high cost to individual liberty. They point out that:

> China's Social Credit System is a unique case as it represents one of the most ambitious attempts in history to use socio-technical means to produce "perfect citizens." It demonstrates not only how new technologies transform citizenship values and institutions, but also indicates future directions of citizenship governance that implement fundamentally different conceptions of freedom, privacy, and due process, and undermine one of the most significant achievements of the Enlightenment—the Kantian rooted idea that human beings should be treated as an end in themselves, and not merely as a means to achieve public goods.[31]

It is important to caution that the position above considers developments in Chinese society within value frameworks that have sprung out of Western society, such as the Enlightenment.[32] From this Western perspective, observers may be concerned and fear the SCS model spreading to other societies, both non-democratic nations around the globe and democratic ones in the Kantian heartlands of Europe.

This fear has fueled depictions of the SCS as a singular state-run panopticon uniformly administered throughout the country. That vision is somewhat inexact. There are, in fact, a variety of commercial and government versions deployed in different ways. Indeed, since the program was announced a somewhat fragmented system has developed. The Mercator Institute for China Studies (MERICS) reports that pilot projects were started in select cities to test the system, and although they operated according to a central guidance, they were all implemented differently according to local needs and priorities. This has led to the existence of multiple versions of the SCS across different regions, cities, and provinces. Even the logic through which points are assigned or deducted, leading to individuals being placed on a black list (bad) or a red list (good), differs depending on location. Additionally, each

---

[31] Orgad, Liav and Wessel Reijers (2020) "How to Make the Perfect Citizen? Lessons from China's Model of Social Credit System," *Robert Schuman Centre for Advanced Studies*, Research Paper No. RSCAS 2020/28, p 2.

[32] To the average Chinese citizen and public official, however, the idea that humans are ends in themselves may appear quite alien. Historically, the individual in China has always been seen to exist primarily within a dynamic web of horizontal relations and vertical responsibilities. Consequently, many citizens in China seem to approve of the SCS. See Kostka, Genia (2019) "China's Social Credit Systems and Public Opinion: Explaining High Levels of Approval," *New Media and Society*, 21/7, 1565–1593.

location may have several and changing red and black lists, depending on the different aspects of life local authorities prefer to focus on.[33]

This leads to a system that does not always make much sense. In the version implemented in the city of Zhengzhou, for example, all personnel working in hospitals handling Covid-19 patients were automatically blacklisted, attributing low "trustworthiness" to people who were essentially just doing their job. The system of punishments and rewards does not always seem proportionate either. There are examples of people banned from public transport for smoking or prohibited from buying plane tickets for unpaid fines.[34] The impression one gets is of a collection of disparate systems manned by well-meaning but small-minded bureaucrats, intent on wielding this new tool for the common good, but quite frankly being overwhelmed by its awesome power and in the meantime creating a lot of frustration for regular people.

China's neighbor India has also embarked upon an ambitious program of sociological data collection that can give us further insight into the evolving global dynamics of political automation. In 2009, a project known as Aadhaar was launched to centralize information about the nation's billion-plus populace. In it, a 12-digit number was assigned to each citizen following the collection of their demographic and biometric data, including fingerprints and iris scans. Indian authorities vaunted the program as a method for the poor and the undocumented to better access government services. Officially, Aadhaar was "a strategic policy tool for social and financial inclusion" that aimed to reform the public sector and to curtail corruption by allowing direct access to welfare benefits. In practice, however, it has been the subject of several controversies, including fears of privacy violations and accusations that a hidden purpose was to identify and deport illegal immigrants (using the welfare delivery intention as a smokescreen).[35]

---

[33] See Donelly, Drew, "An Introduction to the China Social Credit System," *Horizons*, accessed December 11, 2023, https://nhglobalpartners.com/china-social-credit-system-explained/ ; and Drinhausen, Katja and Vincent Brussee (2021) "China's Social Credit System in 2021: From Fragmentation Towards Integration," *Mercator Institute for China Studies (MERICS)*.

[34] See Adelmant, Victoria (2021) "Social Credit in China: Looking Beyond the 'Black Mirror' Nightmare," *Center for Human Rights and Global Justice*, April 20, https://chrgj.org/2021/04/20/social-credit-in-china-looking-beyond-the-black-mirror-nightmare/; and Backer, Larry Catá (2019) "China's Social Credit System: Data-Driven Governance for a 'New Era,'" *Current History*, 9, 209–214.

[35] Shahin, Saif and Pei Zheng (2020) "Big Data and the Illusion of Choice: Comparing the Evolution of India's Aadhaar and China's Social Credit System as Technosocial Discourses," *Social Science Computer Review*, 38/1, 25–41, p 28; see also Sathe, Gopal (2019) "Hacking Democracy: How Stolen Aadhaar Data Of Nearly 10 Cr Voters Was Used To Delete People From Electoral Rolls,"

DIGITIZED BIOGRAPHIES 129

Payal Arora, professor and digital anthropologist at Erasmus University Rotterdam, also questions the benevolent motives of the project, noting that what started as a voluntary program became de facto mandatory in 2012—when various social, governmental, and financial services were denied to those who refused to register.[36] This was challenged in the Supreme Court of India, which ruled that registration should not be mandated and neither should an identification number be required for certain services such as banking. Nonetheless, authorities were able to effectively circumvent the rulings, and by 2017 there were 1.12 billion people registered on Aadhaar, nearly 99 percent of India's entire adult population.[37]

In parallel to the development of Aadhaar, the Indian government also rolled out four interlinked digital surveillance initiatives: CMS, NETRA, NATGRID, and AASMA. The CMS, or Centralized Monitoring System, launched between 2009 and 2013, was motivated in part by the November 2008 terrorist attacks in Mumbai. The CMS sought to strengthen India's internal security structure. According to the Internet Freedom Foundation (IFF), an Indian non-governmental organization that advocates for digital rights, the main innovation introduced with the CMS is that it automates interception of telecommunications (including SMS, social media messaging, and phone calls) without having to ask permission from the individual telecom service providers (TSPs) as was previously required.[38] NATGRID, or the National Intelligence Grid, was also announced in 2009. Its aim is to facilitate better coordination between law enforcement and intelligence agencies and provide real-time information in order to combat crime and national security threats. The IFF described NATGRID as "an integrated IT solution" that permits government agencies "to access data gathered from various databases such as credit and debit cards, tax, telecom, immigration,

---

HuffPost, April 19, www.huffpost.com/archive/in/entry/hacking-democracy-stolen-aadhaar-voter-deletion_in_5cb9afa2e4b068d795cb870c, for how hacked data was used to profile and delete citizens from the electoral rolls.

[36] Arora, Payal (2019) "Benign Dataveillance—the New Kind of Democracy? Examining the Emerging Datafied Governance Systems in India and China" *Communicative Figurations*, Working Paper, 24, 1–19.

[37] Henne, Kathryn (2019) "Surveillance in the Name of Governance: Aadhaar as a Fix for Leaking Systems in India," in Haggart, Blayne, Kathryn Henne, and Natasha Tusikov, eds., *Information, Technology and Control in a Changing World: Understanding Power Structures in the 21st Century*, Springer International, p 229.

[38] Jain, Anushka (2020) "Watch the Watchmen Series Part 2: The Centralized Monitoring System," *Internet Freedom Foundation*, September 14, https://internetfreedom.in/watch-the-watchmen-series-part-2-the-centralised-monitoring-system/.

airlines, and railway tickets" in a centralized fashion.[39] In 2013, the government would further its internet surveillance capacity through NETRA, or Network Traffic Analysis system. This system monitors all text and voice internet traffic, scanning for keywords deemed to be suspicious.[40] The year 2020 saw the introduction of yet another government tool known as AASMA, which stands for Advanced Application for Social Media Analytics. This software runs sentiment analytics on content posted by social media users and alerts authorities accordingly.[41]

Despite challenges to these programs from the Supreme Court of India, by 2021 the government was able to introduce key legislation that would bring virtually all online content under the state's purview, including private encrypted messages (for example those sent on messaging services like WhatsApp)."[42] A report by the German Institute for Global and Area Studies' (GIGA) Institute for Asian Studies finds that several states in India have used the country's new information technology laws and tools "to arrest people for social media posts and to block/takedown web pages and accounts," amounting to "a new form of repression" that has turned social media into a space of surveillance with "a chilling effect on self-expression."[43]

Taken together, these programs, and particularly the ability to have unrestricted access to online communications without going through the intermediary of the TSPs, have caused concern among civil liberty groups and local media.[44] Professor Kathryn Henne, who leads the Justice and

[39] Jain, Anushka (2020) "Watch the Watchmen Series Part 1: The National Intelligence Grid," *Internet Freedom Foundation*, September 2, https://internetfreedom.in/watch-the-watchmen-part-1-the-national-intelligence-grid/.
[40] Parbat, Kalyan (2013) "Government to Launch 'Netra' for Internet Surveillance," *The Economic Times*, December 16, https://economictimes.indiatimes.com/tech/internet/government-to-launch-netra-for-internet-surveillance/articleshow/27438893.cms.
[41] Mahapatra, Sangeeta (2021) "Digital Surveillance and the Threat to Civil Liberties in India," *GIGA Focus Asia*, 3, 1–12, p 5.
[42] The legislation has been challenged in court by tech firms. See Ellis-Peterson, Hannah (2021) "'Wolf in Watchdog's Clothing': India's New Digital Media Laws Spark Fears for Freedoms," *The Guardian*, March 11, www.theguardian.com/world/2021/mar/11/wolf-in-watchdogs-clothing-indias-new-digital-media-laws-spark-censorship-fears; and Ellis-Peterson, Hannah (2021) "WhatsApp Sues Indian Government Over 'Mass Surveillance' Internet Laws," *The Guardian*, May 26, www.theguardian.com/world/2021/may/26/whatsapp-sues-indian-government-over-mass-surveillance-internet-laws.
[43] Mahapatra, "Digital Surveillance," p 5.
[44] See Xynou, Maria (2014) "India's Central Monitoring System (CMS): Something to Worry About?" *The Centre for Internet and Society*, January 30, https://cis-india.org/internet-governance/blog/india-central-monitoring-system-something-to-worry-about; Sankaran, Keerthana (2018) "Big Brother is Here: Amid Snooping Row, Govt Report Says Monitoring System 'Practically Complete'" *The New Indian Express*, December 24, www.newindianexpress.com/nation/2018/dec/24/big-brother-is-here-amid-snooping-row-govt-report-says-monitoring-system-practically-complete-1915866.html; and "Govt Slammed For Social Media Monitoring, SC Says India

Technoscience Lab at Australian National University, points out that Aadhaar and related programs are "not simply about *knowing* subjects, but also about *laying claim* to subjects." This kind of body ownership "continues longer, biopolitical processes of state (co)production" that "are quite explicit about the centrality of biopolitical management to state preservation."[45] This is an important point. As the GIGA report finds, through digital surveillance in India "people are not just observed but are pinpointed and profiled without their consent."[46] Via this act of profiling they are also somehow conjured into a form of bureaucratic being—and thus managed as biopolitical assets—by the state.

Arguably, this same process is also occurring in other parts of the globe. The historical forces underway are far larger than those affecting just one nation. In this review of the different techniques being used globally we see that in all cases a citizen's very identity in the eyes of the state is being transformed via automation. New sociological data collection techniques are radically remaking citizens' identities because they have expanded the scale and nature of information that can be collected about them. In the simplest terms: In the eyes of the state, the person you were, socially and politically, before automation is not the same as the person you are after automation. You may have been a model citizen then, but are a criminal now; or, typically less likely, vice versa. Furthermore, as these systems seem to be implemented unevenly across geographies, even within the same nation, your digital representation may differ from place to place.

Another important commonality is the way that citizens' identities change based on who they associate with. Being friends with people on black lists edges you closer to getting on a black list yourself. Gary Smith, professor at Pomona College, argues in his book *The AI Delusion* that this is where we could see the most pernicious implications for societies. Guilt by association logic creates divides where citizens are rewarded for keeping the potentially guilty out of their social networks.[47] But it is not always so simple to keep those risky people out because definitions of guilt tend to easily shift and expand at certain historical junctures. This is especially the case when paranoia pervades a bureaucracy that perceives itself under siege, as with the

---

Is Becoming A 'Surveillance State,'" (2018) *India Times*, July 13, www.indiatimes.com/news/india/govt-slammed-for-social-media-monitoring-sc-says-india-is-becoming-a-surveillance-state-349302.html.

[45] Henne, "Surveillance in the Name of Governance," p 237.
[46] Mahapatra, "Digital Surveillance," p 2.
[47] Smith, Gary (2018) *The AI Delusion*, Oxford University Press, p 221.

Tsarist Third Department, the Maoist Dang'an, or the US Department of Justice during both postwar Red Scares. We saw this phenomenon at work again to a degree in various NSA metadata collection initiatives in the years following the 9/11 attacks on the World Trade Center and Pentagon.

Definitions of guilt tend to get further diluted by automation as it becomes easier to widen the dragnet. All it takes is for the wrong email address to end up in your contacts book. This leaves black lists vulnerable to compounding individual and political influences; and, more importantly, pries control over a citizen's own prosopography further and further away from their own power. Disparate data about peoples' social life are so bountiful, and processing power to detect patterns so indefatigable, that there are few practical limits to the number of persons that the state can consider guilty in one way or another.[48]

Where may we expect all this to go? What is the overall trajectory? One area to watch is the growing use of government chatbots for public sector service delivery. Already a popular tool used for countless helplines, chatbots are increasingly being deployed for the delivery of government services. Integration with the latest generative AI technologies, such as large language models (LLMs) and retrieval augmented generation is set to improve responsiveness and efficiency.

In the US, a recent review by the Center for Democracy and Technology found that at least five federal agencies may already have incorporated LLMs in their chatbots.[49] The government of Singapore embarked upon an ambitious project to upgrade all their government chatbots to LLM-driven versions as part of their plan to improve public sector services.[50] Other cities around the world are also implementing generative AI chatbot solutions to enhance their interaction with citizens. Argentina's capital Buenos Aires is communicating with residents via an AI chatbot called Boti that serves up to eleven million users every month. Boti connects residents with external

---

[48] What governments then do with the results of the processed data will also increasingly be automated, as we saw with the SCS in China where a person's access to travel is automatically cut off.

[49] Bateyko, Dan (2023) "Let LLMs Do the Talking? Generative AI Issues in Government Chatbots," *Center for Democracy & Technology*, December 13, https://cdt.org/insights/let-llms-do-the-talking-generative-ai-issues-in-government-chatbots/.

[50] Hirdaramani, Yogesh (2023) "Is It Time to Say Goodbye to 'ask Jamie'? Inside Govtech's Refresh Of Government Chatbots," *GovInsider*, September 14, https://govinsider.asia/intl-en/article/is-it-time-to-say-goodbye-to-ask-jamie-inside-govtechs-refresh-of-government-chatbots; and IBM (2023) "Three Ways Foundation Models Promise to Put Generative AI to Work for Governments," *GovInsider*, September 13, https://govinsider.asia/intl-en/article/three-ways-foundation-models-promise-to-put-generative-ai-to-work-for-governments.

services or with a human operator for more sensitive issues.[51] The Indian government is also reported to have plans to launch an ambitious chatbot that can produce conversational responses to queries from citizens in a natural voice format.[52]

While incredibly convenient for citizens and cost-effective for governments, chatbots will also serve as a powerful social listening tool for the state. Most states will not resist the temptation to record and catalog every citizen–chatbot interaction. The cost of storing this data is relatively cheap and the potential benefit significant. Once stored, states will have to resist the temptation to fuse it with other data streams and mine it for predictive signals and other valuable demographic insights into citizens' relations to others, to entities, to ideas. Citizen digital rights frameworks will have to be exceptionally robust to counter both these temptations. In most national contexts there is little evidence to this end.

What is more likely is that citizen–chatbot interaction data will find its way to the ever-evolving prosopographic file defining one's digital double in the eyes of the state. It will simply be layered on to the rest of it: to US citizens' telephone, text, and email metadata collected by the NSA, to the dilating funnel that is China's SCS, or to the demographic and biometric data already linked to the Aadhaar in India. George Lucas, the research professor at the University of Notre Dame cited above, illustrates it best when he describes the result of state data collection as "resembling a constellation or mandala" of intricate nodes that can be mined "to discern meaningful patterns within them."[53]

Another area to watch for future developments is the increased use of geolocation tracking. Sanitation staff in several municipal governments in India have been mandated to trial "Human Efficiency Trackers." These trackers are basically smartwatches that are GPS enabled and equipped with a camera and microphone. Supervisors use them to ensure workers stay within assigned areas. These devices have been described as incredibly intrusive; workers fear being snooped on in their homes as they are required to take the

---

[51] Gilman, Hollie and Sarah Jacob (2024) "Cities Are at the Forefront of AI and Civic Engagement," *Next City*, April 2024, https://nextcity.org/urbanist-news/cities-are-at-the-forefront-of-ai-and-civic-engagement.

[52] Barik, Soumyarendra (2023) "MeitY May Soon Integrate ChatGPT With WhatsApp for Key Government Schemes," Indian Express, February 14, https://indianexpress.com/article/technology/tech-news-technology/meity-may-soon-integrate-chatgpt-with-whatsapp-for-key-government-schemes-8441010/.

[53] Lucas, *Ethics and Cyber Warfare*, p 146.

devices home to charge them, and female workers avoid bathroom breaks for fear of being recorded. This "human tagging program" has no worker consent, no oversight, and no transparency regarding how the data is stored, tracked, and analyzed, nor who has access to it.[54]

In previous chapters we saw that, historically, the most innovative data collection techniques tend to be experimented on the most fragile, or those somehow on the fringes, of society. This was certainly the case with the mass fingerprinting of South African and Chinese Laborers in the British and Japanese empires, or the anthropometric measuring of French and American criminals in Bertillon's time, or the subjecting of German and Scandinavian patients to eugenicist hereditary health laws. It was also the case for travelers in US airports being racially profiled with the aid of automatic emotion detection systems, or the Uyghurs in Xinjiang being stared at by police software that considers the smallest change in the diameter of their facial pores an indication of criminal guilt. The brain-computer interface (BCI) technologies that purportedly read minds, too, are being deployed first on persons with disabilities.

In India today it seems it is the turn of the urban sanitation worker to bear the ugly burden of paving the way for new frontiers in human bio-data collection. This genre of technology will potentially add yet another dimension to the automatically regenerating file discussed above. Sociological data may soon no longer be restricted to the associations, political parties, and religious groups you are a member of, or the people you call and text, but now may also include who you are in actual close physical proximity to. Quite literally, the company you keep. This may be the ultimate sociological data point, and a windfall for the algorithms busy searching for predictive patterns. The pivotal addition here is the capacity to triangulate a citizen's physical location, who they communicate with, and what groups they are connected to socially. Deductive logical frameworks will then automatically reduce that person's future behavior to a handful of likely scenarios. Resources can then be deployed to discourage or encourage hypothesized future actions.

In some nations location information will be gathered directly by state authorities, in others there may be layers of intermediaries. In Western

---

[54] Khaira, Rachna (2020) "Surveillance Slavery: Swachh Bharat Tags Sanitation Workers to Live-Track their Every Move," *HuffPost*, February 18, www.huffpost.com/archive/in/entry/swacch-bharat-tags-sanitation-workers-to-live-track-their-every-move_in_5e4c98a9c5b6b0f6bff11f9b.

democracies, the trend is to circumvent constitutional safeguards by acquiring location information from private data brokers. The Electronic Frontier Foundation warns that in the US "data brokers and federal military, intelligence, and law enforcement agencies have formed a vast, secretive partnership to surveil the movements of millions of people." Location data is gathered mainly from the apps we use on our phones that require our location, like games, or e-commerce, weather, and navigation apps. Private data brokers buy this information and then partner with federal agencies in order to share it.[55] The Brennan Center for Justice states that "by buying data rather than obtaining it pursuant to a subpoena, warrant, or court order, federal agencies are circumventing the basic safeguard against intrusive policing enshrined in the Fourth Amendment."[56]

From one perspective, the leap from justifying states' need to know what social and cultural circles you are subscribed to, for example, to needing to know what persons you actually consort with, is not that big. Some may argue that we could have seen it coming. All that Tsar Nicholas I was lacking in 1826 was the tracking technology. The danger to citizens is now—just as it was for Dostoyevsky when he was charged with reading the wrong books—that the individual is not in control of how that information is interpreted and processed, or the *story* it tells. Let us say a person happens to be walking down a street when a group of activists stage a protest on the same street, and suppose that person is curious and walks in the same direction for a while to learn more. Suddenly, automatically, that person is now considered differently by the algorithm that tracks physical proximity to protestors and triangulates that data point with a host of other data points. All other relational information on that person's file, from the content of their texts and emails, to the websites they visit, to the risk factor of their old acquaintances

---

[55] Cyphers, Bennett (2022) "How the Federal Government Buys Our Cell Phone Location Data," *Electronic Frontier Foundation*, June 13, www.eff.org/deeplinks/2022/06/how-federal-government-buys-our-cell-phone-location-data.

[56] Hecht-Felella, Laura (2021) "Federal Agencies Are Secretly Buying Consumer Data," *Brennan Center For Justice*, April 16, www.brennancenter.org/our-work/analysis-opinion/federal-agencies-are-secretly-buying-consumer-data. For more on government purchasing from data brokers see: Wessler, Nathan (2020) "The US Government Is Secretly Using Cell Phone Location Data to Track Us. We're Suing," *American Civil Liberties Union*, December 2, www.aclu.org/news/immigrants-rights/the-u-s-government-is-secretly-using-cell-phone-location-data-to-track-us-were-suing; Tau, Byron and Michelle Hackman (2020) "Federal Agencies Use Cellphone Location Data for Immigration Enforcement," *The Wall Street Journal*, February 7, www.wsj.com/articles/federal-agencies-use-cellphone-location-data-for-immigration-enforcement-11581078600; Riotta, Chris (2022) "What Does the Federal Government Buy from Data Brokers?" *Federal Computer Week*, August 17, https://fcw.com/congress/2022/08/what-does-federal-government-buy-data-brokers/375963/.

still friends on social media, is now tainted by that chance occurrence. Once again, the file is the evidence.

The historical paths we reviewed in previous chapters for physiological and psychological data collection initiatives revealed that in both cases the future of data collection lays in technologies that get increasingly closer, and in some cases penetrate, the human body. In the case of physiological data, we saw that wearables may soon monitor our vitals in real time, and, in the case of psychological data, technology is being developed to interface directly with our brain's neural activity. The same encroachment is at work here, as the precise location of a citizen's physical body is being added to the sociological data collection mix. In the US it may take the guise of the Funopticon, in places like China it may pass largely uncontested, and in democracies like India it may be unsuccessfully contested, but at the end of the day the overall trajectory will be similar for everyone.

PHOTO SECTION
RELATIONS

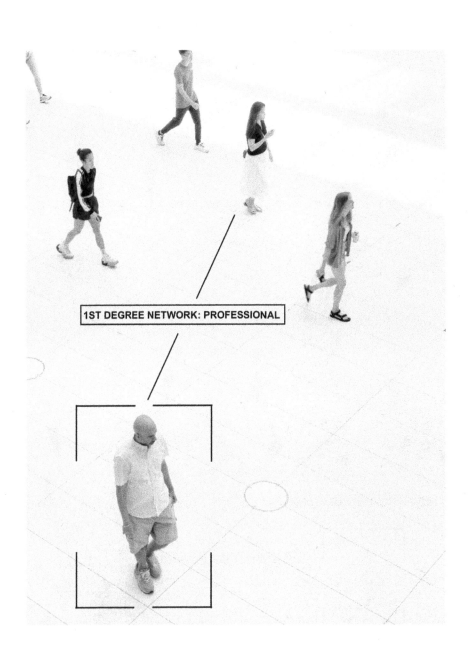

Chapter 8
India

In this chapter we turn our attention to data collection programs in India. With the help of researchers exploring these issues, the chapter will explore the effects of digital surveillance on the rights of citizens and society as a whole in the country. Digital Futures Lab (DFL) is a multidisciplinary research network that examines the interaction between technology and society in the Global South. Their work centers on projects related to AI and society (how algorithmic decision-making is transforming the dynamics of politics, society, and culture), the future of work (how work practices are being altered as a result of new digital technologies), and digital rights (how the legal frameworks required to ensure individual and community rights are protected are changing in emerging digital societies).[1] Anushka Jain is a research associate with DFL as well as a lawyer and policy researcher interested in disruptive technologies such as AI. She previously worked for the Internet Freedom Foundation (IFF), an organization that safeguards online privacy, political freedom, and innovation in India.[2]

Shweta Mohandas is a lawyer and researcher analyzing emerging technologies and their implications for legal regulatory frameworks. She has published extensively in this area, including on the uses of AI and facial recognition technology (FRT). She has also contributed to policy proposals for India's AI, privacy, and data protection regulations. She currently works for the Centre for Internet and Society (CIS), where she highlights the need for improved privacy and data protection legislation. The CIS is a nonprofit organization that performs interdisciplinary research from a policy and academic perspective on internet and digital technologies, including internet governance and online privacy.[3]

---

[1] Digital Futures Lab, "Research," accessed November 9, 2023, https://digitalfutureslab.notion.site/research-e92e224e0c9a49729c1fe3b45f60872d.
[2] Internet Freedom Foundation, "Homepage," accessed November 9, 2023, https://internetfreedom.in/.
[3] Centre for Internet and Society, "Homepage," accessed November 9, 2023, https://cis-india.org/.

The interview with Anushka Jain involves discussion about the use of surveillance technologies in India and the work of DFL, and her previous role with the IFF, which included work on Project Panopticon. This project tracks the number of facial recognition projects in India in an effort to raise public awareness on the presence of the technology. She highlights accuracy issues raised by the Aadhaar digital identity system that can potentially exclude vulnerable citizens and violate their rights. She also discusses the use of geolocation trackers on municipal workers and their potential misuse and negative impact on lower-income communities. Jain touched on the development of technologies that map social relationships, such as family ID systems, and raised concerns about the ethical implications of these technologies and the need for adequate data protection measures.

Shweta Mohandas discusses the use of AI for surveillance in India, focusing on the potential misuse of data by foreign actors and the lack of citizen representation in data collection projects. This can lead to skewed data sets and negatively impact civil liberties. She explains that the recently passed Personal Data Protection Act does begin to address some privacy concerns but that it should be stricter regarding what types of data can be transferred abroad. She also raises the same concerns as Jain about geolocation trackers used on employees from marginalized communities, considering the use of such devices an overreach and a violation of civil rights. She noted that there were no employee surveillance regulations in the new Personal Data Protection Act.[4]

Anushka, can you speak about your work with the IFF and the DFL?

At the IFF I served as the policy counsel, where my main focus was on surveillance technologies. This encompassed a range of technologies including CCTV, facial recognition, emotion recognition, and others closely related to surveillance. The core of my work at IFF revolved around addressing the challenges and implications of these technologies.

A key initiative I led was Project Panoptic. This project, which I conceptualized, launched, and managed, is a live tracker that monitors facial

---

[4] Interviews held via videoconferencing technology on October 11 (Jain) and October 13 (Mohandas), 2023; replies paraphrased by author.

recognition projects implemented by both the central and state governments in India. While Project Panoptic doesn't claim to be exhaustive, it strives to cover as many projects as possible. The data for this project was meticulously gathered through right to information requests, government documents available online, and media reports. The primary aim of Project Panoptic was to raise public awareness and advocacy. This was crucial because surveillance technologies are often developed and deployed covertly, leaving many unaware that they are under constant surveillance.

The project emphasized the importance of public awareness regarding the development and deployment of FRTs. It provided a user-friendly interface; for instance, a resident of Delhi could visit the project's website, select Delhi, and view all the ongoing or planned facial recognition projects in the city. This transparency was aimed at informing the public about what surveillance measures were being taken in their vicinity. In addition to raising awareness the project also advocated for specific policy changes. A major stance of the IFF, which I strongly supported, was the call for a ban on the use of FRT for law enforcement purposes. We launched a petition to gather public support for this cause.

My time at IFF, which spanned approximately four years, primarily revolved around issues of privacy, data protection, and surveillance, although I also contributed to matters related to freedom of speech and internet access. After my tenure at IFF, I transitioned to the DFL. DFL is a research organization that explores the intersection of technology and society, particularly focusing on the Global South. My move to DFL, which occurred just over a month ago, marked a shift in my focus. The work at DFL is centered on envisioning the future of technology, particularly AI, and fostering responsible tech practices. The lab is deeply engaged in exploring the future of work and other related domains, emphasizing the long-term impacts of technology in shaping society.

A quick follow up question about your work on Project Panoptic: what successes and what challenges have you encountered in creating public awareness of these technologies?

Measuring success in public advocacy work is challenging, but the growth of Project Panoptic offers a tangible metric. Initially, the project listed around 34 to 35 facial recognition projects on its website. This number has expanded to 170, illustrating the substantial information we've gathered and presented to the public. This achievement marks a significant milestone for the project.

Beyond mere data collection, the project has significantly influenced the discourse surrounding FRT. Launched in 2020 (around the time when facial recognition began to be integrated into law enforcement in various places), Project Panoptic has played a crucial role in shaping public understanding. As reports of this technology's usage surged, our work provided the public with a critical policy perspective, elucidating the nature of these technologies, their implications, and possible approaches to them. While it may not have single-handedly brought this issue to the national forefront, our efforts have coincided with a growing interest in privacy and surveillance in India, positioning facial recognition as a key topic of concern.

The success of our advocacy was evident during the Covid-19 pandemic. The Indian government initially planned to integrate facial recognition with the Aadhaar digital identity system for vaccine distribution. We raised concerns that this could restrict vaccine access, potentially having fatal consequences during the pandemic. Our advocacy contributed to the government's decision to roll back the use of facial recognition for vaccine distribution, a significant victory in ensuring equitable access to healthcare. The success of Project Panoptic lies in its ability to illuminate aspects of FRT that were previously overlooked or under-discussed. The project has been instrumental in bringing these critical conversations to light, fostering a more informed and engaged public discourse on the issue.

Can you explain how FRT would have restricted vaccine access?

The persistent concern with FRT lies in the collection of massive amounts of biometric data, especially in the absence of robust data protection legislation. This uncertainty around data storage has always been problematic. However, the more immediate and critical risk in this context was the potential impact on vaccine accessibility.

The proposed system required individuals to present an ID, like an Aadhaar identity number, and validating this identity through facial recognition to access the Covid-19 vaccine. This raised concerns. The unreliability of FRT, coupled with the known accuracy issues of India's Aadhaar digital identity system, posed a significant threat. Combining these two flawed systems could have led to severe consequences, particularly in the context of the pandemic, where inaccuracies in identity verification could have had devastating effects on public health. If facial recognition failed to match an individual's identity it could potentially deny them vaccine access.

How is the work of civil society organizations like the IFF and the DFL funded?

The IFF is primarily supported by contributions from everyday citizens and Indian organizations. Lacking a Foreign Contribution Regulation Act license, IFF is unable to receive funds from abroad and hence relies on domestic fundraising from individuals and groups aligned with IFF's mission and values. This support comes from a diverse range of sources, including individuals, companies, and other organizations. Its funding details are transparently displayed on the IFF website. As a nongovernmental entity, the IFF does not receive direct funding from the government. While it may collaborate with various government departments and institutions for its initiatives, the organizations contributing financially to IFF are not government-funded entities, maintaining its independence in operations and advocacy.

What new government regulations and laws in India do you find worrisome from a civil rights perspective?

I think one of the biggest causes of concern right now is the new Information Technology (IT) rules of 2021, which are threatening the principle of intermediary liability protection in India. In India, under the Information Technology Act passed in 2000, section 79 provides for intermediary liability protection, which basically says that a social media company or anybody who is providing a platform is not responsible for what a user is publishing on that platform.

But the IT rules that came in 2021 are trying to decrease this protection and make social media companies responsible for what is being posted on their platform. As a consequence of increasing liability to these platforms, there's a risk of over-compliance. Social media companies, facing the pressure to quickly and thoroughly comply with these regulations, will resort to overly cautious content moderation. This over-compliance could lead to unwarranted censorship, as there may not be sufficient time to carefully assess whether the content in question actually violates free speech norms in India. Such an environment could undermine the principles of free expression, with platforms erring on the side of caution to avoid potential liabilities under the new rules.

Would social media companies have to resort to automated content sorting technologies in order to comply with the new regulations?

The new IT rules include a clause allowing companies to deploy automated tools, or AI, for content moderation. Specifically, this automation can be used for identifying and removing material subject to copyright infringement or for detecting illegal content. While the rules do not specifically mandate the use of automation for identifying hate speech, social media companies might independently employ such methods, as this provision facilitates the use of technology to swiftly identify and address targeted content on digital platforms.

Are there any groups in India that are targeted more than others by digital surveillance tools?

Digital surveillance technologies often reflect and amplify the biases inherent in the systems they are applied to. This is particularly the case in law enforcement. Historically marginalized communities, who have been subject to excessive policing and surveillance, find themselves disproportionately impacted by the implementation of these technologies. This is especially true for lower-income groups, religious minorities, and communities classified as "backward" in India. The intertwining of surveillance with economic power is also evident; areas inhabited by economically weaker religious minorities are more likely to be heavily monitored with CCTVs compared to affluent neighborhoods.

The deployment of surveillance technologies during political protests further targets these marginalized communities. When a particular community protests against injustice or victimization, the act of surveilling the protests amplifies that injustice. This not only intensifies the scrutiny on these already vulnerable groups, but also raises questions about the distribution of societal costs and benefits of surveillance. The pattern observed in India shows that surveillance technologies, rather than being neutral, tend to reinforce existing societal inequalities, highlighting the need for a more considered and fair approach to their use in law enforcement and public monitoring.

Can you describe the Aadhaar digital identity system? How is the population in India responding to its increased use?

Aadhaar, India's vast biometric data collection system, has significant repercussions due to its nationwide application and issues with accuracy at scale. This lack of precision has led to exclusionary consequences, notably in cases where individuals could no longer access essential food assistance programs due to malfunctions in the Aadhaar, resulting in a number of deaths from starvation.

The system's extensive reach, which links individuals' Aadhaar numbers to various aspects of their lives including their bank account details and personal travel itineraries, has raised concerns about potential civil rights violations. Many are uneasy and fear that Aadhaar could enable a comprehensive monitoring of citizens' activities, creating a 360-degree surveillance among the populace. So there are high costs and risks, both in terms of functionality and citizen privacy.

Can you describe the interface between national security, surveillance, and digital rights in India?

The argument that national security justifies extensive surveillance raises critical issues about the balance between security needs and individual rights. While national security is undoubtedly crucial, it cannot be the sole reason for infringing on citizens' fundamental rights, such as privacy, life, and dignity. The use of surveillance technologies in the name of national security necessitates a system of checks and balances. This would ensure that surveillance measures are appropriately justified and regulated, whether it be through judicial oversight or a specialized panel scrutinizing their alignment with actual national security objectives.

Merely citing national security cannot provide carte blanche for all actions. In a democracy, safeguarding citizens' fundamental rights is paramount. Any violation of these rights, even for national security, requires substantial justification. The right to privacy can be limited in certain circumstances and for specific reasons, but this must adhere to established principles and be overseen by judicial decisions. Any deviation from these principles constitutes an illegal violation.

Surveillance measures, especially those involving digital technologies, must not be overly broad or unchecked. Without proper regulation, the risk of transitioning from a democratic state to a surveillance state is real. A democracy demands a balance of power, necessitating mechanisms that hold the government accountable and prevent overreach in the guise of national security. This balance is essential to maintain the democratic fabric, ensuring that government actions are in line with the principles of justice, transparency, and respect for individual rights.

Can you speak about the use of geolocation tracking technologies by municipal authorities in India?

The deployment of tracking technologies, particularly on sanitation workers, who are among the most marginalized in India, raises significant ethical concerns. These devices are perceived as dehumanizing and are disproportionately used on individuals from oppressed castes, marginalized groups, and lower-income sectors. This practice exploits their lack of political and social power, intensifying their vulnerability. In contrast, individuals with greater political or social influence would likely resist such surveillance, and their objections would be taken seriously.

The workers, who are merely earning a wage, should not be subjected to invasive tracking as if they are owned by their employers, be it the government or other institutions. Therefore, use of such devices is not just a physical encroachment but also has social implications. It highlights a feudalistic mindset, where constant monitoring of workers is socially normalized.

There are reports of workers feeling physically unwell due to the constant surveillance. Female workers have expressed concerns about privacy violations, fearing that cameras in these devices might be activated while they use washrooms. These tracking devices not only create a sense of unease and infringement on personal space but also violate the fundamental rights of these workers. They transcend mere workplace monitoring, affecting the social and emotional well-being of individuals who are already facing systemic disadvantages. Addressing these issues requires recognizing the broader social context and the inherent power imbalances that make these technologies a viable idea, calling for a re-evaluation of their existence in line with respecting the dignity and rights of all people.

Is it possible that these types of invasive technologies tend to be first deployed among the most vulnerable, but then in time start to spread to other parts of the population as well?

The gradual expansion of surveillance technologies, beginning with the most vulnerable communities, is a concerning trend. Initially deployed on sanitation workers, these tracking systems may soon extend to those in lower-income government jobs or the private sector. The gig economy already sees widespread use of such technology, driven by the public's desire to monitor the status of their orders and deliveries.

This pattern of first introducing surveillance in lower-income groups sets a precedent for broader normalization. As these practices become more accepted, they start to permeate upward, affecting an increasing number of communities. This incremental expansion poses a serious risk of evolving into a pervasive surveillance society.

The potential for such a "slippery slope" makes it imperative to scrutinize and challenge these deployments at every level. Failing to do so could lead to a gradual erosion of privacy and autonomy, extending from those with limited political power to wider segments of society.

How can new technologies identify relationships between citizens? We have discussed facial recognition and geolocation tracking, but there is also some indication that government databases collect and store information on citizens' relationships, i.e., who they are connected to socially. Can you discuss any developments in India in this regard?

Recently, several states in India have begun implementing "family ID" systems. These assign a single ID to an entire family and map out relationships. This family ID system, which I haven't extensively researched, identifies the number of members in a family and is used to access various government benefits, including food assistance.

Any data collection initiative, lacking sufficient personal data protections, poses potential harm. The aggregation of entire families' information in such exercises is particularly concerning. Without deeper research into the specifics of these systems it is challenging to detail the precise risks or negative consequences that might arise from them.

Shweta, are you aware of any instances of government authorities in India using AI-based surveillance tools to monitor citizens and quell political dissent?

During the Citizenship Amendment Act protests in 2020, there were indications in the media that social media surveillance was conducted on protesters. Additionally, there were unconfirmed reports suggesting the use of FRT to identify individuals participating in these protests. However, the specifics of the tools used remain unclear, and my understanding is based on secondhand information rather than direct research or firsthand accounts.

What are your thoughts regarding the impact of these technologies on civil liberties in India?

AI-based surveillance raises significant concerns, particularly regarding the opacity of decisions derived from such surveillance. Once an AI system makes a decision, it can be incredibly difficult to contest or prove it wrong. Also, technologies like facial and gait recognition collect data whose implications may not be immediately apparent. The harms could manifest years later, making it challenging to trace back, justify, or appeal against the initial recording.

Another concern is the pervasiveness of AI and the ease with which it can operate unbeknownst to individuals. This uncertainty about whether one is being recorded and what decisions are being made about them based on this surveillance is troubling. The outcomes of AI systems, the parameters they operate within, and their potential biases are often unclear. This ambiguity is particularly problematic in India, where there is a lack of diverse data to ensure AI systems are accurately attuned to Indian demographics. This could lead to erroneous decisions when applied to Indian faces and situations.

The challenge of appealing against or questioning AI decisions poses a significant risk. The inability to scrutinize these decisions leaves individuals vulnerable to potential errors and biases embedded within AI systems. This lack of accountability and transparency in AI decision-making processes can have far-reaching implications, particularly in a culture like India where contextual understanding is crucial. The overarching issue is not just limited to civil liberties but extends to the wider impact of the general application of AI technologies in society. The future risks associated with unregulated and unaccountable AI systems highlight the need for more robust oversight and ethical considerations in their deployment.

Have you personally experienced or perceived AI-based surveillance in India?

Although I haven't directly experienced AI-based surveillance, there's a notable shift toward AI utilization in India. This trend isn't strictly surveillance-focused but aligns with the broader drive toward digitalization and subsequent AI adoption. A prime example is the implementation of DigiYatra, a facial recognition system used at airports. This initiative is gaining momentum, encouraging people to register for smoother airport experiences. However, concerns persist about how this data is collected, processed, and used. The transparency around the handling of such sensitive information remains unclear. The growing prominence of FRT in Indian airports exemplifies the increasing reliance on AI solutions in various sectors, raising questions about privacy, data security, and the broader implications of AI integration into everyday life.

How are Indian citizens reacting?

In the Indian context, AI's application in governance is in the nascent phase and goes relatively undetected. However, the proliferation of surveillance cameras is more noticeable, particularly in urban areas. For instance, in my city, there has been a noticeable increase in camera installations over the past two years. This rise in surveillance is often justified by the promise of safety, suggesting a trade-off between privacy and security. The idea is that these cameras can assist in identifying criminals or solving crimes.

The discourse around surveillance in India often oscillates. On one hand, there's an awareness of privacy concerns; on the other, there's a tendency to view technology as offering a trade-off. This trade-off is framed as a choice between relinquishing some privacy for the sake of convenience, safety, and ease of access or movement. Such a perspective is increasingly common as people weigh the benefits of technological advancements against the potential erosion of privacy. This dynamic reflects the complex interplay between embracing modern technology and maintaining individual privacy rights in a rapidly digitizing society.

Furthermore, India has recently finalized its Personal Data Protection Act after numerous revisions over six years. This Act is expected to bring a new dimension to how data protection and privacy rights are discussed and enforced. However, its real-world application and effectiveness in safeguarding privacy rights remain to be seen.

Can you describe how Indian society is dealing with managing the trade-offs between maintaining national security, like terrorism prevention, and maintaining digital and privacy rights?

Understanding the need for advanced technology to prevent terrorism and terror attacks is crucial, especially in today's context. Technologies like facial recognition play a significant role in enhancing security. However, the trade-off involved in these surveillance methods is a point of contention. These technologies survey everyone to identify potential threats, raising concerns about the rights of individuals whose data are being collected but that are not suspected terrorists.

The key challenge is balancing the necessity of surveillance for security purposes with the protection of individual privacy. Ensuring high security standards for the data collected is essential. This means implementing stringent measures to safeguard the data, preventing leaks, and restricting unauthorized access. Keeping the data secure and protected is paramount to maintaining trust in these systems. Transparency in data collection and processing is also vital. People should be informed about the collection of their data, its intended use, and the safeguards in place. This level of transparency can help promote a more informed public debate that permits citizens to understand the reasons for their surveillance.

Another concern is the potential misuse of collected data by third parties, including private companies. There is a risk that this data could be used to train AI systems, which might then be sold back to the government or used in ways that could harm the public. Ensuring that the data does not fall into the hands of nefarious actors or get commercially exploited is another aspect of safeguarding privacy.

While the use of advanced surveillance technologies is necessary for national security, it's crucial to maintain high standards of data security, ensure transparency in data usage, and prevent the misuse of collected data. These measures are key to achieving a balance between the need for security and the protection of individual privacy rights.

Can you explain in more detail the issue of data security? What regulations are in place governing how data are stored and used?

In India, there's a growing emphasis on digitization, particularly for transforming physical records into digital format for easier public access. This shift has significantly benefited citizens, allowing them to access information online that previously required visits to courts or government offices. While it's beneficial to have a centralized repository of public data, it's imperative to ensure high security standards to protect this data.

For instance, in my research on health data, I've come across instances of data leaks due to ransomware or malware attacks on leading health institutions. This underscores the necessity of robust security measures. A centralized system for health data, accessible from anywhere in India, is undoubtedly advantageous, but it must be accompanied by strong security protocols. This is crucial to prevent data from falling into the hands of malicious actors or being misused by companies or startups, especially in scenarios where data might be used to train AI systems without proper consent or awareness of the individuals involved.

The Personal Data Protection Act in India aims to impose greater control and responsibility on data collectors, including the government. However, while the bill mandates reasonable security practices, I believe the requirements should be more stringent and explicit. Both private and public entities handling large volumes of data should adhere to specific, high-standard security practices. This is critical because, even with anonymization, data can potentially be re-identified if cross-referenced with multiple sources.

The focus should be on ensuring that data, while being made more accessible, is also safeguarded against breaches and misuse. High-level security protocols, clear guidelines for data handling, and stringent enforcement of these measures are essential to protect the privacy and security of individuals. This approach is vital to correctly managing the vast amounts of data being digitized and ensuring that the benefits of digitization do not come at the cost of privacy and security.

What can you say about the use of technologies from other countries deployed in India?

India's burgeoning status as a data-rich nation has caught the attention of major global companies, particularly in the context of AI development. The country's AI policies acknowledge this, envisioning India as an AI test bed for international corporations to experiment with their products. This perspective is fueled by India's vast population, a significant portion of which is increasingly accessing the internet and mobile technology, generating copious amounts of data.

However, the utilization of this data by foreign entities poses concerns, particularly in the absence of a fully enforced personal data protection framework. For example, there are questions regarding where the collected information is being utilized. Is it being used locally to improve decision-making processes, or is it serving other purposes? Another issue is when will it be utilized. We are witnessing rapid advancements in AI capabilities, raising questions about how previously collected data can be used by future AI-based decision-making processes.

Yet another issue is context-specific AI applications, especially in language recognition. For instance, Indian languages or slurs may not be accurately identified when transliterated into English by automated systems, indicating a gap in contextual understanding. This highlights the need for AI systems that are attuned to the cultural and linguistic nuances of India.

The implementation of the Data Protection Act marks a step toward addressing these concerns, but its impact remains to be seen, especially in terms of cross-border data transfer. Earlier versions of the bill were stricter regarding the types of data that could be transferred internationally, but recent iterations seem to have relaxed these regulations.

There still is a significant degree of uncertainty about the handling and application of the vast amounts of data being generated in India. As the country positions itself as a global AI test bed, it is crucial to ensure that data protection and privacy are upheld, and that AI systems developed using this data are contextually relevant and respectful of the unique cultural and linguistic landscape of India.

What is the potential utility of all this data for "anticipatory governance"—the practice of creating predictive tools that preempt citizen behavior therefore permitting government to craft policies that are more future oriented? What may be the implications for citizens' rights in India?

This depends on the accuracy and representativeness of the data that is collected. The problem of data collection and its representativeness in India is indeed significant and warrants careful consideration. Although internet and mobile penetration in India are high, this doesn't uniformly translate across the country. Variations in internet reliability, frequent internet shutdowns, and inconsistent electricity supply mean that data collection is not evenly distributed. This unevenness puts into question the representativeness of the data in portraying the nation's pulse.

Several studies have highlighted that often a single mobile phone is shared by an entire household. This means the data collected from one phone could represent multiple users, not just the individual it is registered to. Additionally, there is a gender disparity in mobile phone ownership, with more men owning phones than women. This further skews the data, potentially excluding the perspectives and behaviors of a significant portion of the population.

The concentration of mobile internet users in certain parts of India means that views and data from these areas are overrepresented. This creates a bias, as decisions and analyses based on these data may not accurately reflect the diversity of opinions from the entire country. Such a skewed perspective is problematic when decisions made on this basis are applied nationally.

Furthermore, the process of decision-making based on this data is often top-down, leaving little room for questioning or revising decisions once made, especially at a public or citizen level. This approach is particularly challenging in a country as large and diverse as India, where central decisions may not always resonate with the varied needs and realities of its vast population.

While the volume of data generated in India is significant, its collection and use for any governance initiatives raises concerns. Ensuring that data accurately reflects the diverse demographics, opinions, and needs of the Indian population is crucial, particularly when it informs decisions that affect the future of the entire nation. Addressing these challenges requires a more nuanced and inclusive approach to data collection and analysis, one that acknowledges and compensates for the disparities in access and usage across different segments of society.

Can you explain more about these disparities in access and usage? Are these technologies deployed differently across communities, where certain groups are more vulnerable to potential negative effects?

A study I came across highlights that surveillance cameras are often strategically placed in areas with a history of higher crime rates or where certain demographic groups reside. This leads to a cycle where areas labeled as "problematic" or "less posh" receive heightened surveillance, perpetuating a pattern of increased crime detection in these localities.

The introduction of AI and FRTs in these areas exacerbates the issue. Communities that have been under surveillance historically continue to be disproportionately monitored. Even before the advent of CCTV, these areas were closely watched, and now, with advanced technologies like facial recognition, the scrutiny has intensified.

This approach, largely based on historical preconceptions about certain areas, can lead to a self-fulfilling prophecy where increased surveillance results in more behavior being recorded as criminal in these areas, justifying even more cameras. It also raises concerns about decision-making processes that contribute to the marginalization and continuous surveillance of certain communities. Decisions made based on surveillance-generated data from these areas can further reinforce existing biases, leading to a cycle of increased monitoring and profiling of these communities.

The deployment of AI and surveillance technologies in India tends to follow historical patterns of inequality, leading to increased surveillance in certain areas but not in others. This approach risks further penalizing already marginalized communities. Also, it fails to address the root causes of crime, instead perpetuating a cycle of bias, surveillance, crime, and inequality.

Can you discuss the deployment of geolocation tracking technologies among public sanitation workers in certain Indian cities?

The study I referenced before also sheds light on the issue of workplace surveillance, particularly involving sanitation workers. These workers, primarily women, were required to carry phones equipped with geo-tracking devices. This situation raises several concerns about surveillance and data protection in the workplace.

These devices had to be taken home by the employees, and there was no option to switch them off. The workers had to charge these devices using their own electricity, despite being from marginalized backgrounds where electricity is scarce. The report indicated that this continuous monitoring extended beyond work hours, leading to concerns about privacy invasion and the potential recording of personal conversations.

Such extensive monitoring seems to be an overreach, blurring the lines between professional and personal boundaries. The fact that these workers had to carry the tracking device at home implies that surveillance extended into their private lives. This raises serious questions about civil and human rights violations.

Regarding legislation, the earlier drafts of the Personal Data Protection Act in India included provisions on employee surveillance, but these were absent in the final version. This omission highlights a gap in addressing the complexities of workplace surveillance, especially when it involves geolocation tracking that infringes upon personal privacy.

In essence, the use of geolocation tracking devices in this context represents a concerning trend at the intersection of government overreach, employee surveillance, and civil rights. It showcases how surveillance practices, especially when inadequately regulated, can extend beyond the workplace and significantly impact individuals' dignity and freedoms. This instance underlines the need for more robust legal frameworks that protect employees from excessive and intrusive surveillance, ensuring their fundamental rights are upheld.

Chapter 9
The Eye of Nations

Thus far, we have reviewed data collection technologies that focus on citizens' bodies, minds, and social networks. Yet, one more layer encompasses and surpasses the previous three: citizens' broader environment. This represents the natural next step beyond a person's social relations and includes climatic conditions, economic dynamics, political circumstances, and general popular sentiment about various topics. In the algorithmic gaze of modern bureaucracies, citizens are embedded within this environmental context—which, like everything else, can be quantified. Data about a person's wider environment can be easily collected alongside that person's physiological, psychological, and sociological activity.

Like for a fish in a fish tank, it matters what temperature the water is, its salinity, pH level, and so forth. These elements can change the fish's behavior. Likewise, it is now possible to analyze large amounts of contextual information that may influence human behavior, such as climate-related data (temperature, rainfall, soil moisture, vegetation coverage, water reservoirs), economic data (commodity and food prices, interest rates, wages, inequality, unemployment levels), political indicators (arms stockpiling, conflict events, voting preferences, polarity, numbers of displaced peoples), and data that represents popular moods and cultural trends (fluctuating sentiment toward political matters in social media posts, local news, radio).

Relations between different combinations of these data streams can be unpacked, as can their overall effect on an individual's—or group's—likely future behavior. This includes potentially violent future conduct like terrorist attacks or armed confrontations. Interestingly, the most innovative (public) work in this field is being carried out not at the local or national level of governance but at the multilateral level, and, in particular, within the United Nation's (UN's) conflict prevention and response architecture.

This makes sense. The UN was erected upon the ashes of the League of Nations, whose express purpose was avoiding conflict. Alan Sharp, emeritus professor of international history at Ulster University, points out that although the League never reached the status of the universal body it strived

Political Automation. Eduardo Albrecht, Oxford University Press. © Oxford University Press (2025).
DOI: 10.1093/9780197696989.003.0009

for, it was at the time "the most ambitious of the attempts by the peacemakers in 1919 to ensure that the dreadful experiences of the First World War would not be repeated." Previous attempts at maintaining peace, like the nineteenth-century Concert of Europe, created after the Napoleonic Wars, had failed.[1]

Crucially, the states signing on agreed to discard notions of alliances or balances of power "in favor of a system of collective security." In Article 10 of the League's Covenant, members promised "to respect and preserve as against external aggression the territorial integrity and existing independence of all members of the League." As Sharp observes, "It was a startling commitment, based on the idea that peace was indivisible and that it was the responsibility of all to safeguard the security of each of the members."[2]

For Leonard Smith, a military historian at Oberlin College, "sovereignty within states and sovereignty among them would become two sides of the same coin," and nations could now "conform their interests to those of the global citizenry." To this end, the League would have to develop a new kind of authority; it would have to become "the instrument of the sovereign citizens of the world, maintain surveillance, determining inclusion and exclusion from the international system." Smith describes it as a "panoptical League."[3] Indeed, in Woodrow Wilson's address to the 1919 Paris Peace Conference establishing the League, the US president insisted it be

> not a thing sometimes called into life to meet an exigency, but always functioning in watchful attendance upon the interests of the nations—and that its continuity should be a vital continuity; that it should have functions that are continuing functions and that do not permit an intermission of its watchfulness and of its labor; that it should be the eye of the nations to keep watch upon the common interest, an eye that does not slumber, an eye that is everywhere watchful and attentive.[4]

---

[1] Sharp, Alan (2015) *The Consequences of the Peace: The Versailles Settlement: Aftermath and Legacy 1919–2015*, Haus Publishing, p 48.
[2] Ibid.
[3] Smith, Leonard (2018) *Sovereignty at the Paris Peace Conference of 1919*, Oxford University Press, p 30.
[4] "Woodrow Wilson's Address to the Peace Conference in Paris, January 25, 1919," *The American Presidency Project*, accessed June 7, 2023, www.presidency.ucsb.edu/documents/address-the-peace-conference-paris-france. The League's watchful eye was not slumbering when King Alexander I of Yugoslavia was assassinated in Marseilles in October 1934. Ondřej Ditrych, former director of the Prague Institute of International Relations, notes that the event sparked the first formal debate on the "anarchy and barbarism" of terrorism, a thing that could "overwhelm the civilized world," and "in

A major interest of this "eye of the nations" was to be the production and stockpiling of armaments among member states. Thus commenced a massive data collection exercise in which governments were obliged to exchange "full and frank information as to the scale of their armaments, their military, naval and air programs and the condition of such of their industries as are adaptable to warlike purposes."[5] David Lincove, professor emeritus at Ohio State University, explains that this "would contribute to an environment of greater transparency, international trust, and cooperation," but just as importantly it would also establish "patterns of thinking and organization that emphasized the role of expert, unbiased data collection in international discussions and decision-making on arms limitation and national security."[6]

Other types of data became equally important to assuring peace. In June 1920, League members created the International Statistical Commission (ISC). The ISC, a subsidiary body under the League's Council and ancestor of the UN Statistical Commission created in 1947, was animated by a belief that "technical information could solve problems across borders." It included statistics focusing on "international economics, finance, labor, and industrial production," with the objective of "forecasting, monitoring, and remedying social and economic ills."[7]

Carolyn Biltoft, associate professor of international history at the Graduate Institute Geneva, notes that a significant portion of the League's work "turned in some way on the production, management, or diffusion of information."[8] She asserts that this was part of a broader change in which "geopolitical conflicts began to shift somewhat away from territory and toward controlling networks or circuits of money, markets, [and] knowledge." The production of knowledge became closely intertwined with the production of power.

---

which the most elementary foundations of international peace would inevitably disappear." The conclusion was that a single nation or alliance of nations could not properly defend from such savagery, which meant that "a robust joint action, featuring elements of punishment, surveillance, and discipline was necessary if there was any hope to be left for the 'future of civilization.'" Wilson's eye was not enough, and signatories to the League now sought to establish conventions for the "prevention and punishment of terrorism" and for an international criminal court. See Ditrych, Ondřej (2013) "International Terrorism as Conspiracy: Debating Terrorism in the League of Nations," *Historical Social Research*, 38/1, pp 200–210, 200, 206.

[5] Quoted in Henig, Ruth (2010) *The League of Nations*, Haus Publishing, pp 109–110.

[6] Lincove, David (2018) "Data for Peace: The League of Nations and Disarmament 1920–40," *Peace & Change*, 43/4, pp 498–529, 498–499, 519–520.

[7] Ibid, p 500.

[8] Biltoft, Carolyn (2021) *A Violent Peace: Media, Truth, and Power at the League of Nations*, University of Chicago Press, p 5.

In terms of the power-knowledge nexus, the League continually produced volumes of evidence about various nations' so-called progress and so-called backwardness measured via indicators of income, infrastructure, education, and literacy, and so on ... each nation-state suddenly had to face constant comparisons to a sea of "others"—others often more privileged or more powerful.[9]

Managing and ranking the flow of information became the secret ingredient to governance. In his book *Seeing Like a State*, James Scott, professor of political science and anthropology at Yale University, offers some context for this phenomenon. He observes that twentieth-century states, driven by a desire for scientific certainty and total administrative control, developed a tendency to impose deterministic schemes onto complex natural and social systems. States started to count everything and arrange things into causal relations.[10] It is logical that a league of states should try to do the same but on a global scale. Biltoft describes it as a "wider transference wherein a variety of actors transcribed the desire for absolute certainty onto the world itself."[11]

Yet, while global institutions like the League of Nations might *try* to control the global flow of information, "reality would never hold still; information circuits always carried alternative truths, differing political views, and existential doubts into both households and seats of government." Biltoft usefully reminds us that there will "always be unfamiliar visions and dissonant claims creating doubt and political foment even into the most carefully censored societies."[12] Similarly, Scott describes how despite states' best attempts at deterministic control the stochastic reality of nature meant that they often failed quite spectacularly with detrimental consequences to both the natural environment and human community.[13]

This caveat did not cloud the confidence of Lucien March, ISC member and director of the Statistique Generale in France, when he wrote in 1921 that "a precise knowledge of the economic and social condition of peoples, their strength and productive power, would be the best guarantee for universal peace."[14] Indeed, this belief has remained fundamentally unchanged a

---

[9] Ibid, pp 10–11.
[10] Scott, James (1998) *Seeing Like a State: How Certain Schemes to Improve the Human Condition Have Failed*, Yale University Press.
[11] Biltoft, *A Violent Peace*, p 12.
[12] Ibid, p 13.
[13] Scott, *Seeing Like a State*.
[14] Lincove, "Data for Peace," p 500.

century later. The types of data available have ballooned, and technologies to process it all may have exceeded March's wildest imaginations, but the basic confidence in the order-inducing power of information is the same now as it was then, and continues to enthuse peace practitioners at multilateral organizations inheritors of the League's remit, such as the UN today.

Eleonore Pauwels, a senior fellow at the Global Center on Cooperative Security, notes that "UN agencies use data capture technologies and intelligence collection to map and understand recurrent conflict patterns and forecast potential crises."[15] Since 2014, when the Expert Panel on Technology and Innovation in UN Peacekeeping observed that "information is a political resource," myriad open-source and proprietary data streams have been tapped into for peacekeeping efforts. The panel insisted the UN get creative: "voice, video, and data from commercial satellites, sensor networks, and other technical feeds are available and need to be used by UN decision-makers."[16] In the rest of this chapter we will review the new technologies employed to crunch these environmental data as well as some of the practical, policy, and ethical dilemmas that are arising.[17]

Just like at the local and national levels of governance, technologies used at the multilateral level are either internally generated or sourced via private companies. Various UN entities have built highly sophisticated information repositories and analytic capacities to support their mandates. Other entities have partnered with external private actors to supply predictive analytics based on social media, earth observation,[18] and many other types of digital information generated from both routine human behavior and the natural environment. Often, the UN uses a mix of both in-house and external tools. Whatever the source, when appropriately alloyed, these data streams can give advance insight into future political unrest. Given that to predict is to possibly prevent, the technologies are becoming ever more fundamental to the UN's ability to fulfill its peacekeeping mandates.

There is no shortage of zeal to experiment. Forward-looking pockets within the UN, like the Department of Political and Peacebuilding Affairs'

---

[15] Pauwels, Eleonore (2020) "Artificial Intelligence and Data Capture Technologies in Violence and Conflict Prevention: Opportunities and Challenges for the International Community," *Global Center on Cooperative Security*, pp 3–4, 6.

[16] Wählisch, Martin (2020) "Big Data, New Technologies, and Sustainable Peace: Challenges and Opportunities for the UN," *Journal of Peacebuilding & Development*, 15/1, pp 122–126, 122–123.

[17] Arguments in this part of the chapter also appear in Albrecht, Eduardo (2023) "Predictive Technologies in Conflict Prevention: Practical and Policy Considerations for the Multilateral System," *United Nations University, Centre for Policy Research*.

[18] Images or information about the earth generated via satellites, drones, and sounding ballons.

(DPPA) Innovation Cell, have been exploring multiple scenarios for AI and "its potential to be used for the noble purposes of peace and security," which "could revolutionize the way of how we prevent and solve conflicts globally."[19] Similarly, the DPPA's Mediation Support Unit has developed a "Digital Technologies and Mediation Toolkit" that explains how data analytics and machine learning could "be used for the purpose of conflict analysis, early warning, [and] prediction of conflict." The toolkit further clarifies that mediators could "generate predictions about what conflict stakeholders will do, when and where."[20] The UN Global Pulse, too, has been advancing work around using data for foresight "to become more data-informed and anticipatory in not only strategy, but also planning and implementation."[21]

A leading in-house example is the UN Development Programme's Crisis Risk Dashboard, or CRD. Started in 2016 under the direction of the Crisis Risks and Early Warning team, the CRD "ensures that relevant and updated data is readily available to support processes of monitoring, analysis, and formulation of anticipatory measures and responses." Furthermore, the "team is leveraging innovative technologies as they become available and prove to be relevant and useful." For example, "at a time of increasingly hostile online discourses and hate speech, several CRDs are being developed to use sentiment analysis, machine learning, and predictive technology to find patterns and detect early warning signals to develop effective programs and mitigate violence."[22]

Some internally generated information repositories fall short of becoming full-blown predictive tools. An example of this is the Situational Awareness Geospatial Enterprise (SAGE). Allard Duursma and John Karlsrud, writing for the Norwegian Institute of International Affairs, describe how the tool "allows UN military, police and civilians in UN peace operations (both

[19] Masood, Daanish and Martin Wählisch (2019) "Future Wars Will Be Waged With Robots. But So Might Future Peace," *EuroNews*, March 28.
[20] "UN Digital Toolkit," United Nations, accessed December 11, 2023, https://peacemaker.un.org/digitaltoolkit. To the toolkit creators' credit, they emphasize that these technologies must be handled with care, as output "can be shaped by the cognitive and social biases underlying the programming algorithms." These biases may, in turn, "engender discrimination towards traditionally excluded groups and vulnerable communities." They correctly point out that "context and technical experts would be required to correct and adjust the machine learning process and contribute their knowledge and analysis to improve accuracy."
[21] Smith, Amy Lynn (2023) "Using Imagination, Information, and Insight to Prepare the UN for the Future," *UN Global Pulse*, July 14, https://medium.com/un-global-pulse/using-imagination-information-and-insight-to-prepare-the-un-for-the-future-3296521404e8.
[22] Scognamillo, Corrado and Jonas Gutschke (2021) "Understanding the World through Data: United Nations Development Programme," *UNDP Blog*, November 9, www.undp.org/blog/understanding-world-through-data.

UN peacekeeping operations and special political missions) to log incidents, events, and activities." They also note that this treasure trove of conflict data, combined with machine learning, could potentially "offer a giant step forward in the predictive capability of the UN, and hopefully be translated to preventive action on the ground." The authors detail how predictive analyses could in principle generate "risk maps" where a "color coding of administrative districts indicates the probability of events of interest like armed clashes between the main warring parties, communal violence, or violence against civilians."[23] Yet, to date, this has not occurred.

There are a number of headwinds to tools like SAGE being used in this way. Dirk Druet, a fellow at the International Peace Institute, in a study for the UN Department of Peace Operations (DPO), surveyed a wide array of digital technologies used in peacekeeping and found that in SAGE there are inconsistencies in the quality of the data across space and time. Additionally, the database only records information about events (as opposed to individuals or contextual factors). These characteristics, he says, do not lend themselves well to predictive trend analyses.[24]

Duursma and Karlsrud point to serious potential privacy concerns should UN databases be used for predictive purposes. UN analysts often rely on local informants to gather data in conflict-affected areas as this information is not always available from other sources. Parties to a conflict may attack individuals thought to have given actionable information to the UN. This way, "civilians who are already at risk can face new threats if their personal information is disclosed or reidentified."[25] This would be the case particularly if combatants knew that such information was used to inform preventive approaches resulting in an unfavorable distribution of UN peacekeeping resources. In sum, turning a database into a predictive tool has serious security ramifications.

Similar headwinds may have come upon a tool developed by the UN Global Pulse called Qatalog and another developed by the DPPA called

---

[23] Duursma, Allard and John Karlsrud (2018) "Predictive Peacekeeping: Opportunities and Challenges," *Norwegian Institute of International Affairs*, pp 1–2.

[24] Druet, Dirk (2021) "Thematic Research Paper for the DPO Peacekeeping Technology Strategy: Enhancing the Use of Digital Technology for Integrated Situational Awareness and Peacekeeping-Intelligence," *Department of Peace Operations*, p 10.

[25] Duursma and Karlsrud, "Predictive Peacekeeping," p 3. The UN Peacebuilding Support Office, in fact, explicitly recommends that "any intervention using these technologies must be mindful of the operational and ethical risks associated with using data that can be linked to personally identifiable information." Escobal, Lorena et al. (2018) "Big Data for Peace and Security," *UN Peacebuilding Support Office/SIPA*, pp 5–6.

Sparrow. QataLog uses AI-based language processing technology to automatically "listen" to public radio talk shows and "read" public social media streams in different geographies across the globe. The tool allows UN analysts to personalize machine learning text classifications and extract useful information on trends.[26] Sparrow is a social media scanning tool that separates noise from authentic conversations. We know that a portion of online conversation is intended to sway public opinion in favor of this or that political agenda—often using incorrect facts, sponsored by foreign actors, or fueled by automated systems, i.e., bots. Sparrow addresses this concern as it "allows UN desk officers in New York and in field missions to rapidly analyze Twitter data and separate 'noise' created by bots on social media from authentic political speech," thereby capturing actual sentiment trends in the population.[27] These harvested data, alongside other information on conflict events, could potentially be mined for predictive signals. However, as it stands, Qatalog and Sparrow do not formulate predictions but rather only monitor current and past trends.

UN-contracted private companies supplying data analytics tend to be less lead-footed regarding their products' predictive capacity. Druet, in his survey, notes the use of third-party social media analysis tools such as Dataminr and Predata. These platforms, "in use in pockets of DPO/DPPA headquarters and missions," claim to function as conflict early warning tools. Yet, he finds that several factors limit their actual utility in peacekeeping. For example, internet coverage is likely limited in areas affected by conflict, which can create data blind spots. Also, disparities in local usages of social media can make meaningful analyses across populations difficult. Druet concludes that "few, if any, social media analysis tools can offer predictive insights with sufficient geographic precision in peacekeeping contexts to be tactically actionable."[28] Duursma and Karlsrud similarly cast doubt on the capacity of "automated data extraction algorithms, such as web scraping and signal detection based on social media," to "forecast low-probability conflict events with high temporal and spatial accuracy."[29]

---

[26] "Experimenting with Big Data and Artificial Intelligence to Support Peace and Security," (2018) UN Global Pulse, https://www.unglobalpulse.org/document/experimenting-with-big-data-and-ai-to-support-peace-and-security/.

[27] "'We Use Technology, Not the Other Way Around'—Social Media and Political Analysis" (2021) Politically Speaking, September 30, https://dppa.medium.com/we-use-technology-not-the-other-way-around-social-media-and-political-analysis-e97706ba0465.

[28] Druet, "Thematic Research Paper for the DPO Peacekeeping Technology Strategy," p 10.

[29] Duursma and Karlsrud, "Predictive Peacekeeping," pp 6–8.

We must add that even when and where the tools do work, uptake by peace operators is not always a given. Kristian Hoelscher and Jason Miklian, senior researchers at the Peace Research Institute Oslo, talk about an "expertise gap" that occurs when private technology start-ups jump into the global peacebuilding space. The past years have seen a plethora of such start-ups surface, "often through government and philanthropic funders who believe that cutting-edge technologies can help mitigate political evils." The trouble, they point out, is that "it leads to an expertise gap as start-ups launch peace tools without employing existing peacebuilding knowledge—or worse, don't think that such knowledge is needed at all . . . then, experts dismiss the well-meaning initiatives as being hopelessly naive to complex conflict realities."[30]

Martin Wählisch, a founding member of the DPPA's Innovation Cell, in fact, tempers enthusiasm on the topic of predictive technologies in peacekeeping. He warns straightforwardly that "new technologies cannot be a panacea for any analytical question in conflict prevention or any operational challenge in peacemaking." Even the most advanced technologies can only leverage "diplomatic efforts to a certain extent: Personal experience and gut feeling for political nuances cannot be replaced by machines, yet."[31]

In addition, as Pauwels reminds us, there is always the risk that "technologies built for lawful use can easily be adapted to facilitate surveillance in violation of human rights principles."[32] A desire within the UN system to be respectful of rights can dampen the zest to pick up certain tools even when they are arguably within reach. Then there is the risk of "automation bias." It turns out that humans have a documented tendency to be less critical of suggestions made by automated decision-making systems than they are of their own judgment.[33] This bias can result in an over-reliance on predictive technologies (and an over-confidence in their output), which may complicate the ability to respond effectively in fast-moving and emergent conflict scenarios. The above and related concerns have likely contributed to curbing efforts to turn tools like SAGE, Qatalog, and Sparrow from purely monitoring ones to predictive ones too, and generated skepticism within the UN toward tech companies' out-of-the-box software solutions.

---

[30] Hoelscher, Kristian and Jason Miklian (2017) "Can Innovators be Peacebuilders? A Peace Innovation Action Plan," *Global Policy Journal*, August 1.
[31] Wählisch, "Big Data, New Technologies, and Sustainable Peace," p 123.
[32] Pauwels, "Artificial Intelligence and Data Capture Technologies in Violence and Conflict Prevention," p 11.
[33] Ibid, p 16.

Nevertheless, the past two decades have seen significant technological advances in other parts of the multilateral system, as well as academic and policy areas contiguous to it. While fraught with growing pains, it is clear that these technologies are destined to become an increasingly significant part of the wider multilateral system's work related to government instability, climate change, displacement, terrorism, armed conflict, and international development.[34] The next section of this chapter will review some of the progress made in using environmental data for prevention, and highlight the role of multilateral organization member states and their academic institutions in supporting these advances.

In 2017, the Swiss Foreign Department of Federal Affairs and the Canton of Basel-Stadt launched the Basel Peace Forum. The forum intends to "inspire new and unconventional ideas for peacebuilding." To this end, decision-makers, diplomats, academics, and civil society leaders meet yearly to "rethink peace." As early as the 2017 inception edition, linkages between peace, artificial intelligence, and risk analysis took center stage. David Lanz, head of the Mediation Program at Swisspeace, wrote in a summary of the workshop exploring these linkages that "research around AI needs to be refocused to how the technology can promote peace, rather than wage war."[35] This is no small point. As we have seen in previous chapters the vast majority of state investment in AI and related technologies has gone to advance nations' surveillance, defense, and intelligence apparatuses. Nevertheless, a small number of states have steadily increased investment in AI-fueled early warning projects that can potentially help defend civil liberties, prevent

---

[34] For a review of literature describing developments in the past two decades see Trappl, Robert, ed. (2006) *Programming for Peace: Computer-Aided Methods for International Conflict Resolution and Prevention*, Springer; Goldstone, Jack et al. (2010) "A Global Model for Forecasting Political Instability," *American Journal of Political Science* 5, 190–208; O'Brien, Sean (2010) "Crisis Early Warning and Decision Support: Contemporary Approaches and Thoughts on Future Research," *International Studies Review* 12/1, 87–104; Hegre, Havard et al. (2013) "Predicting Armed Conflict, 2010–2050," *International Studies Quarterly* 57/2, 250–270; Mancini, Franceso, ed. (2013) "New Technology and the Prevention of Violence and Conflict," *International Peace Institute*; Guo, Weisi, Kristian Gleditsch, and Alan Wilson (2018) "Retool AI to Forecast and Limit Wars," *Nature Comment* 562/7727, pp 331–333; Gupta, Ravi and Hugh Brooks (2013) *Using Social Media for Global Security*, Wiley; Reuter, Christian, ed. (2019) *Information Technology for Peace and Security: IT Applications and Infrastructures in Conflicts, Crises, War, and Peace*, Springer; and Petheram, Andre et al. (2020) "Fakes, Files, and Facial Recognition," *Oxford Insights*. For a description of uses in development see Raja, Siddhartha et al. (2018) "People and Data," in *Information and Communications for Development: Data-Driven Development*, Boutheina Guermazi ed, World Bank Group.

[35] Lanz, David (2017) "New Technologies to Prevent Conflict and Build Peace: Critical Reflections of the Basel Peace Forum Workshops on AI, Warfare, Ethics," *Basel Peace Forum*, accessed December 11, 2023, https://basel-peace.org/assets/listitem/Critical-reflections/Basel-Peace-Forum-Critical-Reflections-New-Technologies.pdf.

armed conflict, and avert mass atrocities in various geographies—typically far afield from their national borders.

Much of this investment is carried out in partnership with academia.[36] For example, the Violence Early Warning System (VIEWS) was created by researchers at Uppsala University and the Peace Research Institute Oslo. It can automatically identify future instances of violence in Africa. VIEWS is publicly available, data-driven, and "generates monthly probabilistic assessments of the likelihood that fatal political violence will occur." Its predictions can see up to three years into the future for each 55×55 km grid cell throughout the African continent. The work is funded by the European Research Council, the Swedish Research Council, the UN High Commissioner for Refugees, and the UK Foreign and Commonwealth Office, among others.[37]

A similar example is Conflict Forecast. Investigators here have developed a model that can predict outbreaks of internal armed conflict by automatically parsing through "millions of newspaper articles" published since 1989. The project predicts conflict up to a year in advance in 180 countries worldwide. It is funded by the UK Foreign and Commonwealth Office and the Spanish National Research Council.[38]

Another case of successful academic–government cooperation is the Armed Conflict Location and Event Data Project (ACLED). Its prediction tool, the Conflict Alert System (CAST), forecasts violence events for every country in the world up to six months in the future. The forecasts are made using population statistics and ACLED's own event data—"information on the dates, actors, locations, fatalities, and types of all reported political violence and protest events around the world"—which is a handy resource to practitioners and scholars in itself. The project received funding from the University of Texas at Austin, the European Research Council, the US Department of State, the German Federal Foreign Office, and the Dutch

---

[36] Cooperation with academia is quite common even in the UN. The DPPA's Innovation Cell, for example, cooperated with researchers at Stanford University to explore the correlation between depleting groundwater and civil unrest, and at MIT to better sharpen tools that monitor social media conversations occurring in dialects and less common languages around the world. See Brown, Dalvin (2021) "The United Nations Is Turning to Artificial Intelligence in Search for Peace in War Zones," *The Washington Post*, April 23; and "Getting to Grips with New Tech in Prevention and Peacemaking" (2019) *Politically Speaking*, November 22, https://dppa.medium.com/getting-to-grips-with-new-tech-in-prevention-and-peacemaking-7ee5fc6461ce.

[37] VIEWS, "About," accessed December 11, 2023, https://viewsforecasting.org/about/; and Uppsala University Department of Peace and Conflict Research, "Research," accessed December 11, 2023, www.pcr.uu.se/research/views/; see also Ryan-Mosley, Tate (2019) "We Are Finally Getting Better at Predicting Organised Conflict," *MIT Technology Review*, October 24.

[38] Conflict Forecast, "About," accessed December 11, 2023, https://conflictforecast.org/about.

Ministry of Foreign Affairs. Multilateral support has come via the International Organization for Migration and the Complex Risk Analytics Fund (CRAF'd).[39]

The UN-hosted CRAF'd, launched in collaboration with the World Bank in 2021 and supported by the German, Dutch, US, and Finnish governments, is poised to become a key player in the field and allow multilateral organizations to play a more significant role in advancing this kind of work. The fund is a financing instrument that seeks to "better capabilities to share data, insights, and research more seamlessly; and, over time, predict risks earlier"[40] and "to spur anticipatory action before disasters unfold."[41] To this end, it invests in data analysis tools, forecasting systems, and techniques to examine information from a wide variety of sources.[42]

Other initiatives are funded directly by national governments and then shared. The Turing Group, in partnership with UK government defense and security agencies, developed a technology called Global Urban Analytics for Resilient Defence, or GUARD. This tool enables peacekeepers to predict where urban conflict will likely break out twelve months in advance. Veronica Wardman, a technical partner for the project, states that "different populations and cultures have different dynamics, trigger points, and strategic influence, which must be appreciated and taken into account." One of the main innovations of GUARD is that "it seeks to unpick and understand this space using the latest cutting-edge tools and techniques."[43]

In other cases, projects may start with public research funds but then find further support from the private sector. The free, open-source resource called the Global Database of Events, Language, and Tone, or GDELT, is a good example. Here, work funded in part by US National Science Foundation grants to create a news monitoring and forecasting capacity, was

---

[39] ACLED, "Conflict Alert System," accessed December 11, 2023, https://acleddata.com/early-warning-research-hub/conflict-alert-system/; and ACLED, "About," accessed December 11, 2023, https://acleddata.com/about-acled/.

[40] CRAF'd, "Homepage," accessed September 25, 2024, https://crafd.io/.

[41] "United Nations and Partners Launch Complex Risk Analytic Fund to Unlock Power of Data for Crisis Action" (2021) *United Nations*, October 13, https://press.un.org/en/2021/dev3444.doc.htm.

[42] CRAF'd, "Who We Are," accessed September 25, 2024, https://crafd.io/who-we-are.

[43] "Predicting Conflict a Year in Advance," *The Alan Turing Institute*, accessed December 11, 2023, www.turing.ac.uk/research/research-programmes/artificial-intelligence-ai/safe-and-ethical. Similar initiatives go further back in time. The US military's Integrated Crisis Early Warning System (ICEWS) could automatically monitor and forecast events that affect security interests more than a decade ago. See O'Brien, Sean (2010) "Crisis Early Warning and Decision Support: Contemporary Approaches and Thoughts on Future Research," *International Studies Review*, 12/1, 87–104.

then expanded via support from Jigsaw, a technology incubator created by Google. GDELT "monitors the world's news media from nearly every corner of every country in print, broadcast, and web formats, in over 100 languages, every moment of every day." All global news is translated in real-time into English and categorized according to hundreds of event types, thousands of emotions, and millions of themes. GDELT's Risk Assessment and Global Trends tool offers visibility into emerging conflict risks by identifying key trends in the last forty-eight-hour news cycle and comparing them to the previous forty-eight-hour cycle.[44]

These are only some of the many projects in what has sometimes been referred to as the "peacetech" field. The term, in vogue with the establishment of representative nonprofits like Build Up, PeaceTech Lab, and JustPeace Labs,[45] collectively refers to those initiatives operating at the intersection of data, human rights, and peacebuilding. A New York University Center on International Cooperation (CIC) resource called the Ecosystem Map: Data for Peacebuilding and Prevention provides information on this evolving space. The Ecosystem Map is an interactive digital tool that surveys all existing global organizations (ranging from civil society, to government, to the private sector) working with data for peacebuilding.[46] Developments in the field have been so fast and varied that it can be hard to keep track, making this tool especially valuable to peace practitioners. Paige Arthur, a fellow at the center, and Branka Panic, a visiting scholar, make a strong case for it in a CIC publication that describes how a centralized repository of different data technologies is essential to peacebuilding in the digital era.[47]

As in previous chapters, let us briefly turn to future trends in the field. It is likely that peacetech initiatives will increasingly make use of digital twins in their attempt to better understand the drivers of conflict. Digital twins are

---

[44] The GDELT Project, "Homepage," accessed December 11, 2023, www.gdeltproject.org/. For an example of academia–civil society collaboration see the Early Warning Project (EWP), https://earlywarningproject.ushmm.org/. This system can assess the likelihood of mass atrocities in countries worldwide up to two years in advance. EWP is a joint initiative of the Simon-Skjodt Center for the Prevention of Genocide at the United States Holocaust Memorial Museum and the Dickey Center for International Understanding at Dartmouth College. For a system with a similar objective but with forecasting capacity still under development, see the Sentinel Project, https://thesentinelproject.org/what-we-do/early-warning-system/.
[45] See https://howtobuildup.org/, www.peacetechlab.org/, and https://justpeacelabs.org/.
[46] NYU-CIC, "Data for Peace Map," accessed December 11, 2023, https://cic.nyu.edu/data-for-peace-map.
[47] Panic, Branka and Paige Arthur (2021) "Towards A Prevention and Peacebuilding Data Hub: Scoping the Future of Data Services and Capacity Building," *NYU Center on International Cooperation*, pp 1–5.

virtual replicas that mirror real-world objects or systems, like wind turbines, airplanes, factories, office spaces, government agencies, or even an entire city and the people in it. Creating the digital twin of an environment permits the testing of different hypothetical scenarios. Variables can be tweaked, producing the effect of a time-machine that allows for experimentation with potential solutions.

City administrations are already experimenting with the technology for infrastructure planning. The Planning and Development Agency in Boston changed their plans for a project after seeing the effect on the digital twin landscape they created. Singapore has created a digital twin of the entire city, which contributes valuable information for urban planning. Populations can also be twinned to help authorities "determine the best way to serve the public and better meet the needs of individual citizens," in what amounts to "the mass personalization of government services."[48]

In conflict-affected environments, an entire polity can be replicated and different intervention scenarios tested before real-world deployment of peacekeeping personnel. Even the reactions of citizens to that intervention can be tested through their digital twins. Advances in generative AI technologies will play a significant role here, as the digital twins of citizens will be animated by large language models (LLMs). In a way, the models will become proxies of the real citizens. Indeed, research shows that LLM-powered replicas can already accurately mimic real citizen voting preferences and political stances on a host of issues.

The technique is based on the idea of "AI agents." An agent is a model that has been programmed to behave in a certain way based on preset demographic characteristics and access to limited information environments, like news articles from select outlets. In essence, it is AI that has been instructed to act human. Researchers have set up "populations of thousands of AI agents that respond as if they are individual members of a survey population, like humans on a panel that get called periodically to answer questions."[49] While the technique may not yield perfect results, it has the following key

---

[48] Chenok, Dan (2023) "Three Ways AI-Powered Digital Twins Can Improve Government Services," *The Business of Government*, September 11, www.businessofgovernment.org/blog/three-ways-ai-powered-digital-twins-can-improve-government-services. See also Scoble-Williams, Nic et al. (2024) "How Play And Experimentation In Digital Playgrounds Can Drive Human Performance," *Deloitte Insights*, February 5, www2.deloitte.com/us/en/insights/focus/human-capital-trends/2024/using-digital-playgrounds-to-advance-workplace-technology.html.
[49] Berger, Aaron et al. (2024) "Using AI for Political Polling," *The Ash Center for Democratic Governance and Innovation, Harvard Kennedy School*, June 7, https://ash.harvard.edu/articles/using-ai-for-political-polling/; see also Stahle, Tyler (2023) "Can AI Predict How You Will Vote in the Next

advantages: 1) Unlike human-dependent surveys it can operate indefatigably round-the-clock, 2) It can swiftly incorporate new information ensuring responses remain current, 3) It can replicate millions of respondents far exceeding the scope of traditional surveys, and 4) By eliminating direct human interaction in data collection it is possible to mitigate certain forms of response bias.

Peace practitioners, as well as development and humanitarian relief workers, are set to benefit from this and other technologies reviewed thus far. However, the policy implications that naturally arise when deploying potentially game-changing technologies at the multilateral level of governance remain quite challenging. Some important discussions are starting to surface in the public debate. One organization pushing forward thinking in this area is the Organisation for Economic Cooperation and Development (OECD). Through a series of publications, the OECD has invited reflection on the uses of automation in the public sector and shed light on the policy concerns accompanying the technologies.[50] Among think tanks, the Carnegie Council for Ethics in International Affairs' Artificial Intelligence and Equality Initiative has been raising important questions about the potential for "AI systems [to] exacerbate structural inequalities."[51] JustPeace Labs, a nonprofit, has broached the matter in a document entitled "Ethical Guidelines for PeaceTech" and other publications. They argue for the need to protect communities on the receiving end of the technologies against "the risk of physical harm, shaming, retribution and group harms."[52] Furthermore, they emphasize the importance of deploying technologies hand in hand with local communities in order to create "effective partnerships for peace and human security."[53]

UN institutions, too, are increasingly sensitized to these broader reflections. In a briefing to the Security Council, Rosemary DiCarlo, Under-Secretary for Political and Peacebuilding Affairs, expressed several policy-related concerns about the increased reliance on digital technologies. She

Election?" BYU News, March 27, https://news.byu.edu/intellect/can-ai-predict-how-youll-vote-in-the-next-election-byu-study-says-yes.

[50] OECD (2019) "Hello, World: Artificial Intelligence and its Use in the Public Sector," *OECD Observatory of Public Sector Innovation*; OECD (2019) "Artificial Intelligence in Society," OECD Publishing; and OECD (2020) "Governance Responses to Disinformation: How Open Government Principles can Inform Policy Options," OECD Working Papers on Public Governance.

[51] CCEIA-AIEI, "Homepage," accessed December 11, 2023, www.carnegiecouncil.org/initiatives-issues/artificial-intelligence-and-equality.

[52] "Ethical Guidelines for PeaceTech" (2019) JustPeace Labs.

[53] "Technology in Fragile Contexts: Engagement, Partnerships, and Positive Action" (2021) JustPeace Labs.

brought up, for example, the possibility of automated systems being able to make decisions that impact human lives without humans being directly involved and highlighted the need for a "global digital compact"—as called for in the Secretary-General's Our Common Agenda—to outline principles for an "open, free, and secure digital future for all." The UN, she said, "has a critical opportunity to build consensus on how digital technologies can be used for the good of people and the planet" and stressed that "collective action by Member States remains essential towards this goal."[54]

To this end, in 2018 the UN Secretary-General laid out a roadmap for a "digital revolution throughout the UN system." The DPO, together with the Departments of Operational Support and Management Strategy, Policy, and Compliance subsequently produced a joint *Strategy for the Digital Transformation of UN Peacekeeping*. In it, they recognize that the vast quantity of information now available through digital technologies can play a role in conflict prevention—but that this is "accompanied by a high risk of collective data harms." According to the document, these may include abuses such as "breaches of confidentiality, behavioral surveillance, information disorder, information infrastructure sabotage or disruption." The authors also acknowledge that there are questions around "data ownership, sovereignty and consent, social justice and potential social harm, as well as gender, race or other biases in algorithms for processing and analyzing data." Taken together, these and other risks underscore the "importance of choosing a do-no-harm approach" when using predictive technologies for peace operations.[55]

What does an "open, free, and secure digital future for all" look like in the specific case of conflict-tracking technologies used in multilateral peacekeeping and peacebuilding? What are the challenges to these technologies being used in a way that "chooses a do-no-harm approach"? Dirk Druet, gives us an excellent example of the practical conundrum at hand:

> Moving toward a more automated predictive event analysis system would need to address cognitive and default biases already present in peacekeeping data analysis event taxonomies. For example, a decision to reduce complexity in the MONUSCO SAGE data entry form saw a large number of Mayi-Mayi groups collapsed into a single category for event perpetrator

---

[54] "Political Affairs Chief Spells Out Double-edged Nature of Digital Technologies, in Briefing to Security Council" (2022) *United Nations*, May 23, https://press.un.org/en/2022/sc14899.doc.htm.
[55] "Strategy for the Digital Transformation of UN Peacekeeping" (2021) Department of Peace Operations, pp 7, 13.

attribution, risking the identification of linkages where none exist. Ongoing taxonomy debates have also highlighted the particular challenges of using value- and/or legally-laden terms, such as "terrorism" to describe events in a culturally and politically diverse analytical environment.[56]

Druet makes a critical point, particularly if we are to take at heart the spirit of Our Common Agenda and the views of those communities most likely to be on the receiving end of decisions informed by the predictive models' output. It is a mistake to assume that all stakeholders share the same definitions, categories, and parameters, which are fundamental to how the technology is calibrated. Put simply, these assumptions directly impact the kinds of predictions made and about whom. The slightest shift in taxonomy can change who the model predicts is likely to commit violence in the future. Building consensus around the parameters used to calibrate the models, and ensuring that the process is transparent and inclusive, will therefore be hugely consequential to their fair deployment within a multilateral system which, by definition, is "culturally and politically diverse."

Just as we found in previous chapters that reviewed technologies deployed at the local and national levels (and that utilize data about people's bodies, thoughts, and social lives), tools that are used at the multilateral level (and that use various combinations of environmental data) can only be considered fair if there is consensus regarding their calibration parameters. If not, then it is a clear case of the "power-knowledge nexus" described above by Carolyn Biltoft being exercised by one group at the expense of another.[57] Moreover, they are also very likely to fail in their objective, just like the many twentieth-century schemes described by James Scott in *Seeing like a State* that lacked the humility and context sensitivity to recognize the value of local views.[58] Not addressing this matter head on risks slowing the adoption of new technologies and foregoing the global security benefits that may otherwise accrue. It is pivotal, therefore, for stakeholders to have a shared understanding of the policy dimensions involved when taking these technologies forward.

There are also a number of legal questions that crop up when endowing an international organization with software that can predict future events. For example: What legal liability do civil servants have when they are given

---

[56] Druet, "Thematic Research Paper for the DPO Peacekeeping Technology Strategy," p 16.
[57] Biltoft, *A Violent Peace*, pp 10–11.
[58] Scott, *Seeing Like a State*.

foreknowledge of a probable violent future event, like a terrorist attack, but do not act upon it. Are they responsible toward the victims of that attack when and if it occurs? How can foresight generation affect the balance of sovereignty between major donor nations (that can afford to fund cutting-edge predictive technologies) and conflict-affected nations (that cannot, but are the target of the technology)? What confidential information would institutional users, like UN peace agencies, be handing over to private sector software owners (for example, via a hidden "back door") by the very act of using it in a certain way? Classified political objectives and priorities would become all too clear. It is difficult to scratch the surface of the challenges involved without being drawn into a rabbit hole of sorts.

On one level, the answers to these and related legal quandaries depend on the actors using and supplying the technology. Eleonore Pauwels points out that predictive technologies possess a profound capacity for conflict prevention but can be damaging in the wrong hands. Indeed, she notes that the same tools that can be used for peacemaking can be used by nefarious actors for "social surveillance and control, repression, and racial profiling." Massive data sets encompassing biometric, financial, geolocation, and behavioral information on entire populations introduce "new opportunities for authoritarian states or violent nonstate actors to control populations" and threaten "political participation, peaceful assembly, and freedom of movement."[59] Meg King and Aaron Shull, from the Center for International Governance Innovation, would agree. They argue that regulators, in cooperation with the private sector, must identify bad actors to prevent "behavioral nudging ... and foreign adversarial influence on everything from elections to societal cohesion."[60]

While we must not underestimate the role of bad actors whose intentions may be inimical to democracy, on another, deeper level it may be the technology itself, irrespective of who is using it, that causes legal harm. Rainer Mühlhoff, a research associate at the Technical University of Berlin, raises an interesting point. Predictive analytics, he says, is used to forecast the future behavior of a target group or individual, but this prediction results from an analysis of enormous sets of behavioral data—the vast majority of

---

[59] Pauwels, Eleonore (2022) "Counterterrorism and Violence Prevention: Safeguarding Against the Misuse and Abuse of Artificial Intelligence," *Global Center on Cooperative Security*, pp 2–4.

[60] King, Meg and Aaron Shull (2020) "Introduction: How Can Policy Makers Predict the Unpredictable?," in Modern Conflict and Artificial Intelligence, *Centre for International Governance Innovation*, pp 2–4.

which is *not about them*. In other words, predictions about specific groups or individuals are made "based on the data many unrelated individuals provided." These predictions then inform differential treatment of that person or group.[61]

In a peacekeeping or policing setting it would look something like this: A specific person or group is predicted to have a higher likelihood of engaging in future violence, triggering closer monitoring of their activities or curbing of their legal rights. That prediction, however, is built on statistical modeling of data collected almost entirely about other peoples' activities. Mühlhoff notes how this "gap" between the target of a prediction and the training data "challenges ethical principles such as human dignity and the (liberal) notion of individual privacy." Indeed, "we face situations where an individual's (or group's) privacy is violated using data other individuals provide about themselves, possibly even anonymously."[62] In other words, it is now possible to know something about person or group A by crunching data from persons or groups B, C, and D.[63]

It is worth briefly recalling the deductive frameworks we found to be at work in the technologies covered in chapters 3, 5, and 7. Conflict prediction tools process information about citizens' wider environment in much the same way that policing and national security models process data about peoples' bodies, thoughts, and social lives. All these technologies are rooted in an understanding of events as determined by external causes. From a deductive perspective, it is possible to derive an outcome based on a series of premises (i.e., if all these environmental causes are present, then person or group A will likely engage in conflict). Just as we found with sentiment recognition or social profiling technologies, particular instances of a condition are inferred by reference to a series of general rules. Confidence in this chain of causal links is required for any governance action based on these technologies to be justified, yet this leaves little room for emergent phenomena—things that occur in the world but cannot be measured or explained.

---

[61] Mühlhoff, Rainer (2021) "Predictive Privacy: Towards an Applied Ethics of Data Analytics," *Ethics and Information Technology*, 23, 675–690, p 675.

[62] Ibid, p 687. The author also correctly points out that in this way, by establishing parameters of normalcy and deviance, "predictive systems produce and stabilize precisely the kinds of social differences and inequalities that they claim to merely detect in the world."

[63] Riddles such as these have prompted conversations around the need to redefine the very notion of privacy. For example, given the scenario described above, it may no longer be possible to safeguard individual privacy simply via anonymization or other "blurring" techniques.

Furthermore, we must add to the "target gap" described above a "temporal gap" that exists when acting today based on events that are predicted to occur tomorrow. Consider the difficulty of intervening toward certain groups based on what statistical models (that crunch data on mostly other groups) say they are possibly going to do in the future. The further in the future the prediction, the more this concern is magnified. Any multilateral governance decision based on the output of a prediction model engenders, by definition, a trade-off between a cost paid today and a benefit accrued tomorrow. This is an odd trade-off because it involves comparing apples to oranges; or rather, apples to imaginary oranges. Actions taken in the present are selectively applied, immediate, and quite real, while the benefits are generic, far-off, and only hypothetical. This means that resource distribution today can be dependent on definitions of future benefits that are ultimately not tethered to any factual reality.

This temporal gap makes predictive models vulnerable to manipulation by political and economic interest groups. Anja Kaspersen and Wendell Wallach, senior fellows at the Carnegie Council for Ethics in International Affairs, reflect on this risk in their critique of the idea known as "long-termism." The idea, popularized by philosopher William MacAskill, posits that the current generation should be making sacrifices to avert threats to future generations, and "that the fate of humanity should be our top moral priority." On the surface, few would disagree with such an obvious statement, but when we try to apply the logic to specific cases the trade-offs are not so clear-cut. Kaspersen and Wallach fear that "legitimate concerns can easily be distorted and conflated with personal desires, goals, messianic convictions, and the promotion of deeply embedded political agendas and corporate interests." Groups may discount short-term harms by claiming future benefits will outweigh the costs. Via this mechanism, "the well-intentioned philosophy of long-termism ... risks becoming a Trojan horse for the vested interests of a select few." Or worse, it can give credence to the agendas of "technological elites" pushing developments "that have clearly demonstrated the potential to exacerbate inequalities and harm the wider public interest."[64]

---

[64] Kaspersen, Anja and Wendell Wallach (2022) "Long-termism: An Ethical Trojan Horse," *Carnegie Council for Ethics in International Affairs*. MacAskill's long-termism is a common theme in the 2021 UN Secretary-General's manifesto, Our Common Agenda. The document urges that "now is the time to think for the long term, to deliver more for young people and succeeding generations and to be better prepared for the challenges ahead" and laments that "our dominant political and economic incentives remain weighted heavily in favor of the short term and status quo, prioritizing

At a minimum, affected groups may want to know what data goes into the modeling and how long-term forecasts are made, but they may also want a voice in the ethical debates around trade-offs and how they are defined. MinJi Song, a UN Innovation Cell member, expresses this spirit when pointing to the importance of "democratizing foresight" and the need to "question whose vision of the future are we exploring, testing, and working towards."[65] Ideally, such an approach would collaboratively identify costs and benefits, be culturally and politically inclusive when calibrating models, and satisfy broader citizen questions around the target and temporal gaps inherent in the technology. How this may be practically achieved will be explored in chapter 11.

---

immediate gains at the expense of longer-term human and planetary well-being." To rectify this, the Common Agenda proposes to establish a Futures Laboratory to "support States, subnational authorities and others to build capacity and exchange good practices to enhance long-termism, forward action, and adaptability." UN (2021) "Our Common Agenda—Report of the Secretary-General," pp 4, 38, 45.

[65] Song, MinJi (2021) "What if Uncertainty is the Path to Peace?" *Futuring Peace*, October 8, https://medium.com/futuring-peace/what-if-uncertainty-is-the-path-to-peace-29cfc5cd03d4.

PHOTO SECTION
CONTEXT

Chapter 10
Kenya

In this chapter we revisit Africa to explore developments in Kenya in more depth with the help of Alphonce Shiundu of Africa Check and Lilian Olivia Orero from Safe Online Women Kenya (SOW-Kenya). Africa Check is one of the foremost independent fact-checking organizations in Africa. It assesses thousands of claims made in the public domain, particularly those related to elections, conflict, public health, the economy, and other policy issues.[1] A number of countries have dedicated country desks, and Alphonce Shiundu, award-winning writer and journalist, is the editor for their Kenya office. As well as being the organization's public representative in Kenya, he oversees its day-to-day operations and conducts training on evidence-based decision-making for journalists and on media literacy for civil society. He has personally introduced fact-checking research on Kenya's mainstream print and electronic media.

SOW-Kenya provides digital literacy education for young women and girls in secondary and higher education, empowering them with the skills to navigate online spaces safely. The organization promotes awareness about gender-based violence and cyberbullying, and conducts research on digital threats faced by Kenyan women and girls.[2] SOW-Kenya was founded in 2023 by Lilian Olivia Orero, who is a gender and technology lawyer and an advocate of the High Court of Kenya. She is also involved in research on AI-generated disinformation and gender bias mitigation in AI algorithms.

In the interview with Alphonce Shiundu, he discussed the use of automated disinformation detection tools, and shares his fears about the impact of disinformation—including state-sponsored disinformation—on the quality of public debate. He also described the effect of data-collection technologies on civil rights in Kenya, and the sensitive role of multilateral organizations like the United Nations and the World Bank in both data

---

[1] Africa Check, "Homepage," accessed November 9, 2023, https://africacheck.org/.
[2] Safe Online Women Kenya, "Homepage," accessed November 9, 2023, www.sow-kenya.org/.

Political Automation. Eduardo Albrecht, Oxford University Press. © Oxford University Press (2025).
DOI: 10.1093/9780197696989.003.0010

creation and regulation efforts. The benefits and challenges of government use of predictive technologies are also considered.

In Lilian Olivia Orero's interview she discussed the use of data capture technologies in Africa by foreign countries and international organizations, and the potential misuse of these technologies for surveillance purposes. She also raised concerns about bias in data collection due to the exclusion of local cultural and linguistic frameworks in the design of the technologies, which can lead to the unequal distribution of aid and resources. She also emphasized the need for digital literacy and AI technology regulation in Africa.[3]

Alphonce, can you speak about your work with Africa Check?

Africa Check is an organization dedicated to combating misinformation across the continent. Its mission goes beyond mere fact-checking and encompasses educating and recruiting a network of fact-checkers to foster a well-informed online community. Despite the challenge of low internet penetration in many parts of Africa, Africa Check actively engages with various groups, from primary school students to university scholars, and uses platforms like community radio and national TV to raise awareness about the dangers of false information. This effort is particularly crucial in contexts like health, politics, elections, and the economy, where misinformation can lead to poor decision-making.

The core objective of Africa Check is to promote honest public debate. By ensuring that public figures and decision-makers use data-backed information, the organization aims to inform and elevate public discourse. In this endeavor, AI plays a significant role.

In collaboration with funders like the Google Foundation, and working alongside similar organizations like Chequeado in Argentina and Full Fact in the UK, Africa Check is exploring AI tools to identify potentially false claims. Currently, the project is in the phase where the system can recognize claims that need fact-checking, who made them, and the context. However, the process is ongoing. Automated fact-checking presents its own set of challenges. Fact-checking is not only a process but also involves

---

[3] Interviews held via videoconferencing technology on September 13 (Shiundu) and September 18 (Orero), 2023; replies paraphrased by author.

subjective analysis based on expertise and context. Integrating nuanced decision-making into AI systems is complex and remains a work in progress.

Africa Check operates as a nonprofit, relying on grants from various organizations. Transparency in funding is a key principle, and as mandated by the International Fact-Checking Network, all sponsors and donors are listed on the organization's website. This practice ensures that Africa Check maintains its integrity, avoiding any perception of bias or agenda-pushing.

Africa Check's work is a multifaceted approach to combating misinformation, involving education, community engagement, and the development of AI tools for fact-checking. By promoting data-backed public discourse and working toward advanced AI solutions, Africa Check is at the forefront of the fight against misinformation in Africa, upholding transparency and accuracy in an age where these values are increasingly crucial.

What is a specific example of disinformation in Kenya?

There was a case of misinformation around 2014 during Kenya's involvement in Somalia, where the conflict persisted since 2011. In 2014, an attack occurred in the Kenyan village of Mpeketoni, resulting in many casualties. The incident had all the hallmarks of the militant group Al-Shabaab, operating out of Somalia. However, when the then-president, Uhuru Kenyatta, addressed the public, he denied it was an attack by that group.

Now the context here is most of the people who had been killed belonged to the ethnic community of the former president. They were from the Kikuyu community. The Kikuyu, however, are not the dominant community in the region where the attack took place, which is on the Kenyan coast. They were settled there many years ago, post-independence, during Uhuru Kenyatta's father's time. So when the president denied the attack was done by Al-Shabaab, initially, this denial seemed plausible due to existing tensions related to land disputes and ethnic rivalry in the coastal region.

However, several months later, Al-Shabaab released videos proving their involvement in the Mpeketoni attack, raising questions about the accuracy of intelligence received by the president. This led to speculation whether misleading information exonerating Al-Shabaab benefited certain parties, potentially due to the desire to maintain the narrative of secure borders. It would be in the interest of police forces and security authorities to say it's not Al-Shabaab. The legitimacy of the Somalia operation is based on the fact that you are in Somalia to get rid of Al-Shabaab and to build a buffer zone with Kenya. It looks quite bad if your citizens are being attacked inside the country by the same group. You would have to bring back troops into Kenya. For Al-Shabaab that would be a win because it's furthering their agenda of getting Kenyan troops out of Somalia.

So you don't know whether it's incompetence by the people who are in office to correctly validate intelligence, or self-preservation by the security apparatus, or something else. The fact is that the initial information coming in, filtering all the way to the president, blaming Kenyans for what is an Al-Shabaab attack, and then circulating in the media, was all a bit murky. This example shows just how difficult it can be to fact-check, with or without AI.

So to clarify, what you're pointing at is that sometimes government bureaucracies are also susceptible to generating disinformation

Yes, they are susceptible and sometimes we think of it as state-sponsored disinformation. State-sponsored disinformation because they would know the facts. So if they know the facts, they are deliberately misrepresenting.

What are your thoughts regarding the use of AI-based data collection and surveillance technologies in Kenya?

The apprehension surrounding big brother-like surveillance and the use of AI in governance is a global concern, vividly illustrated in various African nations, including Kenya. These countries have embarked on ambitious projects which aim to track individuals from birth to death by linking personal details such as social security numbers, bank accounts, marital status, and phone numbers. This extensive data collection raises significant privacy and civil liberties concerns.

Even without sophisticated AI or big data analytics, there have been instances of government misuse of telecommunications infrastructure in Kenya. Activists are tracked and detained by law enforcement based on their social media activity, a trend observed not just in Kenya but across the globe. Such practices underscore the risks involved when governments possess extensive control over information infrastructures and data ecosystems.

Another layer of complexity is added by the presence of major global technology platforms like Google and Meta. These companies hold vast amounts of data about people in Kenya and their influence is amplified by weak or nonexistent data protection laws in the country and in the region. The data collected by these platforms is processed outside our borders allowing insights to be drawn and decisions made from afar.

Addressing these challenges requires a nuanced approach. African governments need to collaborate, possibly through the African Union, to establish robust data privacy laws akin to the European Union's model. This collective action is crucial because the power and influence of technology platforms in shaping public opinion and manipulating audiences cannot be understated.

Yet governments, often lacking the necessary expertise and capacity, must find ways to collaborate with the tech platforms. So it is essential to balance control between governments and the private sector. This balance is critical in ensuring AI serves the public interest without becoming an instrument of power for governments.

AI's potential as a tool for oppression, as seen with social media in some African countries, highlights the need for an approach that safeguards civil liberties and human rights while embracing the inevitable progress of AI technology. The key is not to leave AI regulation solely in the hands of governments or private entities. AI is an unstoppable force but its regulation, particularly in countries like Kenya with burgeoning tech communities, needs careful consideration.

What role can multilateral organizations like the United Nations play in this scenario?

The role of multilateral and international organizations in facilitating the responsible use of AI and data in Africa is a complex and multifaceted issue. Taking Kenya as an example, the country lacked regional data, like GDP figures for its forty-seven counties, until the World Bank intervened. Using night light data, the World Bank developed a model to predict county-level GDP, catalyzing the actual collection of data on the ground in partnership with the Kenya National Bureau of Statistics. Such collaborations can foster information sharing and cooperation between countries, especially for predictive modeling in economics or debt analysis.

However, organizations like the United Nations, the International Monetary Fund, and the World Bank often face skepticism due to their perceived Western bias, and are seen as extensions of a neocolonial mindset. This skepticism is exemplified in situations where actual data is scarce. For instance, while certain areas may be suspected to be havens for drug trafficking or other illegal activity, there may still be a significant lack of concrete data to support this. Despite the potential for AI and satellite data to fill these gaps, questions remain about who should handle this sensitive data. The Kenyan government may be hesitant to share such information with these organizations due to historical mistrust.

Also, the capacity of local statistical bodies to produce reliable data varies greatly, which can affect the effectiveness of models developed by outside organizations. For example, many parts of the Kenyan economy are cash-based, with transactions often not reflected in official banking systems, leading to misconceptions about tax evasion and the actual volume of money in circulation.

To address these challenges, it would be beneficial for nations to collaborate and establish an entity akin to the International Telecommunication Union, but especially for AI and data-collection technologies. This body could develop international norms and guidelines for the responsible use of AI. However, enforcing these norms would be challenging due to local constraints, such as limited technological infrastructure, enforcement capacity, and understanding of AI technologies.

While international and multilateral organizations can play a pivotal role in advancing AI use in Africa, it is crucial to navigate the historical, cultural, and economic contexts sensitively. Establishing international standards while empowering local governments to enforce these norms, considering their unique challenges, is key to successfully integrating AI in a way that benefits African nations.

What are your thoughts about utilizing data collection and AI-based technologies for anticipatory governance, i.e., when governments or multilateral organizations make decisions today based on predictions of what may happen in the future?

You mean like early warning systems where they put together intelligence reports and open-source information to identify emerging risks?

Yes, open-source information, as you mentioned, but also social media monitoring, satellite generated earth observation data, econometric and political indicators, and so forth. My question to you is what are the ethical and political challenges that we may encounter with increased deployment of these types of predictive technologies in Kenya?

When considering AI technologies and their application, especially in the African context, it's crucial to recognize that they often operate on historical data to identify patterns and leading indicators, particularly those signaling conflict. The potential of AI to integrate vast data sets, be it from social media or news articles, presents both opportunities and challenges. They can reveal intricate networks and provide insights, which is a valuable asset in various domains. Although some of these software tools are open source, many come with significant licensing fees.

Concerns about who wields this technological power and how it aligns with ongoing privacy debates are paramount. For instance, would it be acceptable for a company like Meta to provide confidential reports to governments for planning around future economic, political, or social events? This question becomes even more pertinent when considering the application of AI in scenarios like protests or other forms of social unrest.

The Covid-19 pandemic illustrated how government use of mobile telecommunications data for contact tracing could lead to heightened surveillance. Instances where individuals who were in proximity to someone who tested positive were quarantined raised questions about privacy and government overreach. Applying such intensive surveillance techniques, powered by the expanding capabilities of AI, could be beneficial but also poses significant risks. The concern is that regimes might use AI to perpetuate their power or suppress opposition.

For example, AI-enhanced social media listening and analysis could easily target opposition influencers by monitoring sentiment, network connections, and trends. Governments could potentially use this technology to suppress dissent, labeling opposition activities as extremist, hate speech, or a threat to public order. This level of precision in targeting opposition could be alarmingly effective.

While I'm not intimately familiar with the full scope of AI's power in predictive analytics, I've observed early warning systems in action. These systems can trigger alerts and provide decision-makers with timely analysis when risk thresholds are exceeded. However, the overarching concern remains the ethical application of AI, especially in a context where government surveillance and control could significantly impact civil liberties and the democratic process.

While AI offers transformative potential for good, particularly in predictive analytics and early warning systems, the balance between leveraging this technology for public benefit and safeguarding against its misuse by governments or other powerful entities is a delicate one. This balance is critical to ensure that AI's advancements contribute positively to society without becoming tools for oppression or political manipulation.

Lilian, how do foreign entities use data-collection technologies in Kenya?

The deployment of surveillance technologies in sub-Saharan Africa, particularly by nations like China, illustrates a trend that can be described as data colonialism. An example of this is the surveillance of the African Union by China, showcasing the strategic use of such technologies for exerting influence.

Biometric technologies, including facial recognition and fingerprinting, enable foreign organizations to amass extensive data on Kenyan citizens. This data can be utilized not just for tracking individual movements but also for anticipating and influencing future behavior. Data governance is always an issue in situations where personal information is collected without adequately informing citizens about its intended use. This lack of transparency was evident when fingerprints and iris scans were taken from individuals without clear communication regarding the purpose and future use of this data. Such practices raise significant concerns, leaving citizens uncertain about how and where their personal information will be utilized.

The term data colonialism aptly describes this phenomenon where control over vast amounts of data equates to a form of systemic, nonphysical violence. It signifies a power dynamic where the entity in possession of the data gains significant influence and control over the subjects of that data. In this context, surveillance technologies are not merely tools for security or administration but instruments of power that can shape future events and policies.

Are there any examples of multilateral organizations engaged in this process?

My experience, particularly with the United Nations and UN Women, focused on addressing technology-facilitated gender-based violence against women and girls. In this project, we analyzed data from eight African countries to understand the prevalence of cyberbullying. The aim was to explore how technologies could be utilized proactively to counteract gender-based cyberbullying before it occurs. This example highlights the potential of using data and technology to preemptively address social issues, specifically cyberbullying. It demonstrates how international organizations are engaging with technology to tackle complex, pervasive problems like online harassment and violence.

An issue is the inherent bias in data collection and utilization. Regions with extensive data availability often have a higher likelihood of receiving aid or grants from multinational organizations. This is because these organizations possess detailed data about these regions, enabling more targeted interventions. In contrast, areas with less data representation might be overlooked for such initiatives.

For instance, in the case of deploying technologies to counter cyberbullying, only the eight countries in sub-Saharan Africa with existing data are likely to benefit from these technologies. Other countries, lacking in data representation, might not receive the same level of attention or resources. This disparity illustrates the impact of data biases on decision-making and resource allocation by international organizations, highlighting the need for more equitable practices.

Is there a potential danger of bias in the way the technologies themselves are created and deployed?

A notable instance involved a mobile app designed to assist women with their sexual and reproductive health. However, the language of the app inadvertently excluded women from other ethnic groups and tribes who did not speak that language. Consequently, these women were unable to access the app and the vital health information it provided. This scenario underscores the importance of considering linguistic and cultural diversity in the development of technology solutions, especially in regions with a multitude of languages and ethnicities, to ensure equitable access to important health resources and information.

Technology, particularly AI, holds immense potential for enhancing our day-to-day lives, but the real challenge arises when it is used unfairly, leading to adverse consequences. To mitigate these risks, digital literacy awareness is crucial. Educating the population about these technologies is imperative, especially in areas where a significant portion of the population may not understand them. This education will enable more people to engage with and benefit from technological advancements responsibly.

From a legal perspective, AI regulation in Kenya is noticeably behind. Many African countries either lack national policies on AI or, if they do exist, they are often overlooked or underemphasized. There is a tendency in the region to look toward Western countries for policy guidance, waiting to adapt and adopt their regulations. However, this approach can be limiting and may not address the unique challenges and context in Kenya.

The need for local experts in AI to develop country-specific regulations and policies is critical. Such initiatives would ensure that the use of AI and related technologies aligns with the national context, addressing specific needs and challenges in Kenya. By taking proactive steps in policy-making and regulation, Kenya can harness the benefits of AI while safeguarding against its potential risks, paving the way for more inclusive and sustainable technological advancement.

Chapter 11
A Third House

At the heart of this book lies a fundamental question: Are political machines consolidating power and curbing citizen participation in governance? The evidence indicates that this is indeed the case—particularly for already vulnerable sections of the population such as migrants and non-dominant political or ethnic groups—but it also points to a matter of a more metaphysical nature. By placing these machines at the center of our lives, we no longer seem to trust our own judgment as humans. It is hard to say what consequences this may have as it has never happened before.

Let us take a step back. Throughout history, organized religions spoke of an omniscient God who could see everything people did. Feudal and clerical bureaucracies used this as a method of social control. The refrain was clear: God sees you, we are in league with God, here are the rules. States later adapted the playbook by replacing God with either the nation or the proletariat. The refrain changed to the people or the workers are watching, we are their representatives, here are the rules. In truth, governments still saw relatively little compared to what they can see today and relied largely on this kind of vicarious surveillance (via God, the people) to project control. It was still far too expensive to actually pry into every citizen's private life.

Whether the official narrative was for Pater or Patria, in the quiet of their minds, people were left to judge themselves. It was their individual conscience that glued them, or not, to the official narrative. Today, it is possible to monitor what goes on in a person's private life. This means there is a reduced political role for organized religion and its otherworldly gaze, or for national and class ideologies and their mythoi of the masses. But it also means there is a substantially reduced role for individual conscience as a means of self-control. The transition from a mostly abstract surveillance to an actual one eliminates the need for individual judgment. It outsources the task of calculating social compliance from one's conscience to a vast network of smart machines.

Political Automation. Eduardo Albrecht, Oxford University Press. © Oxford University Press (2025).
DOI: 10.1093/9780197696989.003.0011

Belief still plays a part. The reduction of the body, human emotion, social relations, and the environment to reams of data requires an act of trust. We must believe that the symbolic representation is the actual thing. We must concede that decisions computed upon those data are the optimal ones and allow them to take precedence over our own discernment. The new refrain is clear: The machine sees you, it actually does, in fact better than you see yourself, so do as it says.

Of course, it is a ruse that it sees you better than you see yourself. It sees a version of you, a ghost trail of numbers you left behind after interacting with hundreds of little data sniffers crowded into your smartphone, car, home appliances, and urban infrastructure. Nonetheless, it is a very sophisticated ruse, and people, by and large, have accepted it as true. Previous chapters illustrate how government decision-makers around the globe have embraced it as valid and how the rest of us—glad as usual to benefit from the increased convenience and security promised—have also largely acquiesced.

What are the consequences of a society no longer needing individual conscience in order to self-regulate? Anthropologically, this is entirely new territory. Hitherto, there was always a certain amount of residual power housed in the intimacy of your mind that served to buffer even the most audacious authoritarians. You could always lie or privately disagree. Now, unfortunately, your browsing/banking/scrolling histories do not allow you to lie. That power, too, is gone, siphoned off from the wet neural networks in your head to the dry ones humming along in the belly of the political machines.

This is not hyperbole and it is likely to intensify. In the book *Shaping the Future of the Fourth Industrial Revolution*, Klaus Schwab and Nicholas Davis of the World Economic Forum speak of an accelerating fusion of our physical, digital, and biological identities. The authors describe how Fourth Industrial Revolution technologies will allow authorities to

> intrude into the hitherto private space of our minds, reading our thoughts and influencing our behavior . . . As capabilities in this area improve, the temptation for law enforcement agencies and courts to use techniques to determine the likelihood of criminal activity, assess guilt or even possibly retrieve memories directly from people's brains will increase. Even crossing a national border might one day involve a detailed brain scan to assess an individual's security risk . . . Fourth Industrial Revolution technologies will not stop at becoming part of the physical world around

us—they will become part of us. Indeed, some of us already feel that our smartphones have become an extension of ourselves. Today's external devices—from wearable computers to virtual reality headsets—will almost certainly become implantable in our bodies and brains.[1]

The technological, business, and governance trends reviewed in this book reveal that this prediction is becoming reality. We have seen how combinations of remote and wearable gadgets are increasingly picking up on unexpressed emotions by sensing our biometrics, vitals, and body chemistries. We learned how appliances are being developed that can observe neural activity. We know that tracking devices embedded in our apps constantly broadcast our physical location. Taken together, these and related developments will further reduce the power harbored in our silent minds and further remove the need for individual judgment on all sorts of matters.

Imagine having a thought on an issue of public concern that you are uncertain about. Before you can make up your mind on it, or rather concomitantly to that process, information streamed from your smartphone and other sensors to the cloud will be processed by sophisticated statistical models that, in turn, will work out the best way to nudge your behavior, and indeed thinking, in the direction statistically most associated with whatever definition of the common good it is working with at that moment.

Nostalgia for the way things were will not stop this trend. The only option now is to participate in the decisions regarding the deployment, design, and regulation of these machines. How? Currently, there are no ways to do that. Legacy representative institutions will not suffice because they were created in a time with very different technological and cultural conditions. Bestriding the Enlightenment, they were forged when individual judgment still played a central political role—a role that was foundational to the development of free media and democratic elections.

---

[1] Schwab, Klaus and Nicholas Davis (2018) *Shaping the Future of the Fourth Industrial Revolution*, Crown Currency, pp 14, 21, 173. See also technology journalist and member of the IEEE Global Initiative on Ethics of Autonomous and Intelligent Systems (A/IS), Susan Fourtané, who writes: "Many predict that by 2030, the lines between *thinking* and *doing* will blur ... By 2030, technology is set to respond to our thoughts, and even share them with others ... Using the brain as an interface could mean the end of keyboards, mice, game controllers, and ultimately user interfaces for any digital device. The user needs to only think about the commands, and they will just happen. Smartphones could even function without touch screens." Fourtané, Susan (2020) "The Internet of Senses: Your Brain Is the User Interface," *Interesting Engineering*, December 14 (referencing Ericsson's 2019 Consumer Trends 2030 report).

As the role of individual judgment fades, so too will these institutions. We will witness the media operate more as a behavioral "nudge unit" for particular interest groups than as a source of information upon which to base an opinion. Similarly, representative officials will perceive their part less as mouthpieces for the electorate and more as caretakers tasked to educate or reform constituents on issues dear to donors. Consequently, elections will simply be less effective. On the surface they will look like virulent culture wars, but in substance electors will note little difference between the parties once in power on key matters such as fiscal and foreign policy.

Decaying legacy institutions will not be able to convey a sense of governance on behalf of the people. Particularly disenfranchised groups may sporadically attempt rebellion, yet political machines, as we have seen in previous chapters, can forecast this and quell it. Violent rebellion is no longer a serious avenue for challenging state power. The ability of state and multilateral organizations to forecast conflict and engage in "anticipatory governance" measures has put an end to this. For this and other reasons, therefore, violence is not an ideal option to assure participation.

The better option is for us to focus on upping participation right where the power is moving to, and that is where the political machines are. As it stands, an amalgam of private and government parties—most of which are well outside the purview of public oversight—are the primary actors participating in the unrolling of political automation. They build systems that observe large swathes of everyday life with the stated purpose of influencing mass behavior in a certain direction. It is often unclear who is involved in their creation or even which parts of government have full knowledge of their existence. Proponents of political machinery are frequently unclear themselves as to what portion of civil society they want to invite to the table and what sort of regulation they envision.

If the future of the polity lies in the power of these machines to think well, then it stands to reason that everyone in that polity should participate in making sure that thinking well is indeed what they are doing. For this, a new institution is needed with the express purpose of doing just that. Not a House of Lords, not a House of Commons, but a Third House through which everyone can contribute equally to the work of the political machines that govern them. A house through which citizens engage with the AI tools used by government, and through which their transparency, accountability, and inclusivity are guaranteed to the people they serve.

What would this house deliberate on? Based on the review conducted in this book, its main task would be ensuring agreed-upon definitions for how political machines categorize things and people. In practice, this revolves around the need to establish a consensus on if-then thresholds. For example, if conditions X, Y, and Z are present in a person's life, then that person can be defined as belonging to category A. What is X, Y, and Z, and what is A? What happens if you are A, or not A? These are not categories that can be decided by any specific group of experts for a nation to stay a republic. They must be agreed upon by all. An institutional space is needed for that deliberation to occur fairly and openly.

This space is also where the public could debate and decide whether or not a particular kind of political machine should ever be deployed. For example, can machines be used to determine a human's intent? Are there limited emergency circumstances where they could override a person's self-description of their intent? Another area of jurisdiction could be determining when the "cognitive security" of specific subgroups justifies the monitoring and possible curbing of the "freedom of reach" of certain types of information to that group. It may seem absurd to humans to have to shield certain persons from certain beliefs, but to an algorithm pouring over countless patterns in disparate data sets and seeking to optimize the security of systems, it may be an obvious course of action.[2] After all, these are the types of quandaries the political machines will face the more we cede knowledge of our private lives while consigning stewardship over our public lives.

It will require a whole new Enlightenment to sort this out, which may take decades if not centuries. In the meantime, however, it is clear that the civil liberties inherited from our forebears are inadequate. The US Constitution, the EU acquis communautaire, and other legal frameworks currently being observed around the globe are not equipped for what is unfolding. Their main limitation is that despite regulatory efforts and new legislation they are incapable of protecting citizens against the massive concentrations of power that are occurring globally.

It is necessary to emphasize once again that the amount of power available today is greater than at any other time in history. It is now possible for

---

[2] One fallacy derived from our tendency to automation bias is to think that every problem has a statistically optimal solution. Technology expert Nicholas Carr, however, notes, "as soon as you allow robots, or software programs, to act freely in the world, they're going to run up against ethically fraught situations and face hard choices that can't be resolved through statistical models." Shank, Jenny (2014) "Nicholas Carr's 'Glass Cage': Automation Will Hurt Society in Long Run," *Mediashift*, November 11.

a sovereign to achieve the previously unattainable condition of ruling over a group of subjects that are not only publicly loyal through verbal or enacted professions of allegiance, but are also privately loyal. Or, if not, that can be identified and one way or another nudged into loyalty. This opens access to novel reserves of power, much like the discovery of fossil fuels revolutionized industrial production. The ability to tap into citizens' private judgment is revolutionizing the production of power on the same scale. Relying on existing legal frameworks to harness this new power is like using a horse to drag forth a motor car. The one is not made for the other.

Radically new legal frameworks and never-before articulated rights are required. Imagine having the right to know immediately and exactly what data the government and its private partners have collected on you, how it was collected, and for what reason. Imagine the right of having it explained to you in a language that you understand. A personalized right of access that any citizen can exercise at any time by quickly opening an app on their smartphone, for example, and consulting an array of user-friendly line graphs, pie charts, and other intuitive visualizations that depict all the data ever collected on them and what it is being used for.[3]

This app would essentially be the public face of the Third House, the main vehicle through which citizens may be able to express preferences, electronically and immediately, on matters regarding the collection of data, its uses, if-then thresholds, and the ethical parameters that govern decision-making processes. For example, it could feature adjustable scales that grant the ability to decide what combination of competing social values (i.e., privacy vs. security, meritocracy vs. equity) one wishes to be given priority in the trade-offs considered by the political machines.[4]

---

[3] This could, for example, be an extension of laws such as the Freedom of Information Act (FOIA), a United States federal law that requires the disclosure of information and documents controlled by the government or other public authority upon request. See the interview referred to in chapter 6 with Kwami Ahiabenu, director of Penplusbytes, a non-profit based in Ghana, for a more detailed discussion of the concept.

[4] For more on this concept see Hijlkema, Fabian, "Political Automata," *Personal Blog*, accessed March 25, 2022, https://fabianhijlkema.nl/political-automata/. In his view: "Since policy is no longer produced by politicians as today would be the case, it [the political automata] does not ask you to vote on a party." Instead, you are asked to move a slider for different ethical parameters like freedom, safety, equality, economic growth, and so on. In other words, you do not vote on either the politician or the law, but on the combination of different ethical parameters you would like to see involved in the enforcement of the law. "When a slider on the controller is moved, the weight is distributed differently . . . [as one] slider is pushed forward the other sliders will automatically slide back and become less important for the algorithm." Once all citizens have had the opportunity to express their preferences, "the collective score on these parameters would be fed into future policy-producing-algorithms."

For this to work, in addition to the right of access, there would need to be a clear right to freedom of thought. The right of access, in fact, is rather pointless without the right to freedom of thought. Existing rights erected around principles of freedom of religion, expression, and speech will have to be retooled to serve the more general—and previously mostly axiomatic— concept of freedom of thought. Ahmed Shaheed, UN Special Rapporteur on Freedom of Religion or Belief, believes that "major developments in digital technology, neuroscience, and cognitive psychology may have unprecedented consequences for the privacy and integrity of our thoughts." Freedom of thought, he points out, albeit mentioned in Article 18 of the Universal Declaration of Human Rights, "is yet a largely unexplored right." He encourages "the UN human rights system to further clarify the freedom's scope and content," and reminds us that "it is foundational for many other rights and it can be neither restricted nor derogated from, even during public emergencies."[5]

Imagine having a right to absolute freedom of thought enshrined in law. This will entail facing head-on tough conversations. Security-minded readers enjoined by the "nothing to hide" crowd will point out that there must be limitations to this right, as we have today for freedom of expression. Are some security threats to the nation, for instance, so severe that it is no longer a matter of banning the expression of particular views but a matter of not permitting them to be thought? As the technology to monitor and influence thoughts progresses, this temptation will certainly arise. Despite collectivist urges that will seek to carve out exceptional circumstances, under no condition should this foundational right be "derogated from"—as it is the basis upon which many other rights can be exercised.

The rights of access and freedom of thought must be framed as liberties and not as entitlements. To be clear, an entitlement, or positive right, is granted under certain conditions (right to shelter, food), but a liberty, or unalienable right, cannot be taken away under any circumstance by the government (right to faith, happiness). Political machines, particularly as they regulate differential access to such resources as public safety, health, transport, and debate, operate under the logic of positive rights. This skews the balance in favor of the state.[6]

---

[5] "Freedom of Thought Increasingly Violated Worldwide, UN Expert Warns" (2021) *OHCHR*, October 20, www.ohchr.org/en/press-releases/2021/10/freedom-thought-increasingly-violated-worldwide-un-expert-warns.

[6] The balance between the two defines the role of the state and the very meaning of freedom (i.e., freedom "from the state" versus freedom "guaranteed by the state"). Both have a role to play.

The looming prospect of significant shifts in legal frameworks and definitions of rights has sparked energetic debate among experts from different fields. Arne Hintz, Lina Dencik, and Karin Wahl-Jorgensen at Cardiff University's School of Journalism, Media, and Culture, for example, ask, "how can we understand citizenship in an age defined by data collection and processing?" In their book *Digital Citizenship in a Datafied Society*, the authors reflect on "a shift which is not merely technological, but also social and political, and it therefore confronts us with questions of power, agency, and control." They point out how:

> Algorithmic decision-making increasingly interacts with human agency, supported by new forms of artificial intelligence, and the growing importance of data-based prediction transforms key social processes and institutions ... The [Snowden] revelations coincided with the digitization of an ever-wider expanse of our social life, driven by the generation, collection and analysis of data, and illustrated the consequences for the inhabitants of these digital environments. In doing so, they crystallized a key turning point in the interplay between digital technologies and notions of citizenship.[7]

This critical turning point, Hintz, Dencik, and Wahl-Jorgensen go on to explain, is that our role as citizens is now not solely determined by our actions but also, and more crucially, "by the data traces that we generate and that are used to categorize and profile us." Although the datafication of persons emerged from a longer history of citizen monitoring (which this book also touched upon), there has since been "a paradigm shift in not only the scale of surveillance but also a reconfiguration of its character and subjects."[8]

This has made "large complex populations manageable to state and corporate actors" who may now more quickly "define inclusion and exclusion" and more easily reproduce and extend "already existing forms of inequality."

Too much freedom from the state can lead to chaos, injustice, and exploitation. Too much freedom guaranteed by the state can lead to tyranny as it centralizes power. The ideal zone is somewhere in the middle. A Third House, based on principles of direct democracy as well as the rights of access and freedom of thought, would counter the risk of centralization and rebalance matters in favor of the citizen.

[7] Hintz, Arne, Lina Dencik, and Karin Wahl-Jorgensen (2018) *Digital Citizenship in a Datafied Society*, Polity Press, pp 2–3.

[8] Ibid, pp 145–146.

Referring to Oscar Gandy's work *The Panoptic Sort: A Political Economy of Personal Information*, the authors conclude:

> Our social identities and practices are thereby reduced to our "data doubles" that can be managed and sorted through the application of algorithmic processes. In the era of datafication, therefore, acts of digital citizenship are both enabled and constrained by structures and processes that remain little understood, and all the more difficult to discuss, govern, and resist. Datafication—while opaque and obscure in its workings—is now a key component of how decisions about us as citizens are made across our social, political, economic, and cultural participation.[9]

The evidence collected in previous chapters of this book supports this assessment, with the proviso that the difficulty to "discuss, govern, and resist" can be overcome with the right institutional structure in place. It must be an entirely new structure precisely because the character of citizenship is entirely new. Legacy institutions were geared for legislating on the physical citizen; a new type of institution is needed for legislating on the digital citizen (the "data double" of the real one). In the long history of republican forms of government—from forums for landowning *nobiles* to extending the franchise to various subgroups of commoners—the next logical step may be to give these digital citizens a forum as well.

It is imperative that real citizens have ownership and command over their digital counterparts. The state already interacts in myriad ways with the digital citizen, but there is no formal connection between the digital citizen and the real one, besides of course the real one being on the receiving end of any decisions made. A Third House would be the institutional conduit through which digital citizens are tethered to the corresponding real ones.

What would this relationship look like? This is a nontrivial question since digital citizens may soon come to have, quite literally, a life of their own. Generative AI allows for digital citizens to be "animated" with a personality and voice. Throughout this book we have seen that governments and private partners are collecting great amounts of physiological, psychological, sociological, and environmental data on citizens. Taken together, this trove of

---

[9] Ibid, pp 146–147, referencing Gandy, Oscar (1993) *The Panoptic Sort: A Political Economy of Personal Information*, Westview.

personal information can be used to give life to digital citizens so that they speak and behave just like those real people.[10]

Governments could interact with these animated digital citizens to gain input and test responses to different policies before real-world deployment. But they could also perform another, less expected, task: digital citizens could end up participating in a new form of virtual deliberation on our behalf. After all, the objective of AI is to offload mental work to machines much like the Industrial Revolution offloaded physical work. In this revolution, all kinds of mental work—including that of participating in political debate, engaging thorny cultural issues, and finding points of agreement for how to manage the public sphere—may be offloaded. These AI "agents" could do some of that heavy lifting for us.

In a way, political automation calls for automated deliberation. Political machines are too fast and too ubiquitous for any human to keep up with. No one has time to dedicate to such a task. Digital citizens, as AI-augmented versions of us, are better equipped to bear the brunt of engaging with the political machines and with the millions of other digital citizens. As such, it is not something that can be stopped, it can only be done in better or worse ways. Today, no commercial farmer plows a field with their own hands, and no profitable factory employs workers for tasks that can be done by machines. Those ships have sailed. Some, of course, will engage in boutique farming or pre-industrial forms of craftsmanship, but most will not. In the same way, some political deliberation will occur in person by real people, but most of it will not.

We may think of digital citizens as our personal emissaries to the Third House. Our work as real citizens should be one of approval and oversight. To

---

[10] LLM-powered agents are already breaching the workforce. Eric Yuan, CEO of videoconferencing platform Zoom, envisages people soon having their own "personal AI digital twin to attend meetings and write emails for them so that they can go to the beach instead." He explains that "AI clones could help shorten the workweek to three or four days" leaving more time for in-person interactions and an improved social life. Altchek, Ana (2024) "Why You Should Be Excited About Getting an AI Clone, According to Zoom's CEO," *Business Insider Africa*, June 4, https://africa.businessinsider.com/news/why-you-should-be-excited-about-getting-an-ai-clone-according-to-zooms-ceo/pz0hp25. Similar agents are being proposed to aid with dating, socialization, and even holding public office. See Naftulin, Julia (2023) "3 Ways ChatGPT Can Improve Your Dating Life, According to A Dating Coach Who Charges $20,000 Per Client," *Business Insider*, July 21, www.businessinsider.com/how-to-use-chatgpt-for-dating-2023-7, Power, Stephanie (2024) "The AI Companions You Can Have Conversations With," *BBC*, February 7, www.bbc.com/news/business-68165762, Vizard, Frank (2024) "AI Companions: Romantic Partners or Just Data Diggers?" *Techstrong.AI*, March 27, https://techstrong.ai/articles/ai-companions-romantic-partners-or-just-data-diggers/, and Grierson, Jamie (2024) "Brighton General Election Candidate Aims to be UK's First AI MP," *The Guardian*, June 10, www.theguardian.com/politics/article/2024/jun/10/brighton-general-election-candidate-uk-first-ai-mp-artificial-intelligence.

do that, we must be able to "drive" the digital citizen—much like the owner of a driverless car can set the car's direction or take control of the wheel when they so wish. Above, we considered an app that would permit citizens to express preferences on data collection and if-then thresholds by political machines. We also envisioned the use of sliding scales to let people weigh in on the competing ethical parameters used to inform decision-making. The relationship between real and digital citizens could be mediated in the same way and in the same app. Intriguingly, this could also be done conversationally.

Real citizens may use it to define the values they want to see prioritized in their digital citizen's thinking. Provided we are in charge in this way, the results of the automated deliberation will ultimately correspond to our real collective needs, and we will have contributed to calibrating the political machines in a way that grants them popular legitimacy.

All this is just a blueprint of an idea. It will take decades (if it happens at all) to realize something of this sort in practice, and it may be adopted to different degrees and in different ways depending on the type of government and regulatory framework already in place. In some places there will be a larger role played by the private sector, in others a smaller one. In some places there will be multiple versions of digital citizens used by different organizations granting different levels of access (for example, public health versus national security), in others it will be more concentrated. Some nations will codify the rights of access and freedom of thought, others will not.

Whatever the case, the stakes are quite high if we do nothing. We may encounter what John Danaher, lecturer in the Law School at the University of Galway, calls the "threat of algocracy." Algocracy, a concept developed by sociologist Aneesh Aneesh, describes a type of government run not by humans but by algorithms.[11] (If we add digital citizens to the mix, it may be more aptly described as government run by algorithms for algorithms.) Danaher is concerned about the moral implications of such a system, which relies on "hiddenness" (referring to how data is collected and utilized without consent) and "opacity" (referring to how the systems "work in ways that are inaccessible or opaque to understanding"). Hiddenness, he

---

[11] See Aneesh, Aneesh (2006) *Virtual Migration: The Programming of Globalization*, Duke University Press.

says, compromises the right to privacy, while opacity undermines political legitimacy.[12]

In the first pages of this book, we hypothesized how differentials in access to political machines would parallel the formation of different de facto classes. Those with access—i.e., those who can see through the opacity and hiddenness—would gravitate toward fine-tuning the political machines in ways that funnel resources and power toward members of their group, having a compounding effect on inequality. For everyone else, as Danaher puts it, "we may be on the cusp of creating a governance system which severely constrains and limits the opportunities for human engagement."[13] Throughout this book we encountered numerous real-life situations in which this was the case, and many of those interviewed highlighted as much.

Yet, while the threat of algocracy is real, the potential societal rewards of getting it right are also real. It is necessary to put things in historical perspective to see this upside. Every past revolution in information technology has led to a renewal in social institutions. The written word brought us prophecy and philosophy; the printed word religious reform and the Enlightenment. These were both revolutions in information technologies. What will the ubiquitous word bring? The main novelty is that information is now incredibly cheap to produce and even cheaper to disseminate. (Additionally, an ever-increasing portion is produced via generative AI, as we have seen above, with the net effect of multiplying the overall amount). In sum, there has never been so much of it, and political machines, at heart, rely primarily on this development.

As with the written and printed word, this evolution in knowledge production will represent a substantial challenge to existing political systems. One obvious inconvenience to existing systems is that information is now widely distributed throughout every nook and cranny of a polity.[14] Some of this information, albeit certainly not all, may flower into knowledge. Applying a Baconian framework, as knowledge is divulged, so

---

[12] Danaher, John (2016) "The Threat of Algocracy: Reality, Resistance and Accommodation," *Philosophy & Technology*, 29, 245–268, pp 245, 247–249. The opacity of political machines also raises the question of who, if anyone, does know how they work. Who are the computer programmers, and who gave them their project "specs"? Danaher notes that having some in the know while others remain in the dark can transform the threat of algocracy into the threat of epistocracy—or rule by those with knowledge. See Estlund, David (2003) "Why Not Epistocracy?" In Naomi Reshotko ed. *Desire, Identity, and Existence: Essays in Honor of T.M. Penner*, Academic Printing and Publishing; and Estlund, David (2008) *Democratic Authority*, Princeton University Press.

[13] Danaher, "The Threat of Algocracy," p 266.

[14] Most of the world's information is now accessible to anybody with an internet connection, outside of places where there are political, technological, and financial limitations to access.

too is power. From the point of view of legacy institutions, this trend must be reversed as it is a direct challenge to their inheritance.

Incidentally, this is another reason we may not expect existing institutions to properly govern this new era but require entirely novel ones. Neither will extensions of the old institutions do, as it is in their DNA to govern a reality in which information is only partially distributed throughout society. Political professionals, whether elected or not, have traditionally relied on an asymmetry of knowledge, a strategy known since Plato's day as the "noble lie," to maintain control. This noble lie, in which the lower strata of society have access to only limited versions of the truth in the interest of social harmony, is no longer available.

Undoubtedly, legacy institutions will scramble to hoover power back up by cordoning off this or that subset of information,[15] but it is a strategy destined to fail in the long run precisely because the political machines being deployed *require* the ubiquity of information to work. You cannot have one without the other. Information must be widely available, and more of it continuously generated, for political machines to work. As mentioned above, some of this ubiquitous information is bound to mature into knowledge and some of this knowledge into power. This mechanism is one of the silver linings silhouetting the introduction of political machines.[16]

In a sense, our current predicament contains within it the kernels of the new institutional structures to come. These kernels must not be resisted but rather understood and carefully cultivated. For example, there is a

---

[15] Authoritarian methods will be used to defend a certain idea of democracy. George Orwell describes the threat in the following way: "There is now a widespread tendency to argue that one can defend democracy only by totalitarian methods. If one loves democracy, the argument runs, one must crush its enemies by no matter what means. And who are its enemies? It always appears that they are not only those who attack it openly and consciously, but those who 'objectively' endanger it by spreading mistaken doctrines. In other words, defending democracy involves destroying all independence of thought ... These people don't see that if you encourage totalitarian methods, the time may come when they will be used against you instead of for you." Orwell, George (1972) "The Freedom of the Press," *New York Times*, October 8 (originally written, but not printed, in 1945).

[16] The statist temptation to hose it all down will be great, but unsuccessful. New institutions typically emerge from the bottom up. If you take away the freedom to err, you take away the possibility that order will emerge naturally from the cooperation of large numbers of humans who are free to do so. Friedrich Hayek spoke about the difference between order imposed from above versus order that grows organically from below. In his theory of "spontaneous order," which permeates his economic and philosophical thinking, he notes that any order imposed from above contradicts the tendency toward order naturally latent in nature and society, and ultimately fails. Hayek, Friedrich (2009) [1944] *The Road to Serfdom*, University of Chicago Press, and Hayek, Friedrich (2011) [1960] *The Constitution of Liberty*, University of Chicago Press.

negentropic force hidden in the entropic effects of excessive information. It is known that too much information in a society shared too quickly can push it toward entropy, or chaos. In fact, a well-established consequence of the ubiquity of information has been increased social polarization and fragmentation,[17] exacerbated by social media companies whose business model is predicated on the ever-increasing excitability of language.[18] But what if fragmentation, as ugly as it is, is *precisely* what is needed to rebalance multiple competing interests, to revive deliberative politics, and to find order again?

The shattering of nations into micro-polities of one may be the unexpected path to finding a new equilibrium. Indeed, for the political machines to work societies need to be splintered into countless single individuals in ever-shifting constellations of coalitions. In the era of the "data double," however, these coalitions are not what they used to be. It is vital to understand that groupings are not solely drawn along typical markers like geography, demography, or culture, but along myriad additional lines drawn by the political machines themselves. The machines will lump people together into new blended groups or separate previously cohesive ones into many subgroups based on their classifiers' logic.[19]

---

[17] Social polarization has been further exacerbated by labor polarization. Labor polarization is when the workforce is characterized by high paying-high skill jobs at one end, an abundance of low paying-low skill jobs at the other, and a shrinking pool of middle-class professional jobs in between. A report by the McKinsey Global Institute shows that automation and globalization have contributed to a marked acceleration of this polarization phenomenon in recent decades (see Lund, Susan et al. "The Future of Work in America: People and Places, Today and Tomorrow" (2019) *McKinsey Global Institute*). The net result is a massive downward mobility of highly educated individuals from previously well-resourced communities. As the two polarization trends converge, you see many educated but disenfranchised people joining an already very polarized public square, contributing to political chaos and accruing strain on the existing system.

[18] See Faroohar, Rana (2019) "How to Take Back Control From the Big Tech Barons," *The Financial Times*, December 8. Not surprisingly, the influence of these social media corporations has also expanded, to the point that they can undermine legislatures' ability to regulate them. See Philippon, Thomas (2019) *The Great Reversal: How America Gave Up on Free Markets*, Harvard University Press. It is not unthinkable that in some nations social media will become a public utility like water or transportation infrastructure. An analogy may be drawn with the freedom of the seas argument made by Hugo Grotius in 1609. Grotius, a Dutchman, posited that the Portuguese had no right to monopolize sea lanes because the seas, by natural right, belonged to all. Similarly, citizens in some nations may come to the conclusion that they have a natural right to a public social media platform. See Grotius, Hugo (2017) [1609] *The Freedom of the Seas*, The Lawbook Exchange.

[19] As we have seen in previous chapters, this logic is typically generated by algorithmic technologies that are developed through private–public partnerships, and that may involve various state, academic, non-profit, and international organization apparatuses. As it stands, most of these technologies have only a tiny number of people involved in the calibration process and are generally shielded behind various layers of intellectual property protection.

One person can and will be a member of many, overlapping, and contradictory groupings, constantly floating between different mandalas of affiliations, not all of which they will be entirely conscious of belonging to. Yet that particular mandala of affiliations, which is different for everyone, will be how they are defined as citizens in the eyes of the state and will determine what privileges and resources they have access to, and, conversely, what freedoms they do not have.[20] For this reason the Third House must be a direct democracy. Political machines hyper-personalize government services. It makes sense that every citizen have a personal connection back to them. As such, it must be a place-less and time-less institution.

Representative democracy is a product of its being place and time-bound. In order to meet and discuss matters, representatives of a constituency have to travel to a far-away capital. Not all can go, so some have to be elected to represent the rest. Once in the capital, they are not immediately reachable, so on trust they are expected to be more or less faithful to the policies agreed upon until the time of re-election. The Third House does not need to be restricted in this way. There is no reason it should be place or time-bound. Preferences can be expressed at any time, by anyone, on any matter—automatically green-lighting and calibrating policies on a rolling basis.

It is easier to see these historical trajectories if we shift our interpretative framework from an industrial one to an anthropological one. The digital revolution has misguidedly been characterized as an industrial revolution (apparently the fourth), while it is much more than that. The great arc starting with the internet, big data, AI, and now agents is a gear shift moment in how humankind relates to itself, similar to what occurred with the advent of writing and then later with printing.

Those past gear changes in the way information was produced also transformed the way humankind related to itself. It had inevitable consequences for social institutions. Writing helped erect massive religious bureaucracies, and printing helped splinter them through the spread of reform. The

---

[20] This has prompted some to talk about group rights as a corollary to increased datafication. For example, Linnet Taylor and Bart van der Sloot of Tilburg University, along with Luciano Floridi at the University of Oxford, have debated in an edited volume the need to start thinking about protecting the privacy rights of groups as a central consequence of emerging technologies. They clarify that group privacy should be considered "as an enhancement and safeguard for the individual right to privacy, rather than as a potential substitute for it." Taylor, Linnet, Luciano Floridi, and Bart van der Sloot, eds. (2017) *Group Privacy: New Challenges of Data Technologies*, Springer, p 235.

kind of relationship that individuals have with themselves is the foundational building block for the kind of institutions they ultimately accept for themselves.

This time around the change may be all the more pronounced since some of that information (knowledge?) is not even produced by us, but by various applications of generative AI. Humankind is relating to itself in ways that can no longer be contained nor explained by existing institutions. So, what is this relationship like today? How *do* we relate to ourselves? This is the crux of the matter and the true nature of the crisis of individual judgment we addressed at the start of this chapter. The introduction of political machines that can judge things for us whether we want it or not, know it or not, has unhinged humankind's relationship to itself.

What if this reshuffling is a necessary thing? What if it is necessary to destroy one kind of relation to the self to make room for a completely new one? It is not easy to see the light of dawn at dusk, but let us hold for a moment the possibility that the relation of humankind to itself based on individual judgment must recede to make room for a new type of relation based on a kind of *augmented* judgment. The former was a precondition for representative democracy in the industrial era, the latter may be a precondition for direct democracy in the digital era.[21]

In a representative democracy a citizen must vote for the official who best represents their individual interests within a constituency. Individual judgment is sufficient for that. In a place-less, time-less, and hyper-personalized direct democracy each individual must be able to interact with millions of other citizens and with an ever-expanding multitude of political machines continuously making decisions that impact their lives. They cannot do this unless their individual judgment is somehow supported, amplified, and augmented technologically.[22]

The challenge will be to do that without compromising the authenticity of one's own thinking. Indeed, it only works if it is the individual that is driving the augmentation, and not the other way around. This is where the rights of access and freedom of thought come in. They must be the main legal pillars around which political automation occurs and around which any institutional oversight mechanisms like the Third House are erected. If we get it

---

[21] Over the long run, legacy representative institutions may come take on a more limited, ceremonial role, not too dissimilar to some monarchies today.

[22] The classic era's relation to self was focused on virtue, the medieval on the sacred, and the modern on rationality. It may now be the turn of the hyper-self.

right, the entirety of society will become an institution of government, and ordinary citizens, leaving their digital versions and the political machines to bear the brunt of deliberation and decision-making, will be free to ponder higher-order concerns such as the direction society should be moving toward.

Fabian Hijlkema, a designer and artist based in the Netherlands, explains that once we trust "that the principles that constitute the working of self-learning machines and algorithms might make them better suited to take humane and righteous decisions than humans themselves," then we will see a separation between the "act" and the "art" of politics. In other words, as political machines relieve us from the minutiae of formulating optimal decisions (the "act" of politics) we are left to debate more abstract matters like the meaning of it all (the "art" of politics). This shift entails that politics will "move closer towards what is now considered the field of philosophy in order to deal with the larger questions that lie in front of it."[23] Provided there is a way for us all to participate, that is a good deal.

---

[23] Hijlkema, Fabian, "The Separation of Politics and Policy Making," *Personal Blog*, accessed March 25, 2022, https://fabianhijlkema.nl/the-separation-of-politics-and-policy-making/.

APPENDIX I

Further Reading by Scholars

If any of the themes touched upon in this book have piqued your interest and you would like to research them in more depth, here you will find a list of scholars who have made important contributions and written extensively on these subjects. They are arranged alphabetically within the following six broad categories to facilitate research:

- AI Governance/Democracy/Politics/Citizenship   212
- Computer Science/Machine Learning/Statistics   221
- Ethics/Law/Privacy/Surveillance   225
- Media/Communication/Culture   235
- Peacebuilding/Conflict Prevention   244
- Social Sciences/Philosophy   249

AI Governance/Democracy/Politics/Citizenship

Allan Dafoe—University of Oxford

Allan Dafoe, a senior research fellow at Oxford University's Future of Humanity Institute, directs and serves on the board of the Governance of AI Program (GovAI), an independent nonprofit that he founded. His research focuses on the global governance of artificial intelligence, aiming to steer AI development toward the common good. He also works at Google DeepMind as a senior staff research scientist. His earlier research delved into liberal peace, reputation, honor in war, and the development of statistical tools for credible causal inference.

Annelise Russell—University of Kentucky

Annelise Russell, with over a dozen years of experience at the intersection of public policy, communication, and public affairs, is recognized as an expert in digital political communication. Recently a research fellow at the Library of Congress, Russell worked on detailing the evolution of digital politics in Congress, focusing on its impact on congressional capacity, media relations, and political reputation-making. At the University of Kentucky's Martin School for Public Policy, she researches public policy within Congress, emphasizing how new media platforms influence policymaking. Her book, *Tweeting is Leading*, analyzes senators' communication strategies on Twitter, linking their digital behavior to political agendas.

Arne Hintz—Cardiff University

Arne Hintz, a reader at Cardiff University's School of Journalism, Media, and Culture, also serves as the director of postgraduate research and co-director of the Data Justice

Lab. His research examines digital citizenship, encompassing media activism, communication policy, and datafication. His recent projects focus on citizen participation in data and AI governance. He has published extensively in this field, including several coauthored and coedited books such as *Data Justice* and *Digital Citizenship in a Datafied Society*.

Becky Faith—University of Sussex

Becky Faith, a research fellow in the digital and technology cluster at the University of Sussex, co-leads research in the Digital Futures at Work Research Centre. Her expertise lies in gender and technology, digital inequalities, mobile communication, human–computer interaction, and technology for social change. She began her career in digital start-ups in the 1990s, working on the UK's inaugural e-commerce platforms, and subsequently worked for over fifteen years in human rights and technology.

Brian Tse—University of Oxford

Brian Tse, a policy affiliate at Oxford University's Centre for the governance of AI, has contributed significantly to AI research, including translating the OpenAI Charter into Chinese and advising on international cooperation. Fluent in three Chinese languages, his expertise spans working in China's AI hardware start-up sector and investment banking in fintech. Brian's academic journey includes studies at Harvard University, Tsinghua University, and the University of Hong Kong.

Cristian Vaccari—University of Edinburgh

Cristian Vaccari, chair in future governance, public policy, and technology at the University of Edinburgh, is affiliated with the Department of Politics and International Relations and the Edinburgh Futures Institute. He directs the MSc future governance program and specializes in political communication, particularly in the context of digital media. His research explores digital media engagement among political parties, campaign organizations, and citizens, examining how they negotiate power dynamics. He collaborated with Augusto Valeriani on the book *Outside the Bubble: Social Media and Political Participation in Western Democracies*, analyzing the impact of social media on political participation in Western democracies.

Daniel Gayo-Avello—University of Oviedo

Daniel Gayo-Avello is an associate professor at the University of Oviedo in the Department of Computer Science. His research interests lie in web mining and social media, with publications on those topics in various prestigious journals. He coedited a special issue of *Internet Research* on social media's predictive power, and contributed a chapter to *Twitter: A Digital Socioscope*. He also coauthored *Retooling Politics: How Digital Media Are Shaping Democracy*, and is involved in the EU-funded ActEU project which aims to strengthen trust in democracy.

Daniel Kreiss—University of North Carolina Chapel Hill

Daniel Kreiss, a professor at the University of North Carolina (UNC), is a principal researcher at the UNC Center for Information, Technology, and Public Life and holds the Edgar Thomas Cato Distinguished Professorship. His work examines the impact of the internet and platforms on campaigning, information dissemination, and political communication. Kreiss' research also explores the roles of social identities in political communication, advocating for stronger democratic systems and more accountable platforms. He has authored several influential books including *Prototype Politics: Technology-Intensive Campaigning and the Data of Democracy*, which analyzes the use of technology by the two main political parties in the US.

Darrell West—Brookings Institution

Darrell West, a senior fellow at the Center for Technology Innovation within the Governance Studies program at Brookings, focuses his research on AI, robotics, and the future of work. Previously at Brown University, his publications address critical issues in digital technology and public policy. His books include *Turning Point: Policymaking in the Era of Artificial Intelligence*, *The Future of Work: Robots, AI, and Automation*, *The Next Wave: Using Digital Technology to Further Social and Political Innovation*, and numerous other notable works.

Diana Dajer—University of Oxford

Diana Dajer, an Oxford University alumna, has worked extensively in strengthening democracy through citizen participation and government innovation. Her experience ranges from research on Colombia's armed conflict to managing democracy-enhancing projects in Latin America. Dajer's aim to understand policymaking led her to Oxford's Master of Public Policy program and subsequently a DPhil. She founded Policéntrico, a start-up supporting public and social innovation in Colombia, and continues to explore participatory democracy opportunities.

Eleonore Fournier-Tombs—United Nations University

Eleonore Fournier-Tombs is head of the Anticipatory Action and Innovation Pillar at the United Nations University Centre for Policy Research, and Research Lead for the United Nations' (UN) High-Level Advisory Body on Artificial Intelligence. Her diverse career background includes data science roles across the UN. Her Ph.D. from the University of Geneva involved developing a machine learning method to assess online political deliberations. Subsequent research at McGill University and work at the UN Office for the Coordination of Humanitarian Affairs and at the World Bank, focused on diverse issues from public health modeling to climate policy. In 2021, she established a research lab at the University of Ottawa, contributing to AI research for Covid-19 in Senegal and Mali.

Eleonore Pauwels—Global Center on Cooperative Security

Eleonore Pauwels, a senior fellow at the Global Center on Cooperative Security, researches the security and governance challenges posed by AI and related technologies. She has provided expertise to organizations like the World Bank and the UN on AI-cyber prevention and global security. Previously, she was a research fellow at the United Nations University's Centre for Policy Research and spent a decade at the Woodrow Wilson International Center for Scholars. Pauwels also contributes to the International Association for Responsible Research and Innovation in Genome-Editing and has held positions within the European Commission.

Emma Briant—George Washington University

Emma Briant, a researcher at George Washington University's School of Media and Public Affairs, specializes in the study of propaganda and political communication. Her interests primarily focus on the evolving technologies and their effects on democracy, international security, inequality, and human rights. She authored *Propaganda and Counter-Terrorism: Strategies for Global Change*, which explored the increasing impact of digital defense propaganda, and coauthored *Bad News for Refugees*, which examined UK media and political discourse on migration before Brexit. Currently, she is collaborating on *What's Wrong with the Democrats? Media Bias, Inequality and the rise of Donald Trump*, and is developing a long-term book project, *Propaganda Machine: The Hidden Story of Cambridge Analytica and the Digital Influence Industry*.

Emmanuel Letouzé—Data-Pop Alliance

Emmanuel Letouzé, adjunct associate professor of international and public affairs at Columbia University, is director and co-founder of Data-Pop Alliance, an NGO established in partnership with the MIT Media Lab and Harvard Humanitarian Initiative (HHI). The Data-Pop Alliance focuses on data and AI's applications and implications in human development, humanitarian action, and democracy, especially in the Global South. As a visiting researcher at HHI, he has contributed significantly to the field, including co-founding the Open Algorithms initiative. He was notably the lead author on the chapter "AI for the SDGs—and Beyond? Towards a Human AI Culture for Development and Democracy" in *Missing Links in AI Governance*, published by UNESCO and the Montreal Institute of Learning Algorithms.

Espen Geelmuyden Rød—Uppsala University

A political scientist with over ten years of experience, Espen Geelmuyden Rød at the Department of Peace and Conflict Research at Uppsala University focuses on democratization, political violence, and digital technology. An award-winning author, their work *The Internet and Political Protest in Autocracies* examines the internet's influence on protest movements in dictatorships, analyzing the link between the internet and rebellion against dictators across sixty countries. Rød is engaged in several projects, including "Protest, Democratization and Escalation to Political Violence," and "ViEWS: An Early-Warning System for Political Violence," contributing significant insights to the field of political science and digital technology.

George Zarkadakis—Author

George Zarkadakis, an accomplished writer, science communicator, AI engineer, and futurist, is known for his contributions to the understanding and advancement of the Fourth Industrial Revolution. His multidisciplinary approach blends arts, humanities, sciences, and engineering. Zarkadakis authored *In Our Own Image: The History and Future of Artificial Intelligence*, and has been a prolific contributor to publications like Aeon and Wired. In *Cyber Republic*, he proposes a vision for utilizing technology in enhancing liberal democracies and creating a more equitable digital economy, positioning this work as a guiding framework for the Fourth Industrial Revolution and the post-pandemic era.

Gregory Treverton—University of Southern California

Gregory Treverton is professor of the practice of international relations and spatial sciences at the University of Southern California. A renowned international political economist, he possesses extensive experience in both government and private sectors. His expertise covers a wide range of topics including economics, political-military affairs, terrorism, and cyber issues, with a particular focus on global strategic planning and security and risk analysis. Treverton's prolific career is marked by the publication of over thirty books and numerous articles, including *National Intelligence and Science: Beyond the Great Divide in Analysis and Policy*, which analyzes the science and intelligence domains and the consequences of their integration.

Jennifer Forestal—Loyola University Chicago

Jennifer Forestal, the Helen Houlahan Rigali Assistant Professor of Political Science at Loyola University Chicago, draws from American political thought to study digital technologies' impact on democratic practices. Her work, integrating insights from political theory, architecture, and computer science, investigates how UX design and software development processes influence democratic engagements in digital spaces. Her book, *Designing for Democracy: How to Build Community in Digital Environments*, examines the role of design in creating democratic social media platforms, contributing significantly to understanding the interplay between digital technologies and democracy.

Jennifer Halen—Harvard University

Jennifer Halen, a postdoctoral college fellow in Harvard University's Department of Government, holds a Ph.D. in Political Science from the University of Minnesota. Her research explores the interplay between emerging technologies and politics. Her past affiliations include the Berkman Klein Center for Internet and Society at Harvard, and the National Science Foundation Graduate Research Fellowship, showcasing her commitment to studying the evolving relationship between technology and political structures.

Jessica Baldwin-Philippi—Fordham University

Jessica Baldwin-Philippi, an associate professor at Fordham University in the communication and media studies department, focuses her research on digital political participation and citizenship. Her work examines political campaigns and municipal governments' innovation efforts, exploring how digital technologies restructure political participation and notions of citizenship. Her current research delves into data campaigning, building on her first book, *Using Technology, Building Democracy: Digital Campaigning and the Construction of Citizenship*, which outlined how digital media used by political campaigns shapes political participation and citizen expectations.

Joel Penney—Montclair State University

Joel Penney, an associate professor in the School of Communication and Media at Montclair State University, specializes in new media, critical/cultural studies, and political communication and theory. His research delves into the use of participatory and digital media for social and political advocacy and the construction of collective identities. In *The Citizen Marketer: Promoting Political Opinion in the Social Media Age*, Penney examines the role of everyday people in promoting political media messages, proposing the concept of the citizen marketer. This work explores the active role of individuals in circulating media to influence political discourse and shape public opinion.

Johanna Dunaway—Syracuse University

Johanna Dunaway, a professor of political science at the Maxwell School of Citizenship and Public Affairs at Syracuse University and research director for the Institute for Democracy, Journalism, and Citizenship, conducts research on news media and politics, political communication, and the influence of communication technologies on media effects, public opinion, and political behavior. Her work addresses civic literacy and engagement, focusing on how contemporary communication impacts political polarization and news engagement. Coauthored with Kathleen Searles, her book *News and Democratic Citizens in the Mobile Era* investigates the effects of mobile news consumption on democratic citizenship.

Joshua Scacco—University of South Florida

Joshua Scacco, an associate professor and associate chair of the Department of Communication at the University of South Florida, is also the director of the Center for Sustainable Democracy. His research focuses on the effective and ethical use of communication technologies to strengthen democratic governance. His work emphasizes partnerships that enhance democratic representation and governance practices. In *The Ubiquitous Presidency: Presidential Communication and Digital Democracy in Tumultuous Times*, coauthored with Kevin Coe, they explore presidential communication, employing various research methods to analyze the relationship between the president, media, and public.

Karin Wahl-Jorgensen—Cardiff University

Karin Wahl-Jorgensen, the current University Dean of Research Environment and Culture at Cardiff University, focuses her research on the interrelation between citizenship, media, and emotion in the context of technological change and innovation. Her recent work includes in-depth studies on local news entrepreneurs and projects addressing right-wing populist media and misinformation. Her publications include *Emotions, Media and Politics* and *Digital Citizenship in a Datafied Society*, and demonstrate her commitment to understanding the evolving media landscape and its implications for democratic engagement.

Kevin Coe—University of Utah

Kevin Coe, a professor in the Department of Communication at the University of Utah, specializes in political communication, news media, and public opinion. Coauthoring *The Ubiquitous Presidency: Presidential Communication and Digital Democracy in Tumultuous Times* with Joshua Scacco, they examine presidential communication using diverse methodologies, ranging from surveys and content analysis to network analyses. His teaching repertoire includes media, strategic communication, political communication, and content analysis.

Liav Orgad—European University Institute

Liav Orgad serves as the director of the Global Citizenship Law Project at the European University Institute, a European Research Council–funded project that pioneers the subfield of international citizenship law and explores innovative concepts like "blockchain membership" and citizenship algorithms, challenging conventional views of citizenship in a globalized, technological world. His academic journey includes fellowships at Harvard University's Edmond J. Safra Center for Ethics and a visiting professorship at Columbia Law School. He is a member of the Global Young Academy and leader of its Global Migration and Human Rights working group, and the author of *The Cultural Defense of Nations: A Liberal Theory of Majority Rights*.

Linnet Taylor—Tilberg University

Linnet Taylor, a professor at Tilburg University's Institute for Law, Technology, and Society, heads the Global Data Justice project. Her work focuses on the integration of social justice objectives with technology governance, conducting research in collaboration with academic and civil society organizations globally. She is a member of the Dutch Young Academy, and has previously held positions at the University of Amsterdam and the Oxford Internet Institute. Her research interests include data governance, deliberative democracy, and technology's role in sustainable development.

Muzammil Hussain—University of Michigan

Muzammil Hussain, assistant professor of communication and media at the University of Michigan, specializes in global communication, social analytics, and technology governance. His interdisciplinary research focuses on the intersections of global ICT politics, innovation, and policy. Hussain's teaching includes digital politics and global innovation. He authored *Democracy's Fourth Wave?: Digital Media and the Arab Spring*, exploring the evolution of digital activism in the Arab region.

Nanjala Nyabola—Kenyan Journalist

Nanjala Nyabola, a Nairobi-based writer, political analyst, and activist, writes extensively on African politics, technology, international law, and feminism. Her influential book, *Digital Democracy, Analogue Politics: How the Internet Era is Transforming Kenya*, is highly regarded in the field. A former Rhodes Scholar at the University of Oxford and an inaugural participant in the Foreign Policy Interrupted Fellowship, she also serves on the board of Amnesty International Kenya, contributing significantly to discussions on African society and political landscapes.

Nils Weidmann—University of Konstanz

Nils Weidmann, a political science professor at the University of Konstanz since 2015, currently leads the Centre for Human | Data | Society. His postdoctoral research at Princeton, Yale, and the Peace Research Institute Oslo, along with his role at the German Association for Peace and Conflict Studies, underlines his expertise in political violence and social science data. His research delves into the impact of information and communication technology on political mobilization, especially in non-democratic contexts and unconventional political actions like protests and violent conflicts.

Philip Howard—Oxford Internet Institute

Philip Howard is professor of internet studies at the Oxford Internet Institute, and director of Oxford University's program on democracy and technology. A prominent social scientist, known for his expertise in technology, public policy, and international affairs, his role as a visiting fellow at Harvard University's Carr Center for Human Rights further highlights his interdisciplinary approach. An award-winning author, he recently penned *Lie Machines: How to Save Democracy from Troll Armies, Deceitful Robots, Junk News Operations, and Political Operatives*, investigates and reveals the technologies that put political discourse and democracies at risk.

Rachel Gibson—University of Manchester

Rachel Gibson, professor of politics at the University of Manchester, examines how digital technologies transform election campaigns. Her comparative work includes studies in the UK, US, Germany, Australia, and France. In *When the Nerds Go Marching In*, she discusses the evolution of digital technology in political campaigns. She currently directs the European Research Council–funded study "Digital Campaigning and Electoral Democracy" and is a principal investigator on the Norface project on Data-Driven Campaigning.

Rongbin Han—University of Georgia

Rongbin Han, an associate professor at the University of Georgia, specializes in social activism, media politics, political participation, and democratization with a focus on China. His Ph.D. from the University of California, Berkeley, and publications on diverse topics like rural democracy and internet politics in China, reinforce his expertise. His book, *Contesting Cyberspace in China: Online Expression and Authoritarian Resilience*, presents a nuanced view of internet governance in China, arguing for the coexistence of an emancipatory internet with the Chinese state, emphasizing the pluralization of online expression and the rise of pro-state nationalism.

Steven Feldstein—Carnegie Endowment for International Peace

Steven Feldstein, a senior fellow at the Carnegie Endowment for International Peace in the democracy, conflict, and governance program, focuses his research on the intersection of technology and politics. His book, *The Rise of Digital Repression: How Technology is Reshaping Power, Politics, and Resistance*, which was awarded the 2023 Grawemeyer Award, explores the impact of digital technology on political dynamics. His research covers topics like AI's role in repression, technology's geopolitics, China's digital authoritarianism, and patterns of internet shutdowns. His educational background includes times at Princeton University and Berkeley Law.

Taylor Owen—McGill University

Taylor Owen, the Beaverbrook Chair in Media, Ethics and Communications and founding director of the Center for Media, Technology and Democracy at McGill University, is a prominent figure in media and public policy. Hosting the *Big Tech* podcast, and holding fellowships at various institutions, his academic record includes a doctorate from the University of Oxford. He authored *Disruptive Power: The Crisis of the State in the Digital Age* and coedited several influential works. His research at the intersection of media, technology, and public policy is widely recognized, including with awards like the 2016 Public Policy Forum Emerging Leader award.

Zizi Papacharissi—University of Illinois Chicago

Zizi Papacharissi, professor and head of the communication department and professor of political science at the University of Illinois Chicago, focuses on the social and political consequences of online media. She has authored nine books and numerous articles, and is the editor of the journal *Social Media & Society*. She has collaborated with major tech companies and consulted on political campaigns. Her book, *After Democracy: Imagining Our Political Future* explores the evolution of governments in the digital era.

Computer Science/Machine Learning/Statistics

Aaron Roth—University of Pennsylvania

Aaron Roth, the Henry Salvatori Professor at the University of Pennsylvania, engages in research focused on private data analysis, fairness in machine learning, and game theory. Roth's work spans several areas within computer science and cognitive science. His career includes a postdoc at Microsoft Research and a Ph.D. from Carnegie Mellon University. He was also previously involved in advisory and consulting work in the fields of differential privacy, machine learning, and algorithmic fairness, including with Facebook and Apple.

Adrian Cheok—City University London

As chair professor of pervasive computing at City University London, Adrian Cheok leads research in mixed reality, human–computer interfaces, and ubiquitous computing. As the founder and director of the Mixed Reality Lab in Singapore, he has garnered significant funding for projects in wearable computers and mixed reality. His extensive research has yielded numerous academic papers and media articles and has been recognized with multiple awards, including the Hitachi Fellowship and the Young Global Leader award by the World Economic Forum.

Bruce Desmarais—Pennsylvania State University

Bruce Desmarais, is a professor of the Department of Political Science and the Institute for Computational and Data Sciences at Pennsylvania State University. He specializes in the development and application of statistical methods for analyzing complex social and political systems. His work primarily utilizes network analysis, focusing on areas like international conflict and cooperation, political networks, digital communication in local government, policy diffusion, and the nexus between scientific research and regulatory policymaking. Supported by grants from the National Science Foundation and the Russell Sage Foundation, he earned his Ph.D. from the University of North Carolina at Chapel Hill and previously served at the University of Massachusetts Amherst.

Carlo Schwarz—Università Bocconi

Carlo Schwarz, assistant professor at Università Bocconi, holds a Ph.D. from the University of Warwick. His research in applied microeconomics emphasizes policy-relevant issues, integrating causal inference strategies with text analysis, machine learning, and data science techniques. His recent projects investigated social media's role in propagating hate crimes, anti-minority sentiments, polarization, and electoral outcomes.

Corinne Cath—University of Delft

Corinne Cath is a postdoctoral researcher at the Multi-Actor Systems section of Delft University of Technology. An anthropologist by training, Cath's research revolves around the politics of internet infrastructure. Her past roles include Vice President of Research at the Open Tech Fund and completing a Ph.D. at the Oxford Internet Institute. Her postdoctoral work, part of the Gravitation Program Public Values in the Algorithmic Society, focuses on computational infrastructure in justice administration, and particularly the impact of cloud computing on public institutions and technology policy.

David Crandall—Indiana University

David Crandall, is a full professor in the School of Informatics, Computing, and Engineering at Indiana University, and director of the Luddy Artificial Intelligence Center and Center for Machine Learning. He specializes in computer vision, aiming to create algorithms capable of visual understanding. With a Ph.D. in computer science from

Cornell University, his interests also encompass analyzing large volumes of uncertain data, including mining web and social networking data. His tenure at Eastman Kodak Company and as a postdoctoral associate at Cornell University further highlight his expertise in these areas.

Erik Larson—Discovery Institute

Erik Larson, a fellow at the Technology and Democracy Project of the Discovery Institute, is an author concerned with the ethics of computational technology and intelligence with a background in natural language processing. His work critiques the overselling of AI. His experience spans various roles, including as the founder of a software company specializing in AI research, an engineer at Cycorp, and a research scientist at the IC2 Institute at The University of Texas Austin.

Gary Smith—Pomona College

Gary Smith is a professor at Pomona College who focuses on data misuse in statistical analysis, and engages in economic consulting and analysis, with a particular interest in the realistic applications and limitations of AI in decision-making processes. In his book *Standard Deviation: Flawed Assumptions, Tortured Data, and Other Ways to Lie with Statistics* he warns of the pitfalls of confusing correlation with causation. He has also published numerous academic papers and other books including *The AI Delusion*, which contends that in the era of big data, the true peril lies not in computers surpassing our intelligence, but in our tendency to overestimate their capabilities, leading us to place undue trust in them for critical decision-making.

Gretchen Greene—Meta

Gretchen Greene, an attorney, computer vision scientist, machine learning engineer, and senior privacy and public policy manager at Meta, leverages a diverse background to address technological challenges. Her work spans legal, scientific, and engineering disciplines, assisting clients from start-ups to government agencies. A former US national lab mathematician, she has contributed to scientific and policy journals and has been featured in major media outlets.

Hannah Fry—University College London

Hannah Fry, an associate professor at University College London specializing in the mathematics of cities, applies mathematical models to study patterns in human behavior. Her work encompasses collaborations with governments, police forces, health analysts, and supermarkets. She is known for her engaging TED talks, television documentaries, and co-hosting the BBC science podcast "The Curious Cases of Rutherford & Fry," making complex mathematical concepts accessible to a broader audience.

Markus Enenkel—Harvard Humanitarian Initiative

Markus Enenkel's work at the Harvard Humanitarian Initiative involves using earth observation data to identify and forecast interactions between extreme weather events, social conflict, food security, and migration. Contributing to World Bank projects and NASA's Black Marble Alliance, Enenkel's innovative approach combines satellite information with socioeconomic assessments for enhanced decision support in disaster risk management. His academic background includes a Ph.D. in microwave remote sensing and postdoctoral research at Columbia University, focusing on integrating risk perception into disaster management strategies.

Michael Colaresi—University of Pittsburgh

Michael Colaresi, the William S. Dietrich II chair of political science and associate vice provost for data science at the University of Pittsburgh, applies computational tools, including machine learning and Bayesian methods, to issues of national security, political violence, and human rights. His work involves developing tools for collaborative computational research and is affiliated with the Violence Early-Warning Project at the University of Uppsala and the Pitt Institute for cyber law, policy, and security. His book *Democracy Declassified: The Secrecy Dilemma in National Security* examines the balance between state secrecy and public accountability, evaluating the roles of legislative oversight, information laws, and media in liberal democracies.

Michael Kearns—University of Pennsylvania

Michael Kearns, the National Center Chair in the computer and information science department at the University of Pennsylvania, is active in diverse academic fields, including economics, statistics, and data science. As a faculty founder of the Warren Center for Network and Data Sciences, Kearns focuses on machine learning, artificial intelligence, and algorithmic game theory. His research encompasses private data analysis, fairness in machine learning, and computational social science.

Sameer Maskey—Columbia University

Sameer Maskey pioneers work developing software for customer service automation. An ex-IBM research scientist and adjunct assistant professor at Columbia University, his research includes speech translation and summarization evaluation. Maskey's expertise encompasses natural language processing, speech-to-speech translation, and machine learning for language processing. He is founder and CEO of FuseMachines Inc., an advanced machine learning company creating advanced software robots for automating customer service, with the City Government of New York as a major client.

Sascha Meinrath—Penn State University

Sascha Meinrath, the Palmer Chair in Telecommunications at Penn State and director of X-Lab, is recognized for his contributions to technology policy. His career includes founding the Open Technology Institute and the Commotion Wireless Project. His advocacy against governmental spying programs and leadership in developing public interest tech policy initiatives mark him as a prominent figure in the field. Meinrath's research focuses on broadband connectivity, telecommunications policy, and the societal impacts of disruptive technologies.

Timandra Harkness—Author

Timandra Harkness, a writer, comedian, and broadcaster, specializes in scientific and statistical topics. With contributions to various media, including BBC Radio 4, and authorship of *Big Data: Does Size Matter?*, she leads the Data Debate series, collaborating with the Alan Turing Institute and the British Library. Her unique blend of humor and insight into scientific topics makes her a distinct voice in the communication of complex concepts to a broader audience.

Ethics/Law/Privacy/Surveillance
Alexandra Chouldechova—Carnegie Mellon University

Alexandra Chouldechova, the Estella Loomis McCandless assistant professor at Carnegie Mellon University, focuses on algorithmic fairness and accountability within data-driven systems, especially in criminal justice and human services. Her research, funded by organizations like the Hillman Foundation and the National Science Foundation Program on Fairness in Artificial Intelligence, involves examining algorithmic bias in risk assessment tools and developing fair learning algorithms. She also explores the dynamics of human-in-the-loop systems, studying the influence of algorithmic tools on decision-making and user perceptions.

Andrea Loreggia—University of Brescia

Andrea Loreggia, an assistant professor at the University of Brescia, is engaged in artificial intelligence research, focusing on computational social choice and deep learning. His work involves designing artificial agents capable of understanding and reasoning with ethical principles and moral values. Previously he worked on incorporating ethical principles in AI for the Future of Life Institute. He is an associate editor for *AI Magazine* and co-invented a framework for algorithm portfolios that IBM patented in 2017.

Anu Bradford—Columbia Law School

Anu Bradford, a leading scholar in EU regulatory power and digital regulation, is renowned for coining the term the "Brussels Effect" to describe the EU's global market influence. Her book, *Digital Empires: The Global Battle to Regulate Technology*, recognized by the *Financial Times* as a standout publication, reflects her expertise in international antitrust law. She spearheads the Comparative Competition Law Project, creating a comprehensive global data set of antitrust laws, significantly contributing to empirical research on antitrust regimes and market regulation.

Brianna Rosen—University of Oxford

Brianna Rosen, a strategy and policy fellow at the Blavatnik School of Government, University of Oxford, specializes in the governance and ethics of emerging technologies. She is also a senior fellow at Just Security, and research affiliate at the Australian National University's Machine Intelligence and Normative Theory Lab. Her previous roles include positions in the United States government, where she contributed extensively to national security issues for a decade. She holds a doctorate in public policy from the University of Oxford as a Clarendon Scholar.

Carissa Véliz—University of Oxford

Carissa Véliz, an associate professor at the University of Oxford's Faculty of Philosophy and the Institute for Ethics in AI, teaches moral philosophy, ethics, philosophy of mind, and AI ethics. Her research focuses on technology ethics, moral and political philosophy, and public policy. She authored the acclaimed *Privacy Is Power*, and edits the *Oxford Handbook of Digital Ethics*. Her most recent work, *The Ethics of Privacy and Surveillance*, is a philosophical study of privacy that suggests ways forward for policy and private life.

Céline Castets-Renard—University of Ottawa

Céline Castets-Renard, the University Research Chair on accountable artificial intelligence at the University of Ottawa, focuses on digital law and regulation. Her research covers a range of private law areas impacted by technology, from contract and civil liability, to intellectual property and data protection. She was previously appointed to the French Government Research Chair at the Artificial and Natural Intelligence Toulouse Institute where she investigated the protection of indigenous knowledge. During a five-year appointment with the prestigious Institut Universitaire de France, she completed a research residency at Fordham Law School as a Fulbright Scholar, and at Yale University's Internet Society Project.

Chris Gilliard—Macomb Community College

Chris Gilliard, professor of English at Macomb Community College, and a writer and speaker, concentrates his scholarship on digital privacy, surveillance, and the intersections of race, class, and technology. His advocacy for critical and equity-focused technology approaches in education is reflected in his writings for prominent publications. He is currently part of the first Just Tech Fellowship, where he will create a classification scheme to identify and assess risks and social impact of novel surveillance technologies on marginalized groups. He is also a visiting research fellow at the Harvard Kennedy School Shorenstein Center and member of the Surveillance Technology Oversight Project.

David Kaye—University of California Irvine

David Kaye, a clinical professor of law at the University of California, Irvine, previously served as the UN Special Rapporteur on Freedom of Opinion and Expression. His 2019 book, *Speech Police: The Global Struggle to Govern the Internet*, examines the challenges in regulating online expression. He is a member of the Council on Foreign Relations, and was the 2023–2024 Fulbright Distinguished Scholar at the Raoul Wallenberg Institute. He actively participates in international dialogues on internet governance and human rights, contributing significantly to understanding the interplay between technology, law, and freedom of expression.

Emma Ruttkamp-Bloem—University of Pretoria

Emma Ruttkamp-Bloem, professor and head of the Department of Philosophy at the University of Pretoria, leads AI ethics research at the Centre for Artificial Intelligence Research. As a member of the African Union Development Agency—New Partnership for Africa's Development Consultative Roundtable and UNESCO's World Commission for Ethics of Scientific Knowledge and Technology, her research intersects scientific realism and the structure of scientific theories in the philosophy of science. Her focus on culturally sensitive policies for AI emphasizes the need for global regulation and trustworthy technology, reflecting her commitment to ethical AI development.

Fabio Pietrosanti—Hermes Center

Fabio Pietrosanti's career in technology and security spans from early hacking endeavors to entrepreneurship. Engaging in cyber security since 2000, he co-founded the Hermes Center for Transparency and Digital Human Rights in 2011. As its president, he combines management, fundraising, and technical expertise on projects like GlobaLeaks and Tor2web. His focus on laws and policies affecting the information society and digital rights illustrates a commitment to the ethical and legal dimensions of technology.

Firmin DeBrabander—Maryland Institute College of Art

Firmin DeBrabander is a professor of philosophy at the Maryland Institute College of Art, who specializes in political philosophy. He teaches at the intersection of various philosophical disciplines. He is known for his work on gun rights, and his latest book, *Life After Privacy: Reclaiming Democracy in a Surveillance Society*, explores the threat to privacy in the digital age. He also contributes political and social commentary to major national publications, establishing him as a thought leader in contemporary philosophical discourse.

Frank Pasquale—Cornell University

Frank Pasquale, a professor of law at Cornell Tech and Cornell Law School, specializes in the law of AI, algorithms, and machine learning. Authoring influential works like *The Black Box Society* and *New Laws of Robotics*, his research informs legal perspectives on AI in various professional fields. He also coedited *The Oxford Handbook of Ethics of AI* and *Transparent Data Mining*, playing a pivotal role in shaping the legal framework around AI and digital technologies.

Hélèn Landemore—Yale University

Hélèn Landemore, a full professor at Yale University, focuses on democratic theory, political epistemology, and the ethics and politics of AI. Involved with Yale's Institution for Social and Policy Studies and the Institute for Ethics in AI at Oxford University, she advises on AI ethics at OpenAI and DemocracyNext. Her current research is supported by Schmidt Futures through the AI2050 program, highlighting her significant impact on the discourse around democracy and technology in the modern world.

Jake Goldenfein—University of Melbourne

Jake Goldenfein, a scholar at Melbourne Law School, serves as a chief investigator in the Australian Research Centre's Centre of Excellence for Automated Decision-Making and Society. His academic career includes a postdoctoral fellowship at Cornell Tech's Digital Life Initiative. His research encompasses platform regulation, data governance, digital surveillance, and automated decision-making governance. His first monograph, *Monitoring Laws*, investigates the role of the law in shaping the data economy and digital surveillance. Admitted to practice law in Australia, he has previously worked in the fields of privacy and administrative law.

John Basl—Northeastern University

John Basl, an associate professor of philosophy at Northeastern University, specializes in moral philosophy and applied ethics, particularly concerning emerging technologies like

AI and synthetic biology. His research employs applied contexts to reflect on theoretical problems in philosophy and ethics or to apply these theories in resolving practical issues. His notable works include *The Death of the Ethic of Life* and collaborative reports on ethical challenges in AI and big data analytics.

John McGinnis—Northwestern University

John McGinnis is a professor at the Pritzker School of Law at Northwestern University, and is a Harvard College and Harvard Law School alumnus, with an MA from Balliol College, Oxford University. He previously clerked for the United States Court of Appeals and served in the Department of Justice. An author of notable works like *Accelerating Democracy: Transforming Government Through Technology* and *Originalism and the Good Constitution*, he is recognized for his contributions to legal scholarship, including receiving the Paul Bator award from the Federalist Society. He is also listed as a potential panelist for World Trade Organization disputes.

John Zerilli—University of Cambridge/Oxford

John Zerilli is a philosopher with interests in cognitive science, AI, and law. He holds positions as the Chancellor's Fellow in AI, data, and the rule of law at the University of Edinburgh, as a research associate at Oxford University's Oxford Institute for Ethics in AI, and is an associate fellow in the Centre for the Future of Intelligence at Cambridge University. Previously he was called to the Sydney bar in 2011. His recent publications include *The Adaptable Mind* and *A Citizen's Guide to Artificial Intelligence*, which reflect his multidisciplinary approach to understanding AI and its legal and cognitive aspects.

Kate Crawford—University of Southern California Annenberg

Kate Crawford, a research professor at the University of Southern California Annenberg, explores the social and political implications of AI. She is also the senior principal researcher at the Microsoft Research Lab in New York City. Her research examines AI's impact on human aspects like gender, race, and class, arguing against the neutrality of AI systems and highlighting their role in perpetuating existing power structures. Her latest book, *Atlas of AI: Power, Politics, and the Planetary Costs of Artificial Intelligence*, explores these themes.

Kathryn Henne—Australian National University

Kathryn Henne, director of RegNet at Australian National University's School of Regulation and Global Governance and leads the Justice and Technoscience Lab (JusTech). Previously holding a Canada Research Chair at the University of Waterloo, her research spans automated decision-making, policing technologies and surveillance, and sport regulation. Her work has been supported by numerous grants and she is currently authoring a book on traumatic brain injury in sports. Her recent publications include "Creating a new normal? Technosocial relations, mundane governance and pandemic-related disruption in everyday life," coauthored with Aleks Deejay.

Marc Schuilenburg—Erasmus University Rotterdam

Marc Schuilenburg, professor of digital surveillance at Erasmus University Rotterdam, focuses on the expansion of surveillance technologies and their alignment with democratic values. He emphasizes understanding AI technologies from the perspectives of various actors and their impacts on security programs. His latest book, *Making Surveillance Public: Why You Should Be More Woke About AI and Algorithms*, advocates for a digital criminology centered on power, knowledge, and AI experiences, contributing significantly to the discourse on surveillance and technology.

Markus Dubber—University of Toronto

Markus Dubber, a professor of law at the University of Toronto, specializes in criminal law theory, comparative law, and legal history. He has authored several books, including *The Oxford Handbook of Ethics of AI*. As the former director of the University of Toronto's Centre for Ethics, he initiated projects like the "Ethics of AI Lab," illustrating his commitment to interdisciplinary approaches in legal and ethical studies.

Meredith Broussard—New York University

Meredith Broussard, an associate professor at New York University, focuses her research on AI in investigative reporting. Her books *Artificial Unintelligence* and *More than a Glitch* have received significant recognition, including the Prose Award and the Hacker Prize from the Society for the History of Technology. Her work emphasizes the use of data analysis for social good and critically examines the limitations and biases inherent in technology.

Molly Land—University of Connecticut

Molly Land, a scholar in international law and human rights, joined the University of Connecticut law faculty in 2013 and was named associate dean for academic affairs in 2023. Her scholarship intersects human rights, science, technology, and innovation. Her recent book, *New Technologies for Human Rights Law and Practice*, offers insights into technology's relationship with human rights law. Her current research aims to develop a human rights–based framework for addressing online speech harms, balancing freedom of expression and privacy protections.

Nathaniel Persily—Stanford University

Nathaniel Persily, the James B. McClatchy Professor of Law at Stanford Law School, specializes in American election law. His interdisciplinary role spans the departments of political science, communication, and the Freeman Spogli Institute for International Studies. Persily's esteemed career includes positions at Columbia, the University of Pennsylvania, and visiting roles at several global universities. His work, recognized through prestigious fellowships, examines the intersection of technology with political communication and election administration. As co-director of various Stanford initiatives, he played a pivotal role in supporting election officials during the Covid-19 pandemic and contributed to the Kofi Annan Commission on Elections and Democracy in the Digital Age.

Nita Farahany—Duke University

Nita Farahany, a leading scholar on the ethical, legal, and social implications of emerging technologies, holds the position of Robinson O. Everett Distinguished Professor of Law & Philosophy at Duke Law School. She is also the founding director of Duke Science & Society. Her research spans neuroscience, genomics, AI, pandemic-related bioethics, and criminal law's intersection with science and technology. A frequent presenter at prestigious forums, she is also an author, and her latest book *The Battle for Your Brain: Defending Your Right to Think Freely in the Age of Neurotechnology*, focuses on neurotechnology's ethical implications.

Petra Saskia Bayerl—Sheffield Hallam University

Petra Saskia Bayerl is a professor of digital communication and security and head of research at the Centre of Excellence in Terrorism, Resilience, Intelligence and Organised Crime Research at Sheffield Hallam University. Prior to this, she co-directed the Centre of Excellence on Public Safety Management at Erasmus University. She holds degrees in psychology, linguistics, and organizational dynamics, and completed her Ph.D. at Delft University of Technology. Her research focuses on the societal implications of emerging technologies in security, contributing to international journals and books, including coauthoring *Application of Big Data for National Security: A Practitioner's Guide to Emerging Technologies*. She has also played a pivotal role in EU-funded security projects, emphasizing the intersection of technology, security, and society.

Randolph Lewis—University of Texas Austin

Randolph Lewis, a professor and chair in the Department of American studies at University of Texas Austin, focuses his research on surveillance, documentary expression, public scholarship, and the intersection of art and politics. His book *Under Surveillance: Being*

Watched in Modern America delves into surveillance in the United States. He also leads digital humanities projects like "The End of Austin," exploring urban identity. His teaching interests include public scholarship and urban studies, emphasizing the connection between academia and public audiences.

Renée Cummings—University of Virginia

Renée Cummings is an AI, data, and tech ethicist, a professor of practice in data science and first Data Activist-in-Residence at University of Virginia's School of Data Science. She is a senior fellow at the Brookings Institution and involved in various global forums. Her work spans AI ethics, data justice, algorithmic policing, and AI for criminal justice reform, focusing on inclusivity, ethical resilience, and responsible AI development. She is also the 2023 VentureBeat AI Innovator Award winner.

Robert Reich—Stanford University

Robert Reich, a professor of political science with courtesy appointments in philosophy and education at Stanford University, co-directs the Center on Philanthropy and Civil Society and is the associate director of the Institute for Human-Centered Artificial Intelligence. His scholarship, bridging political theory with social science and engineering, focuses on ethics and AI. His recent publications include *System Error* and *Digital Technology and Democratic Theory*, emphasizing ethical considerations in the digital age.

Ronald Sandler—Northeastern University

Ronald Sandler, a professor and chair in the Department of Philosophy and Religion at Northeastern University, is affiliated with the Digital, Analytics, Technology and Automation Initiative. Sandler's research encompasses ethics in emerging technologies, environmental ethics, and moral philosophy. His work in AI and information ethics includes exploring content labeling and building ethical capacities in organizations. Sandler has authored several books, including *Ethics and Emerging Technologies*, contributing significantly to discourse in environmental and technology ethics.

Salomé Viljoen—Michigan Law School

Salomé Viljoen, an assistant professor of law at Michigan Law School, teaches courses on contracts, privacy, commercial surveillance, and data governance. As a former fellow and current faculty associate at Harvard University's Berkman Klein Center for Internet and Society, she explores the law and political economy of data and AI. Her research interests include platform power, information law's role in structuring inequality, and legal theories on social data. Her work, appearing in publications like the Yale Law Journal and the

Columbia Law Review, develops theories on affirmative uses of social data and public agencies' roles in governing it.

Samir Chopra—City University of New York

Samir Chopra, professor emeritus of philosophy at Brooklyn College of the City University of New York, has a diverse academic career, where he began as a logician. His written works cover topics from the politics of technology and the legal theory of artificial intelligence to cricket, reflecting a broad range of interests. He coauthored *A Legal Theory for Autonomous Artificial Agents*, which discusses how current laws can be applied to progressively advanced AI. He is also certified as a philosophical counselor.

Sean Kanuck—Stanford University

Sean Kanuck, an international attorney and intelligence analyst, advises on the future of information technology. As an affiliate of Stanford University's Center for International Security and Cooperation, he brings extensive experience in cybersecurity and international information security. His academic and professional background includes contributions to White House cybersecurity policy, involvement with national and international security councils, and teaching roles at George Washington University and George Mason University, focusing on AI's security implications and ethics in national security law.

Seth Lazar—Australian National University

Seth Lazar, professor of philosophy at the Australian National University, leads the Machine Intelligence and Normative Theory Lab. His research, supported by multiple foundations, explores the moral and political philosophy of AI. His involvement in significant conferences and his contributions to a study by the United States National Academies of Science on responsible computing research demonstrate his leadership in the field. He has delivered notable lectures at Harvard University and Stanford University, underscoring his expertise in AI ethics.

S. Matthew Liao—New York University

S. Matthew Liao, holding the Arthur Zitrin Chair in bioethics and directing the Center for Bioethics at New York University, focuses on the philosophical study of biomedical innovations. A speaker at TEDxCERN, he has discussed ethical considerations in memory modification. His authorship includes *Ethics of Artificial Intelligence* and several books that offer comprehensive insights into human rights and bioethics. His interdisciplinary teaching approach covers medical and environmental ethics, exploring the ethical dimensions of new medical technologies and their societal implications.

Stefaan Verhulst—New York University GovLab

Stefaan Verhulst, co-founder and chief research and development officer at GovLab, founded by New York University, and director of its data program, is a leading figure in data policy. As editor-in-chief of open-access journal *Data & Policy* and with his involvement in numerous research and advisory roles, his work has a significant global impact. His recognition as an influential academic in digital government and his leadership in various data-focused initiatives reflect his commitment to enhancing data use in decision-making and policymaking.

Stephen Cave—University of Cambridge

Stephen Cave, director of the Institute for Technology and Humanity and the Leverhulme Centre for the Future of Intelligence at the University of Cambridge, has a background in philosophy and diplomacy. His research focuses on the ethics of AI, robotics, life-extension, and immortality. Cave has authored and edited several books including *Imagining AI: How the World Sees Intelligent Machines*, which he coedited with Kanta Dihal. His work has garnered significant media attention, and he regularly appears on television and radio discussing philosophical and ethical aspects of technology.

Valère Ndior—Université de Bretagne Occidentale

Valère Ndior, a full professor of law at the Université de Bretagne occidentale, and a junior member of the prestigious Institut Universitaire de France, specializes in international and digital law. As president of the Francophone Network of International Law and a board member of the International Law Association's French branch, his research interests include social media governance and regulation. His scholarly contributions, such as editing the French language *Dictionary of International Current Affairs* and coediting *International Issues of Digital Activities*, also in French, focus on digital diplomacy, online moderation, and cybersecurity.

Victoria Adelmant—New York University School of Law

Victoria Adelmant directs the Center for Human Rights and Global Justice's technology and human rights initiatives through the Digital Welfare State and Human Rights Project, which focuses on the digital transformation's impact on human rights. As an adjunct professor at New York University School of Law, she teaches courses related to emerging technologies and digitalization. Her research examines the human rights implications of digital state transformations, particularly in welfare services. Her forthcoming book, coauthored with Christiaan van Veen and Philip Alston, delves into these topics. Her professional background includes roles in international human rights organizations and grassroots service organizations.

Virginia Dignum—Umeå University

Virginia Dignum is a professor in responsible artificial intelligence and director of the AI Policy Lab at Umeå University. Her research explores the ethical, societal, and legal impacts of AI, focusing on how AI can be responsibly integrated into society. She addresses the moral and regulatory aspects of autonomous intelligent agents, contributing to international policy and strategy guidelines for AI research and applications. She also serves in various international AI advisory roles, including the Global Partnership on AI, and the High-Level Expert Group on the Implementation of the UNESCO AI Ethics Recommendation.

Yong Jin Park—Howard University

Yong Jin Park, a professor at Howard University's School of Communications, specializes in the societal and policy implications of emerging AI technologies. His research, including his book *The Future of Digital Surveillance*, examines the intersection of AI, algorithms, and personal data in perpetuating social and racial inequalities. His recent work, supported by grants from various foundations, explores strategies to debias AI modeling, demonstrating his commitment to addressing the challenges posed by AI in society.

Media/Communication/Culture

Andreas Jungherr—University of Bamberg

Andreas Jungherr, a professor of political science specializing in digital transformation at the University of Bamberg, focuses his research on society's engagement with AI and digital technology. His notable publications include *Digital Transformations of the Public Arena* and *Retooling Politics*, which explore the impact of digital media on politics and public discourse. His research extends to the implications of AI on democracy, political communication, and contemporary media systems. He is currently authoring a book about the integration of social sciences with computer science in AI.

Andrew Chadwick—Loughborough University

Andrew Chadwick, professor of political communication at Loughborough University, is also director of the Online Civic Culture Centre. His research examines the internet and new media's influence on political mobilization, engagement, news, and misinformation. He wrote *The Hybrid Media System: Politics and Power*, introducing the concept into social science, impacting various fields. He is the founding editor of the *Oxford Studies in Digital Politics* book series, which has significantly contributed to digital politics research since its inception in 2010.

Anne Kaun—Södertörn University

Anne Kaun, a professor at Södertörn University in Stockholm, Sweden, specializes in media and communication studies. Her research interests encompass media theory, mediated temporalities, and the humanistic social science perspective on automation and AI. Previous projects investigated media practices in protest movements, exploring how media technologies evolve movement tactics over time. Additionally, she focuses on media memories and their transformation in the context of social media, questioning how online public and connected remembering via platforms like Facebook impact the nature of memory.

Augusto Valeriani—Università di Bologna

Augusto Valeriani, an associate professor in sociology of culture and communication at the University of Bologna in Italy, specializes in digital media and social networking platforms. His research encompasses political and corporate communication, citizen engagement, journalism, and storytelling practices. He coauthored *Outside the Bubble*, which focuses on social media and citizen participation, and has received accolades from organizations like the International Communication Association and the American Political Science Association.

Ben Epstein—DePaul University

Ben Epstein, an associate professor at DePaul University since 2018, specializes in American politics, particularly focusing on the interplay of the internet, politics, media, and political behavior. His research encompasses the evolution of American political communication and its effects on political participation. His notable work includes *The Only Constant is Change: Technology, Political Communication, and Innovation Over Time*, examining the evolution of political communication and the innovation of political strategies over time.

Chris Wells—Boston University

Chris Wells, associate professor in emerging media studies at Boston University, uses a blend of conventional and computational methods in his research. His focus includes the dynamics of news media coverage, citizen learning about politics, and participation patterns. His work, particularly *The Civic Organization and the Digital Citizen: Communicating Engagement in a Networked Age*, investigates the interplay of citizens, civic groups, and digital media, shedding light on democratic culture and citizenship in the digital era.

David Karpf—George Washington University

David Karpf, an associate professor at the George Washington University's School of Media and Public Affairs, explores strategic communication practices of political associations with a focus on internet strategies. His award-winning books, *The MoveOn Effect* and *Analytic Activism*, analyze how digital media transforms political advocacy and activist organizations. His background as an environmental organizer and former Sierra Club board member enriches his research and teaching with practical perspectives.

Francesco Marconi—Applied XL

Francesco Marconi, a computational journalist and co-founder of Applied XL, has previously led research and development at the *Wall Street Journal* and managed strategy at the Associated Press, focusing on content automation and AI. Recognized for his contributions to digital media innovation, he is affiliated with academic institutions such as MIT and Columbia University. His book *Newsmakers: Artificial Intelligence and the Future of Journalism*, examines the evolving landscape of journalism in the age of AI.

Francis Lee—Chinese University of Hong Kong

Francis Lee, director and professor at the School of Journalism and Communication, Chinese University of Hong Kong, specializes in journalism studies, political communication, and public opinion research. His notable works include *Memories of Tiananmen*, *Media and Protest Logics in the Digital Era*, and *Talk Radio, the Mainstream Press and Public Opinion in Hong Kong*. As chief editor of the *Chinese Journal of Communication* and an elected fellow of the International Communication Association, his research significantly contributes to media and social movements studies.

Hyunjin Seo—University of Kansas

Hyunjin Seo, the Oscar Stauffer Professor and associate dean at the University of Kansas, focuses her research on the impact of digital communication technologies on social change. Author of *Networked Collective Actions: The Making of an Impeachment*, she examines the dynamics of political movements facilitated by networked communication. As a faculty associate at Harvard's Berkman Klein Center, her interdisciplinary work spans over fifty publications, contributing to a deeper understanding of digital inclusion and technology's role in societal transformations.

Jason Gainous—University of Sharjah

Jason Gainous, a professor in the Department of Mass Communication at the University of Sharjah, specializes in political communication, digital media, and public opinion. His scholarly work includes *Tweeting to Power* and *Directed Digital Dissidence in Autocracies*, examining the intersection of digital media with political processes. He is also coeditor-in-chief of the *Journal of Information Technology & Politics*, contributing significantly to the field of political science and digital media studies.

Jason Hannan—University of Winnipeg

Jason Hannan, associate professor in the Department of Rhetoric, Writing, and Communications at the University of Winnipeg, focuses on the intersections of rhetoric, political theory, and digital democracy. His research includes explorations into trolling, disinformation, and conspiracy theory in digital media. Author of *Trolling Ourselves to Death*, he investigates the historical roots of trolling and its implications for public discourse in the digital age.

Jason Rittenberg—Author

Jason Rittenberg, as the director of research and advisory services for the Council of Development Finance Agencies, oversees the council's extensive research activities. His prior experience includes a role as a social sciences research specialist at the Ohio Department of Job and Family Services. Holding a Master's in Communication from the University of Illinois and a bachelor's from Ohio University, he coauthored *News on the Internet: Information and Citizenship in the 21st Century*, which examines the impact of online news on individual and societal levels.

Jennifer Stromer-Galley—Syracuse University

Jennifer Stromer-Galley, professor of information studies at Syracuse University, and director of the Center for Computational and Data Sciences, has a distinguished career in digital media research. She served as the president of the Association of Internet Researchers and was a fellow at the Tow Center for Digital Journalism at Columbia University. Her book *Presidential Campaigning in the Internet Age* won the 2015 Roderick P. Hart Top Book Award. Her research, funded by over $15 million in grants, includes over seventy publications, and examines online interaction and strategic communication across various digital contexts.

Jessa Lingel—University of Pennsylvania

Jessa Lingel, an associate professor at the University of Pennsylvania researches digital culture, particularly the power dynamics in technology relationships and their potential for social change. Her research uses qualitative methods to explore three areas: alterations in technology by marginalized groups, the political nature of infrastructure, and technological activism. Her books, including *The Gentrification of the Internet: How to Reclaim Our Digital Freedom*, contribute to the understanding of socio-technical practices in relation to social justice projects.

Jiang Min—University of North Carolina Charlotte

Jiang Min, a professor of communication studies at the University of North Carolina Charlotte and an affiliate faculty of international studies, is renowned for her interdisciplinary research on Chinese internet technologies and politics. As a Secretariat member of the Chinese Internet Research Conference and a CyberBRICS visiting professor, her work spans new media studies, political communication, and legal studies. Her research is instrumental in understanding the impact of Chinese technologies and policies on global communication, particularly in the Global South.

Joseph Chan—Chinese University of Hong Kong

Joseph Chan, emeritus professor at the School of Journalism and Communication at the Chinese University of Hong Kong, has an extensive publication record in media and social movements, journalism, and comparative communication. His book, coauthored with Francis L.F. Lee, *Media and Protest Logics in the Digital Era: The Umbrella Movement in Hong Kong*, connects the Umbrella Movement to contemporary social movement theories. He is also an elected fellow of the International Communication Association and a recipient of the Changjiang Chair Professorship from China's Ministry of Education.

Joshua Tucker—New York University

Joshua Tucker, a professor of politics with affiliations in Russian and Slavic studies and data science at New York University (NYU), directs the Jordan Center for Advanced Study of Russia and co-directs the NYU Center for Social Media and Politics. His initial research in comparative politics evolved into studying the intersection of social media and politics, employing innovative methods to analyze various aspects of political behavior. He coedited *Social Media and Democracy: The State of the Field*, and is at the forefront of research on online political behavior, disinformation, and the effects of social media on political knowledge.

Kanta Dihal—University of Cambridge

Kanta Dihal, a senior research fellow at the University of Cambridge's Leverhulme Centre for the Future of Intelligence, investigates the cultural narratives of intelligent machines. She leads the Global AI Narratives project and is the project development lead on

Decolonizing AI. Her interdisciplinary work in science communication and science fiction examines AI ethics and biases. Her coedited books, *AI Narratives* and *Imagining AI*, along with her papers, contribute significantly to understanding AI's societal impacts. She has also advised international organizations on AI perceptions and narratives.

Kate Starbird—University of Washington

Kate Starbird is an associate professor at the University of Washington and a co-founder of the Center for an Informed Public, which aims to strengthen democratic discourse and counter misinformation. Her research in human–computer interaction and crisis informatics focuses on social media use in crisis events and the spread of disinformation. She examines the role of online platforms in information dissemination and the challenges posed by misinformation in crisis situations.

Kevin Roose—The New York Times

Kevin Roose, a technology columnist for *The New York Times* and co-host of the "Hard Fork" podcast, has reported on technology for over a decade, covering the impact of various technologies, including AI, on society and culture. He is also an author, with his latest book *Futureproof* focusing on adapting to the age of AI. His journalistic career includes production of the "Real Future" documentary series, emphasizing his expertise in technology and its societal implications.

Lina Dencik—Goldsmiths, University of London

Lina Dencik, professor in digital communication and society at Goldsmiths, University of London, co-founded and directs the Data Justice Lab. Her research addresses the dynamics between media developments, social change, and data politics. She leads several projects, including the European Research Council–funded DATAJUSTICE, and has worked on topics ranging from political mobilization to media memories in social media. Her publications, including *Data Justice*, contribute to understanding data's role in societal transformations and governance.

Meredith Clark—Northeastern University

Meredith Clark, associate professor in the School of Journalism and the Department of Communication Studies at Northeastern University, focuses her research on the intersections of race, media, and power across digital, social, and news media. Her experience as a newsroom editor, writer, and columnist informs her work, including her manuscript *We Tried to Tell Y'all: Black Twitter & Black Digital Resistance*. She also leads "Documenting the Now," a Mellon Foundation–supported project aiding community activists in digital archiving.

Minna Ruckenstein—University of Helsinki

Minna Ruckenstein, a professor in emerging technologies in society at the University of Helsinki, leads the Datafied Life Collaboratory. This research group explores digitalization and datafication processes, integrating perspectives from technological anthropology, science and technology studies, communication, and consumer economics. Current projects focus on automated decision-making, algorithmic culture, and algorithmic interactions in Helsinki, Shanghai, and Hangzhou. Her research, including her book *The Feel of Algorithms*, investigates the emotional, social, political, and economic dimensions of data practices in various fields like health and social work.

Nick Seaver—Tufts University

Nick Seaver, assistant professor of anthropology at Tufts University, studies cultural engagement with technology among technology creators. His book *Computing Taste* is based on ethnographic research with developers of algorithmic music recommendation systems in the United States. His current research explores the technocultural aspects of attention, particularly how engineers and developers perceive and navigate public concerns about technologies designed to manipulate users' attention. This project includes professionals working in machine learning, facial recognition, and online advertising.

Payal Arora—Utrecht University

Payal Arora, full professor and chair in inclusive AI cultures at Utrecht University, co-founded FemLab, focusing on the feminist future of work. With expertise in cross-cultural values, inequality, and inclusive design, particularly in the Global South, her work in digital anthropology spans two decades. Her research examines how youth in resource-constrained contexts interact with digital tools and informs the design of equitable systems. Her award-winning book *The Next Billion Users* highlights her contributions to understanding digital cultures.

Rahaf Harfoush—Oxford Internet Institute

Rahaf Harfoush, a visiting policy fellow at the Oxford Internet Institute, specializes in the intersections of technology, innovation, and digital culture. As the executive director of the Red Thread Institute of Digital Culture and an educator at Sciences Politiques School of Management and Innovation in Paris, France, her research encompasses digital culture, cybersecurity, social media, and AI. Her influence in digital culture is evident in her recognition as an innovative leader in France and her contributions to major publications and international forums.

Rasmus Kleis Nielsen—University of Oxford

Rasmus Kleis Nielsen, professor of political communication and director at the Reuters Institute for the Study of Journalism at Oxford University, researches news media organizations, digital media use in political contexts, and political communication. His book *The Power of Platforms: Shaping Media and Society* with Sarah Anne Ganter discusses technology platforms' influence over news and media. His interests include the future of news, the journalism business, digital media, and civic engagement in a digital context.

Richard Waters—Financial Times

Richard Waters, the West Coast editor of the *Financial Times* (FT) based in San Francisco, leads a team focusing on Silicon Valley's technology sector. He writes extensively about the tech industry, including on topics like AI and the influence of major US tech platforms. His career at the FT has spanned various finance and technology roles in London and New York, reflecting his expertise in analyzing the impacts of technology and finance on society.

Sahana Udupa—Ludwig Maximilian University of Munich

Sahana Udupa, a professor of media anthropology at the Ludwig Maximilian University of Munich, and a Joan Shorenstein Fellow at Harvard University, received a significant European Research Council grant for her project on digital media politics. Her work explores online extreme speech and its implications, leading to a European Research Council Proof of Concept award for an AI-assisted model to address this issue. Her publications, including *Digital Hate* and *Digital Unsettling*, examine the global dimensions of online speech and platform politics.

Saif Shahin—Tilburg University

Saif Shahin, assistant professor of digital culture at Tilburg University, critically examines data and technology as sociocultural phenomena. His methodological expertise spans qualitative, quantitative, and computational approaches, including machine learning and network analysis. His research, published in high-impact journals, delves into the production of power in digital discourses and online identity politics. He also serves as associate editor of the *Journal of Information Technology & Politics*.

Samuel Woolley—University of Texas Austin

Samuel Woolley, an assistant professor of journalism and media, and program director of the Propaganda Research Lab at the University of Texas Austin, focuses on how emergent technologies are used in global political communication. His research on computational propaganda reveals the manipulation of public opinion through social media. His book *The Reality Game* explores the manipulation of reality through technology. He also coauthored *Bots* and coedited *Computational Propaganda*.

Sarah Sobieraj—Tufts University

Sarah Sobieraj, professor of sociology at Tufts University and director of the Digital Sexism Project, specializes in political culture in the United States, incivility, and digital abuse. Her book *Credible Threat: Attacks Against Women Online and the Future of Democracy* addresses the impact of digital abuse on women's participation in discourse. She also coauthored *The Outrage Industry* and wrote *Soundbitten*. Her work has won recognition for its focus on the mediated information environment and its effects on democracy and social interactions.

Stefan Helmreich—Massachusetts Institute of Technology

Stefan Helmreich, professor of anthropology at the Massachusetts Institute of Technology, studies scientists' conceptualizations of their study objects in oceanography, biology, acoustics, and computer science. His book *Silicon Second Nature* explores computer modeling in life sciences and won the Diana Forsythe Book Prize. His courses, such as "Cultures of Computing," examine computers anthropologically, exploring their historical, capitalist, and social dimensions, and their impact on society.

Taina Bucher—University of Oslo

Taina Bucher, associate professor in the Department of Media and Communication at the University of Oslo, teaches digital media topics, including social media, digital infrastructure, and AI. She focuses on algorithmic power and politics, and studies the relationships between algorithms, social concerns, and cultural perceptions of digital technology and AI. Her research includes digital infrastructure, algorithmic temporalities, and platform power, particularly Facebook. Her book, *If . . . Then: Algorithmic Power and Politics*, provides an in-depth look at algorithms and their everyday implications.

Tamar Mitts—Columbia University

Tamar Mitts, an assistant professor at Columbia University's School of International and Public Affairs, researches technology and security intersections. Her work focuses on digital platforms' role in militant and hate group mobilization, state and non-state actors' media manipulation, and trust and safety on technology platforms. Her book *Moderating Extremism* investigates the persistence of violent actors on social media despite increased content moderation, drawing on extensive empirical data to reveal underlying mechanisms.

Tarleton Gillespie—Cornell University

Tarleton Gillespie is currently a principal researcher at Microsoft Research, New England, and adjunct associate professor with the Department of Communication at Cornell University. His research delves into the controversies surrounding digital media and commercial providers, focusing on the political and cultural implications of technical solutions to copyright and the role of online media platforms in cultural and political discourse. His most recent book is *Custodians of the Internet: Platforms, Content Moderation, and the Hidden Decisions That Shape Social Media*, which investigates how social media platforms moderate what is posted online.

William Dutton—University of Southern California

William Dutton, an independent researcher and emeritus professor at the University of Southern California, was the Oxford Internet Institute's founding director. His research spans the internet and society, digital divides, digital choice, the Fifth Estate, and network society. His latest book, *The Fifth Estate: The Power Shift of the Digital Age*, delves into the influential role of the Fifth Estate in the digital era. His career includes being a Fulbright Scholar and National Director of the UK's Programme on Information and Communication Technologies.

Peacebuilding/Conflict Prevention

Allard Duursma—ETH Zurich

Allard Duursma, an assistant professor in conflict management and international relations at ETH Zurich, specializes in mediation, peacekeeping, patronage politics, and political order. Holding a Ph.D. from the University of Oxford, his research has included developing the African peace processes data set and conducting field interviews with conflict parties and stakeholders. His academic contributions are recognized through his role as deputy editor at *International Peacekeeping* and as a coordinator for the Conflict Research Society Book of the Year Prize.

Alexander Kjærum—Danish Refugee Council

Alexander Kjærum is a global advisor and senior analyst with the Danish Refugee Council. He is leading the work on enhancing the use of data and analysis for strategic planning, programming, and advocacy. He is also the lead on the use of predictive analytics and author on the flagship Global Displacement Forecast report.

Ali Rebaie—Kiangle AI, Portugal

Ali Rebaie, a distinguished AI phenomenologist and anthropologist, is renowned as a global keynote speaker. He established Rebaie Analytics Group in his early twenties, rapidly gaining a clientele of Fortune 500 companies. Recognized consistently among the top 100 AI Influencers worldwide, his expertise lies in exploring AI's complex impact on society, economics, and personal spheres. His approach integrates philosophy and anthropology, examining AI's role while guiding businesses toward ethical and strategic adaptability in the face of future challenges. Rebaie's AI-based multi-method scenario planning and strategic foresight assist leaders in making informed decisions for sustainable and ethical growth.

Anastasiia Aizenshtat—Centre for Alternative Conflict Resolution

Anastasiia Aizenshtat, founder and CEO of the Centre for Alternative Conflict Resolution, leads this nonprofit organization in leveraging technology for innovative conflict resolution. The Centre's methodology blends AI, macroeconomic models, and game theory to improve outcome predictions and conflict resolution strategies. With a background as a UN analyst and a Master's degree from King's College London, she commits the organization to groundbreaking diplomacy and international cooperation.

Andrea Pellandra—United Nations High Commissioner for Refugees (UNHCR)

Andrea Pellandra, a senior data scientist at the Global Data Service for the UNHCR, focuses on the integration of big data and advanced statistical methods to enhance the quality and timeliness of forced displacement statistics. Leading the dissemination of microdata on the UNHCR Microdata Library, she has authored impactful articles covering topics such as climate-induced displacement, refugee population nowcasting, and responsible data sharing.

Andreas Hirblinger—Geneva Graduate Institute

Andreas Hirblinger, a senior researcher at the Geneva Graduate Institute's Centre on Conflict, Development and Peacebuilding, conducts research on digital peacebuilding. His current project examines digital and political influences on peacebuilding. His publications in notable journals address the intersection of digital technology with peacebuilding processes. He has directed several multidisciplinary projects, focusing on the strategic use of digital technologies in inclusive peace mediation.

Branka Panic—New York University Center on International Cooperation

Branka Panic, a political scientist with expertise in international security and peacebuilding, is a New York University Center on International Cooperation non-resident fellow. Her research centers on data-driven approaches to peacebuilding, conflict early warning, and the creation of a Peacebuilding Data Hub. As an advocate for positive peace, her current focus is on the ethical implications of exponential technologies. She founded AI for Peace, promoting AI's benefits for peace, security, and sustainable development, and is a board member of the Center for Exponential Technologies, contributing to the intersection of policy and technology.

Christian Reuter—Technical University of Darmstadt

Christian Reuter, a university professor and dean at the Technical University of Darmstadt in Germany, combines peace and security research with computer science. With doctoral degrees in business informatics and security policy, his interdisciplinary work bridges cybersecurity, peace and conflict research, peace informatics, crisis informatics, and usable security, and privacy.and human–computer interaction. He has edited several key texts in these fields, including *Security and Safety-Critical Human-Computer-Interaction* and *Information Technology for Peace and Security*.

Clionadh Raleigh—ACLED and University of Sussex

Clionadh Raleigh is the creator of the Armed Conflict Location & Event Data Project (ACLED) and professor of political violence and geography at the University of Sussex. She is an expert in conflict and violence dynamics, with a focus on African political environments and elite networks. Her research addresses subnational power dynamics and their role in violent movements, as well as the impact of environmental change on violence patterns.

Doug Bond—Harvard University

Doug Bond, who has conducted research at Harvard University since 1988, serves as an international relations research advisor and lecturer in the Extension School. Specializing in international relations and social science research, his work involves monitoring global news using event-coding technology. His research contributions include developing the Integrated Events Data Analysis protocol for conflict tracking and designing security incident and peace monitoring systems. He also founded Virtual Research Associates, Inc. to advance automated language parsing systems, focusing on conflict analysis.

Eric Dunford—Georgetown University

Eric Dunford, an assistant teaching professor at Georgetown University, teaches data science and quantitative methodology, and researches political violence and conflict reduction strategies. His ongoing projects explore violent tactics used by armed actors and develop computational tools for conflict analysis. His research, published in notable journals, includes affiliations with the Massive Data Institute and the Interdisciplinary Laboratory of Computational Social Science.

Frank Witmer—University of Alaska Anchorage

Frank Witmer, an associate professor in the Department of Computer Science and Engineering at the University of Alaska Anchorage, is a computational geographer researching violent conflict and human–environment interactions. Utilizing spatial statistical methods and remote sensing data, his work includes immersive visualization in environmental studies. His teaching spans computer science and geomatics, focusing on human–environment geography, immersive visualization, remote sensing, and sociodemographic and environmental change analysis.

Hannes Mueller—Barcelona Graduate School of Economics

Hannes Mueller, a tenured researcher at the Institute for Economic Analysis and an associate research professor at the Barcelona Graduate School of Economics, leads the data science for decision making program. His research spans machine learning, political economy, development economics, and conflict studies, focusing on the economic effects of violent conflict. He employs supervised and unsupervised machine learning techniques to analyze conflict using newspaper archives and satellite images. He collaborates on projects with the Bank of Spain and conducts capacity-building missions for various international organizations, private firms, and governments.

Håvard Hegre—Uppsala University

Håvard Hegre, a professor of peace and conflict research at Uppsala University and research professor at the Peace Research Institute Oslo, investigates the role of democratic institutions in preventing armed conflict. His research examines the interplay between institutions and violence, considering socioeconomic factors like poverty reduction and education. He has directed the Violence & Impacts Early-Warning System project since 2017, which contributes significantly to conflict forecasting methodologies.

John Karlsrud—Norwegian Institute of International Affairs

John Karlsrud, research professor and head of the research group on peace, conflict, and development at the Norwegian Institute of International Affairs, focuses on norm change, peacekeeping, peacebuilding, and humanitarian issues. His diverse experience includes roles as a Visiting Fulbright Fellow and a visiting research fellow at renowned institutions including New York University. He has served with the United Nations and the UN Development Programme, conducting field research and missions in various conflict-affected regions.

Joseph Bock—Kennesaw State University

Joseph Bock, former director of the School of Conflict Management, Peacebuilding, and Development at Kennesaw State University, has extensive experience in humanitarian work. His work includes directing programs in conflict-affected regions for Catholic Relief Services and overseeing programs for the American Refugee Committee. He is an expert in violence prevention, particularly in South Asia, and his most recent humanitarian work was as a Fulbright Specialist in Athens, Greece, assisting with the influx of migrants and refugees. His publications focus on technology and violence prevention, including the book *The Technology of Nonviolence: Social Media and Violence Prevention*.

Marc-André Kaufhold—Technical University of Darmstadt

Marc-André Kaufhold, a postdoctoral researcher at the Technical University of Darmstadt in Germany, specializes in mobile apps and social media design and evaluation in crisis and security contexts. His interdisciplinary research, recognized through multiple awards, encompasses over ninety scientific articles. His work spans domains such as cybersecurity, crisis informatics, and human–computer interaction, contributing significantly to the field of usable security in crisis management.

Martin Wählisch—UN Department of Political and Peacebuilding Affairs

Martin Wählisch leads the Innovation Cell in the Policy and Mediation Division of the UN Department of Political and Peacebuilding Affairs. His team specializes in utilizing new technologies, tools, and practices in conflict prevention, mediation, and peacebuilding. He publishes work spanning national dialogues, peace process design, conflict prevention, policy initiatives, and systemic change in peacemaking and innovation, including the coedited volume *Rethinking Peace Mediation Challenges of Contemporary Peacemaking Practice*.

Patrick Vinck—Harvard Humanitarian Initiative

Patrick Vinck is the research director of the Harvard Humanitarian Initiative and an assistant professor at Harvard Medical School and the Harvard T.H. Chan School of Public Health. His research explores resilience and peacebuilding in conflict and disaster contexts, and the ethics of data and technology in these fields. He co-founded KoBoToolbox and the Data-Pop Alliance, contributing significantly to data collection and analysis in humanitarian efforts. His work extends to international development and food security, informed by his background in applied biological sciences and international development.

Roisin Read—University of Manchester

Roisin Read, senior lecturer in peace and conflict studies at the University of Manchester, researches the politics of international interventions in conflict, particularly in Sudan and South Sudan. Her interests include humanitarian system reform, technology in humanitarianism, and the role of visual representations in humanitarian identity. Previously, she worked on a project focusing on the African Union/United Nations mission in Darfur, Sudan, examining the implications of security incident data collection and analysis.

Thomas Chadefaux—Trinity College Dublin

Thomas Chadefaux, a professor in political science at Trinity College Dublin, focuses on interstate conflict causes and predictions. Utilizing large-scale spatial and temporal data, including newspapers and satellite images, he seeks to identify early-warning signals for war. Holding a Ph.D. from the University of Michigan and an M.A. from the Graduate Institute of International Studies, Chadefaux has also held positions at the University of Rochester and ETH Zurich, enriching his academic journey in political science.

Weisi Guo—Cranfield University

Weisi Guo, head of the Human Machine Intelligence Group at Cranfield, obtained his two Masters and Ph.D. degrees from the University of Cambridge. His award-winning research team focuses on connected intelligence, integrating data science, communication systems, and machine learning. His research addresses socio-cyber-physical ecosystems, exploring AI and information systems' design for challenging environments, and has been recognized with several awards and fellowships. He has published over 140 journal papers and serves as an editor for several journals.

Social Sciences/Philosophy

Adam Russell—University of Southern California

Adam Russell is an anthropologist and the director of the Artificial Intelligence Division at the University of Southern California. He was formerly a research scientist at the University of Maryland's Applied Research Laboratory for Intelligence and Security, as well as a program manager at Intelligence Advanced Research Projects Activity and the Defense Advanced Research Projects Agency. His work focused on enhancing the United States government's human domain capabilities to better understand and anticipate human social behavior. His academic background includes a D.Phil. from Oxford University as a Rhodes Scholar.

Brendan McQuade—University of Southern Maine

Brendan McQuade, an associate professor in the Department of Criminology at the University of Southern Maine, has a background in historical sociology and state theory. His research interests encompass state security apparatuses and social movements. He previously taught at DePaul University and the State University of New York Cortland. He has contributed significantly to the fields of international studies and sociology/anthropology, including with the book *Pacifying the Homeland: Intelligence Fusion and Mass Supervision*.

Catherine Besteman—Colby College

Catherine Besteman, a professor of anthropology at Colby College, focuses on the intersection of race, mobility, security, neoliberalism, and carcerality. Her recent book, *Militarized Global Apartheid*, examines security regimes and their parallels to South Africa's apartheid, earning the Public Anthropologist Prize in 2022. Her research is presented in other works, including *Transforming Cape Town* and *Unraveling Somalia*, exploring themes of security, border militarization, and algorithmic risk assessment technologies.

César Rendueles—Complutense University of Madrid

César Rendueles, a doctoral assistant professor in the Department of Sociology at the Complutense University of Madrid, has a background in cultural intervention and the coordination of cultural programs at the Círculo de Bellas Artes of Madrid. His publications include *Sociophobia: Political Change in the Age of Digital Utopia* and *Rogue Capitalism*, reflecting his expertise in digital culture and historical materialism. His work also involves editing classical texts by influential authors like Karl Marx and Walter Benjamin.

Christopher Anderson—University of Milan

Christopher Anderson, a full professor of sociology at the University of Milan, delves into the production and legitimacy of institutional knowledge under digital conditions. His research focuses on the mediation and construction of expertise, especially in non-elite and quasi-professional settings. In *Apostles of Certainty: Data Journalism and the Politics of Doubt*, he examines the historical use of quantitative information in American journalism, and he is currently engaged in multiple projects including a social history of ideology and bad citizenship.

Clarissa Rios Rojas—University of Cambridge

Clarissa Rios Rojas is a research affiliate at Cambridge University's Centre for the Study of Existential Risk, and is working on the project "A Science of Global Risk," focusing on science diplomacy and sustainable development goals. Recognized as an Eisenhower

Fellow and a UN Women Champion for Change, her expertise includes foresight and science diplomacy. Her involvement with the Global Young Academy, particularly in the Science Advice working group, and various leadership roles, including at the Women Economic Forum, showcases her commitment to managing global risks including the misuse of AI, and promoting education for sustainable development.

David Gunkel—Northern Illinois University

David Gunkel is a professor in the Department of Communication at Northern Illinois University and an award-winning author specializing in the ethics of emerging technology. He co-founded and manages the *International Journal of Žižek Studies* and serves as coeditor of the Indiana University Press series in Digital Game Studies. He has authored over eighty scholarly articles and numerous books including *An Introduction to Communication and Artificial Intelligence* and, most recently, *Person, Thing, Robot: A Moral and Legal Ontology for the 21st Century and Beyond*, which aspires to answer the question of how to classify a robot.

Didier Bigo—King's College London

Didier Bigo, a professor at Sciences-Po Paris-CERI and a part-time professor at King's College London, directs the Centre for the Study of Conflicts, Liberty, and Security. His research interests encompass international political sociology, focusing on democratic boundaries, data politics, and surveillance in the digital age. His work on border controls, biometrics, and anti-terrorist policies has been pivotal in understanding the sociopolitical dynamics of security and freedom. He also edits the international journal *Cultures & Conflits*, contributing extensively to academic discourse in his field.

Fabian Hijlkema—Designer

Fabian Hijlkema, a designer based in Amsterdam, engages in a wide range of design activities, from graphic design projects to political installations. His work, known for its stylistic simplicity and focus on technology's impact, reflects his expertise as a designer and hacker. Hijlkema also teaches interaction design and moving design at Minerva, Groningen, and Artez, Zwolle, contributing to the education of future designers.

Florian Schneider—Leiden University Institute for Area Studies

Florian Schneider, senior lecturer in the politics of modern China at Leiden University Institute for Area Studies, has research interests encompassing governance and public administration in China, Taiwan, and Hong Kong, and the political content of popular Chinese entertainment. As managing editor of Asiascape: Digital Asia and director of the Leiden Asia Centre, Schneider's work over the past fifteen years has focused on political communication and media in contemporary China. His book *Digital Nationalism in China* critically examines online nationalism and the digital construction of Sino-Japanese historiography.

Gonzalo Rivero—Pew Research Center

Gonzalo Rivero, the associate director of Data Labs at the Pew Research Center, is recognized for his expertise in social research methodology, focusing on computational social science and reproducibility. His research encompasses public opinion, political behavior, and representation within the digital political landscape. Before joining the Pew Research Center in 2021, Rivero worked at Westat and YouGov as a statistician and data scientist. He earned his doctorate in politics from New York University and coauthored *Retooling Politics: How Digital Media Are Shaping Democracy*, which reflected his extensive research in the field.

Hugh Gusterson—University of British Columbia

Hugh Gusterson, holding joint appointments in public policy and global affairs and anthropology at the University of British Columbia, specializes in militarism, the anthropology of science, neoliberalism, ethics, and nuclear policy. His previous positions include roles at MIT, George Mason University, George Washington University, and the Georgia Institute of Technology. His research interests have led to coediting books such as *Cultures of Insecurity* and *Life by Algorithms*, focusing on the societal impacts of technology and militarization.

Jack Parkin—Western Sydney University

Jack Parkin, a digital economist at Western Sydney University, specializes in the study of human–machine interaction and its societal effects. His academic pursuits are complemented by his consultancy in the decentralized ledger technology industry. His recent project involved working with a major Australian bank to identify automation trends in finance and the evolving skills required for staff. His comprehensive report discussed the macroeconomic impact of new labor dynamics, offered insights into human–machine interactions in financial sectors, and proposed training curricula to enhance workforce efficiency and resilience. He is also known for his book *Money Code Space: Hidden Power in Bitcoin, Blockchain, and Decentralisation*, which critically examines the contradictions and power asymmetries inherent in blockchain technology.

Jay Aronson—Carnegie Mellon University

Jay Aronson, founder and director of the Center for Human Rights Science at Carnegie Mellon University, also holds a professorship in science, technology, and society. His research delves into the intersections of these fields with law and human rights. His current focus is on documenting police-involved fatalities and deaths in custody in the US. He collaborates with computer scientists and human rights practitioners to improve digital evidence use in human rights investigations, supported by grants from notable foundations.

Jessica L. Beyer—University of Washington

Jessica L. Beyer, is an assistant teaching professor and a lead of the Cybersecurity Initiative at the Henry M. Jackson School of International Studies at the University of Washington. Her research spans international technology politics, online communities, and dis/misinformation. She focuses on understanding Covid-19 information dissemination on Twitter during the pandemic's first year in Louisiana and Washington states. As a member of the Cybersecurity in the Built Environment Lab, she is currently investigating politically significant information spread in informal online spaces. Her past research explored political mobilization in online communities, as presented in her book *Expect Us: Online Communities and Political Mobilization*.

Jian Wang—University of Southern California

Jian (Jay) Wang, a scholar and consultant specializing in strategic communication and public diplomacy, currently serves as the director of the Center on Public Diplomacy and an associate professor at the University of Southern California Annenberg. With a background in consulting at McKinsey & Company, he has extensively researched the role of communication in globalization. His publications include *Debating Public Diplomacy: Now and Next*, and *Shaping China's Global Imagination*. His contributions extend to multiple editorial boards and collaborations with prominent organizations, reflecting his expertise in public diplomacy, digital advocacy, and international communication.

Kathleen Searles—Louisiana State University

Kathleen Searles, associate professor of political communication at Louisiana State University, has a joint appointment in the Manship School of Mass Communication and the Department of Political Science. Her research interests include news media, campaign advertising, and political psychology. Her work examines partisan news content, poll coverage, and the emotional appeals in campaign ads, employing biometrics to understand the effects of political television ads and direct mail. Coauthoring *News and Democratic Citizens in the Mobile Era* with Johanna Dunaway, she offers insights into adapting news media for a connected world.

Kevin Hernandez—UK Institute of Development Studies

Kevin Hernandez, a research officer at the Institute of Development Studies' digital and technology cluster, is devoted to exploring the societal implications of technology through comprehensive research and policy development. His expertise spans digital inclusion, digital inequalities, e-government, the future of work, and the societal and developmental impacts of emerging technologies like AI, Blockchain, and IoT. At the Digital Futures at Work Research Centre, He contributes significantly to the "connecting the disconnected worker" research theme. His diverse collaborations range from academic research to providing technical assistance to governments, NGOs, and INGOs in policy and digital strategy development.

Mark Duffield—University of Bristol

Mark Duffield is an emeritus professor in the School of Sociology, Politics and International Studies at the University of Bristol. His scholarly work encompasses catastrophe politics, probing into liberal interventionism and its humanitarian aspects, and the role of development in governance. He examines the political philosophy of permanent emergency, focusing on the datafication of global crises and the expansion of remote management systems. His work, involving field studies in diverse regions such as Africa and Asia, critiques current approaches to risk and collective security, emphasizing the role of complex, privatized infrastructure and its intersection with ecological and social elements. His latest publication, *Post-Humanitarianism: Governing Precarity in the Digital World*, analyzes the datafication of international aid, highlighting the growing detachment from global realities due to this digital shift.

Mark Taylor—Columbia University

Mark Taylor, a professor of religion at Columbia University, explores the intersections of religion with art, financial markets, and AI. His prolific authorship includes over thirty books, with recent works like *Smart Things Smart Bodies* delving into the impact of AI on medical treatments. Taylor's contributions to online education and his artistic pursuits, showcased in exhibitions, demonstrate his multidisciplinary approach to academia and technology.

Mohamed Zayani—Georgetown University

Mohamed Zayani, professor of critical theory at Georgetown University in Qatar, is an expert in culture and politics. His most recent work is *The Digital Double Bind*, coauthored with Joe Khalil, which provides an extensive and subtle account of digital transformations in the Middle East. He also authored *Digital Middle East* and *Networked Publics and Digital Contention*, which discusses how digital media in the Arab world affects state-citizen relationships, and received numerous awards, including from the International Studies Association and the American Sociological Association.

Nick Bostrom—University of Oxford

Nick Bostrom, professor in the Faculty of Philosophy at Oxford University, is a renowned scholar and founding director of the Future of Humanity Institute. His research encompasses existential risk, the simulation argument, anthropics, transhumanism, and the foundations of consequentialism. He has authored influential works, including *Superintelligence*, and is working on a book addressing the intelligence explosion and machine superintelligence. His academic contributions extend to over 200 publications, shaping discourse in multiple critical areas of future technology impact.

Ross Anderson—The Atlantic

Ross Andersen, a senior editor at *The Atlantic*, oversees the science, technology, and health sections of the publication. Before joining *The Atlantic*, he was the deputy editor at *Aeon* magazine and the science editor at the *Los Angeles Review of Books*. Known for his feature essays blending philosophy, technology, science, history, and the arts, His work as an editor and writer has earned him recognition in the field of science and technology journalism.

Safiya Noble—University of California Los Angeles

Safiya Noble, the David O. Sears Presidential Endowed Chair of Social Sciences at the University of California Los Angeles, holds professorships in gender studies, African American studies, and information studies. As director of the Center on Race & Digital Justice and co-director of the Minderoo Initiative on Tech & Power, she leads critical research in data studies. Noble authored the influential *Algorithms of Oppression: How Search Engines Reinforce Racism*, garnering widespread acclaim. Her board membership at the Cyber Civil Rights Initiative and affiliation with the Oxford Internet Institute underscore her commitment to examining the societal impacts of digital media, focusing on race, gender, culture, power, and technology.

Sarah Brayne—University of Texas Austin

Sarah Brayne, an associate professor of sociology at the University of Texas Austin, investigates the social consequences of data-intensive surveillance practices. Her research, grounded in both qualitative and quantitative methods, examines the transformations and continuities in social structures and stratification mechanisms resulting from these practices. Her first book, *Predict and Surveil*, based on ethnographic research within the Los Angeles Police Department, explores the social implications of predictive analytics and new surveillance technologies in law enforcement.

Tony Roberts—Institute of Development Studies

Tony Roberts, a research fellow at the Institute of Development Studies, intersects digital technologies with international development and social justice. His career, spanning over three decades, includes roles as a volunteer, lecturer, practitioner, and researcher. His extensive field experience informs his doctoral research on digital development, which he further advanced during his tenure at the United Nations University, Computing and

Society Research Institute in Macau. His work emphasizes participatory methods and gender considerations in technology within developmental contexts.

Virginia Eubanks—The State University of New York Albany

Virginia Eubanks, an associate professor of political science at the State University of New York Albany, focuses on the intersection of technology and social justice. Her notable works, including *Automating Inequality*, highlight the impact of high-tech tools on marginalized communities. Eubanks' two-decade-long engagement in community technology and economic justice movements reflects her dedication to addressing technology-driven social issues. She is also a founding member of the "Our Data Bodies" project and a fellow at New America, contributing to the discourse on data rights and digital equity.

Zachary Steinert-Threlkeld—University of California Los Angeles

Zachary Steinert-Threlkeld, an associate professor of public policy at University of California Los Angeles' Luskin School, focuses his research on understanding protest dynamics through natural language processing, computer vision, and comprehensive simulations. He has extensively analyzed protests globally, including the Arab Spring, East Asia, and the Americas. His latest research delves into topics like circumventing China's Great Firewall during Covid-19, social media signaling in the Syrian civil war, and the impact of state violence on protest sizes. His findings have been featured in top journals and received attention from high-profile media outlets.

Zeynep Tufekci—University of North Carolina Chapel Hill

Zeynep Tufekci's research intersects technology and society. An associate professor at University of North Carolina Chapel Hill, with affiliations at Harvard and Princeton, her work examines social movements, privacy, and the impact of digital technologies on society. A former programmer, her transition to academia brings a unique perspective to the study of digital technology's role in social, political, and cultural dynamics. Her book *Beautiful Teargas: The Ecstatic, Fragile Politics of Networked Protest in the 21st Century*, examines the strengths and weaknesses of twenty-first-century social movements.

APPENDIX II

Further Reading by Organizations

This list contains the names and a brief description of organizations conducting research or policy work in AI governance and contiguous fields. They may provide more in-depth knowledge and expertise on various subjects covered in this book. Names are arranged alphabetically and links to websites are included to facilitate further research.

<A+> Alliance for Inclusive Algorithms

The <A+> Alliance, spearheaded by Women@theTable and the Instituto Tecnológico de Costa Rica, constitutes a global, multidisciplinary feminist coalition. The Alliance, encompassing academics, activists, and technologists, aims to prototype AI and automated decision-making technologies that promote gender equality and inclusivity, ensuring no woman or girl is left behind.
https://aplusalliance.org/

AI for Good

The United Nations (UN) platform AI for Good, organized by the International Telecommunication Union (ITU) in partnership with forty UN agencies and Switzerland, aims to identify and scale practical applications of AI to advance the UN Sustainable Development Goals. With less than ten years remaining to achieve the goals, AI for Good capitalizes on unprecedented quantities of data across areas like health and migration to find impactful AI solutions.
https://aiforgood.itu.int/

AI for Peace

The organization AI for Peace believes that constructive dialogue between academia, industry, and civil society is critical to ensure AI's potential to rapidly improve human welfare and also respects rights and security. By informing and including peace-builders, humanitarians, and human rights advocates, AI for Peace seeks to maximize AI's benefits while minimizing risks to democracy and human rights.
www.aiforpeace.org/

AI for the People

The AI for the People initiative promotes the shaping of artificial intelligence around human needs based on the anthropocentric principle that technology should serve people. To narrow gaps in knowledge, action, and tools for change between civil society and technical experts, AI for the People analyzes AI's social impacts, pursues democratizing

AI policies, and conducts projects demonstrating how AI can be leveraged for the greater good. Its diverse team aims to bring AI policy to the public to create positive societal change through and for people.
www.aiforpeople.org/

Alan Turing Institute

The Alan Turing Institute, created in 2015 as the UK's national institute for data science and expanded in 2017 to include artificial intelligence, is named for mathematics and computing pioneer Alan Turing. Jointly established by five founding universities and the Engineering and Physical Sciences Research Council, the London-based institute added eight additional university partners in 2018 and launched an open university network in 2023 to engage all interested UK institutions. The Institute has been primarily funded through government, university, and partnership grants since its founding.
www.turing.ac.uk/

Algorithmic Transparency Institute

The Algorithmic Transparency Institute (ATI) operates as a program within the National Conference on Citizenship, a nonpartisan nonprofit dedicated to strengthening civic life. ATI aims to increase transparency surrounding digital platforms impacting civic discourse by developing technologies, amassing data, and enabling analysis that furthers public comprehension of how digital media spreads harmful content and impacts society. ATI has an established record of creating public digital infrastructure projects, including the platform Junkipedia used by over 100 groups to document problematic online content across subjects like the 2020 US census and election. ATI has also fostered partnerships with civil rights nonprofits, coordinating thousands of volunteers in civic listening efforts on social media to identify and categorize harmful content within Junkipedia.
https://ati.io/

American University: Tech, Law, and Security Program

The Tech, Law, and Security Program at American University Washington College of Law comprises leading experts addressing technological advancements' implications on democracy, freedom of speech, and privacy. The program fosters policy and practice solutions for emerging technology challenges.
www.wcl.american.edu/impact/initiatives-programs/techlaw/

Annenberg Public Policy Center: FactCheck.org

FactCheck.org, a project of the Annenberg Public Policy Center (APPC), is a nonpartisan consumer advocate for United States voters that strives to diminish deception in politics. Monitoring accuracy in various political communications, it employs journalistic and

scholarly best practices to enhance public understanding. Post-election, it often collaborates with the APPC to highlight campaign advertising and electoral strategy trends, offering insights into modern campaign mechanics.
www.annenbergpublicpolicycenter.org/political-communication/factcheck-org/

ARTICLE 19

ARTICLE 19, an international think-and-do organization, champions freedom of expression worldwide. It conducts innovative research, policy analysis, and frontline work through its nine regional hubs, addressing themes like media independence, journalist protection, censorship, the right to information, digital rights, privacy and surveillance, and human rights in digital spaces. Inspired by the Universal Declaration of Human Rights, ARTICLE 19's efforts are dedicated to amplifying voices globally.
www.article19.org/

Aspen Institute: Aspen Digital

The Aspen Institute, a global nonprofit established in 1949, is dedicated to fostering a free, just, and equitable society. Aspen Digital is an affiliated program of the Aspen Institute, assembling global thought leaders and doers to generate new ideas and initiatives that strengthen democracy and empower communities. They engage with a plurality of opinions from government, civil society, and industry to seek clarity and collaborate on the best way forward.
www.aspendigital.org/

Atlantic Council: Digital Forensics Research Lab

The Atlantic Council focuses on promoting constructive international engagement, emphasizing the Atlantic Community's role in addressing twenty-first-century challenges. It functions as a key forum for global leaders, generating policies and strategies to create a safer, freer, and more prosperous world, shaping policy through its influential network. The Digital Forensic Research Lab at the Atlantic Council, founded in 2016, combines technical and policy expertise on disinformation and digital rights. It produces open-source research, sets research standards, and crafts policy recommendations to shape the global information ecosystem.
https://dfrlab.org/

Atlantic Council: GeoTech Center

The GeoTech Center is a program of the Atlantic Council that facilitates the widespread adoption of emerging technologies worldwide for the public good. Simultaneously, it focuses on identifying and addressing potential societal and geopolitical risks associated with these technologies.
www.atlanticcouncil.org/programs/geotech-center/

Berggruen Institute: Decoding Digital Authoritarianism

The Berggruen Institute, formed in 2010 by Nicolas Berggruen and Nathan Gardels, is a think tank that addresses global challenges. It focuses on themes like democracy renovation, universal capital, and the interplay between humans, technology, and the planet, aiming to develop systemic solutions through a global network of thinkers. Decoding Digital Authoritarianism is a project of the institute that aims to re-evaluate conventional foreign policy topics within the context of digital authoritarianism, encompassing security, economics, finance, media, values, and emerging technologies.

https://berggruen.org/projects/decoding-digital-authoritarianism

Brown University: Information Futures Lab

The Information Futures Lab, co-directed by experienced communication experts at Brown University, aims to transform information spaces and build trust through innovation and technology. It fosters collaboration and global research to mitigate misinformation, considering diverse cultural contexts and the multifaceted nature of information channels.

https://sites.brown.edu/informationfutures/

Build Up

Build Up transforms conflict in the digital age by combining peacebuilding, participation, and technology to identify and address threats to peace. It supports peace innovators globally to implement technology interventions into peacebuilding processes and conducts research and stages interventions to address polarization on social and digital media across contexts like active conflicts, post-conflicts, and emerging divisions. Build Up also fosters critical examination of digital age conflict through the annual Build Peace conference convening peacebuilding, technology, and creative arts practitioners.

https://howtobuildup.org/

Carnegie Council for Ethics in International Affairs: AI and Equality Initiative

The Carnegie Council believes ethics to be central to addressing major global challenges and that discovering common values and interests leads to a better future. Founded over a century ago, the Carnegie Council sets the global ethical agenda and works toward an ethical future by convening experts, producing resources, and catalyzing solutions to global problems. It aims to empower ethics and address critical ethical issues of today and tomorrow as countries retreat from multilateralism, embrace nationalism, attack democratic norms, and grapple with climate change and emerging technologies' societal

impacts. The Council's Artificial Intelligence & Equality Initiative is a forward-thinking, impact-driven community dedicated to comprehending the multifaceted effects of AI on equality. Its mission centers on promoting ethical AI deployment, ensuring it contributes to justice, responsibility, and inclusivity.
www.carnegiecouncil.org/initiatives-issues/artificial-intelligence-and-equality

Carter Center: Digital Threats to Democracy Initiative

Guided by its founders' commitment to human rights and alleviating suffering, The Carter Center works to prevent and resolve conflicts, enhance freedom and democracy, and improve health. It assists people in improving their lives by providing skills, knowledge, and access to resources. The Center has also created the Digital Threats to Democracy Initiative to devise strategies and technological resources for tracking disinformation, hate speech, harassment, coordinated inauthentic actions, and covert online advertising in a number of countries around the world, including Myanmar, South Africa, and Tunisia.
www.cartercenter.org/

Center for AI and Digital Policy

The Center for AI and Digital Policy promotes AI and digital policies, furthering a more fair, just, and accountable society based on rights, institutions, and law. As an independent research organization, it assesses AI policies and practices, trains leaders, and advocates democratic AI values.
www.caidp.org/

Centre for Artificial Intelligence, Data, and Conflict

The Centre for Artificial Intelligence, Data, and Conflict (CAIDAC), pioneers AI tools to analyze the weaponization of social media in conflicts and political violence. Founded by experts with first-hand experience in conflict-affected communities, CAIDAC seeks to understand the transformative role of social media in conflict dynamics, providing a comprehensive record of online and real-world events.
www.tracesofconflict.com/

Center for Democracy and Technology

The Center for Democracy and Technology, a leading nonpartisan nonprofit established in 1994, champions civil rights and liberties in the digital age. It influences technology policy, governance, and design, prioritizing equity and democratic values, making it a trusted advocate for digital rights since the internet's inception.
https://cdt.org/

Chatham House: Digital Society Initiative

Chatham House, established in 1920, pioneers research in international affairs, influencing global politics and fostering international understanding. It seeks to build a secure, prosperous, and just world through dialogue, analysis, and empowering future generations, addressing complex changes in governance, power, and technology against existential planetary risks. The Digital Society Initiative is a department of Chatham House that serves as a bridge between policy and technology communities, fostering collaboration to tackle the opportunities and challenges posed by the swift evolution of technology in both domestic and international politics.
www.chathamhouse.org/about-us/our-departments/digital-society-initiative-dsi

Clemson University: Media Forensics Hub

The Media Forensics Hub at Clemson University, within the Watt Family Innovation Center, enhances understanding of modern media through interdisciplinary collaboration. It develops techniques for media analysis, connecting experts, students, and the public across disciplines and perspectives, combining AI and machine learning, lab experiments and fieldwork, and history and case studies.
www.clemson.edu/centers-institutes/watt/hub/index.html

Code for Africa

Code for Africa leverages technology and open data to foster digital democracies, empowering citizens with information for decision-making and tools for accountability. It liberates data from governments and corporations, supports civic watchdogs and media, and promotes active citizenry and evidence-based discourse, operating in over thirty African countries and globally.
https://github.com/CodeForAfrica

Columbia University: Data Science Institute

The Data Science Institute at Columbia University, founded in 2012, aims to advance data science and its application across various sectors. It combines expertise in computer science, statistics, and industrial engineering to foster innovative technology development, train data scientists, and address societal challenges.
https://datascience.columbia.edu/

Copernicani

Copernicani, established in 2018 as a nonprofit, cross-party advocacy group, champions digital innovation in Italy. With diverse backgrounds, its members advocate for a future-oriented vision, emphasizing the importance of science and technology. Copernicani's initiatives, including budget.g0v.it and the International Forum on Digital and

Democracy, facilitate dialogue between politicians and academics on digital technology's impact on democracy.
https://copernicani.it/?lang=en

Council on Foreign Relations: Digital and Cyberspace Policy Program

The Council on Foreign Relations (CFR), founded in 1921, is an independent, nonpartisan organization comprising a think tank, a membership body, and a publisher. It serves as a resource for various stakeholders, including government officials, business executives, and educators, to deepen their understanding of global affairs and foreign policy challenges faced by the United States and other nations. The CFR's Digital and Cyberspace Policy program plays a pivotal role in enhancing understanding about the intricacies of cyberspace politics among policymakers, business leaders, and the wider public. It actively promotes dialogue and collaboration between the public and private sectors, contributing to the formulation of United States policy and the development of global rules and norms governing cyberspace.
www.cfr.org/programs/digital-and-cyberspace-policy-program

Credibility Coalition

The Credibility Coalition seeks to establish common standards for information credibility. Comprising journalists, researchers, academics, policymakers, technologists, and engaged individuals, the Coalition fosters collaborative approaches to assess online information's veracity, quality, and credibility, essential for civil society.
https://credibilitycoalition.org/

Data for Peace and Security

The Data for Peace and Security consultancy contributes to the resolution of peaceful conflicts. Serving clients like the United Nations Development Programme (UNDP) and NATO, it offers services in early warning, policy analysis, and innovation by leveraging data, technology, and AI, and creating automated and data-driven solutions. The consultancy upholds values of equality, solidarity, and progress, operating conflict-sensitively and promoting human rights.
www.d4ps.com/

Data-Pop Alliance

The Data-Pop Alliance, a nonprofit "think-and-do-tank" established in 2013, collaborates with various entities to harness data and AI for societal betterment. It focuses on diagnosing human problems, mobilizing capacities, and transforming societal systems, particularly in the Global South.
https://datapopalliance.org/

Datasphere Initiative

The Datasphere Initiative is a nonprofit dedicated to global collaboration on data governance challenges. It connects stakeholders, conducts research on data challenges, experiments with policy and technical solutions, and influences data governance narratives and policies.
www.thedatasphere.org/

Digital Futures Lab

The Digital Futures Lab examines technology-society interactions in the Global South through research, foresight, and public engagement, aiming to foster equitable, safe, and caring digital futures. It focuses on creating independent, collaborative inquiry platforms that consider social impacts of technology.
https://digitalfutureslab.in/

Digital Peace Now

Digital Peace Now advocates for ending cyberwarfare, urging governments to prevent state-sponsored cyberattacks. It emphasizes the need for global agreements to curb cyberwarfare, highlighting the risks to infrastructure, elections, and civilian safety, and advocates for accountability and guidelines similar to those relevant to armed conflicts.
https://digitalpeacenow.org/

Electronic Frontier Foundation

The Electronic Frontier Foundation, founded in 1990, defends civil liberties in the digital world. It engages in litigation, policy analysis, activism, and technology development, advocating for free speech, privacy, and innovation, and educates the public and policymakers through comprehensive analysis and workshops.
www.eff.org/

EU DisinfoLab

The EU DisinfoLab, an independent nonprofit organization, consolidates expertise on disinformation in Europe. It integrates research, investigation, and policy insight, supporting a broad community engaged in detecting and countering information disorders that threaten citizen integrity, peaceful coexistence, and democratic values.
www.disinfo.eu/

European Commission: INFORM

INFORM, a collaboration led by the Joint Research Center of the European Commission, develops quantitative analysis for humanitarian crises and disasters. It involves various

organizations, providing decision-making tools across the disaster management cycle, including climate adaptation and disaster prevention.
https://drmkc.jrc.ec.europa.eu/inform-index

Freedom House

Freedom House has evolved for over fifty years as a premier American organization advocating for, and tracking threats to democracy globally. It engages in research and programs across political divides, supporting activists and advocates in democratic transformation. Freedom House's research is pivotal for policymakers and civil society in promoting freedom, particularly its annual Freedom on the Net survey and analysis of internet freedom around the globe. They also produce an Election Watch for the Digital Age report, which tracks the confluence of elections, internet platforms, and human rights worldwide.
https://freedomhouse.org/

Geneva Digital Atlas

The Geneva Digital Atlas is a comprehensive resource that maps digital policy actors and the internet governance scene in Geneva. It offers detailed analysis of over forty actors' policy processes and events, contributing significantly to the understanding of digital governance.
https://dig.watch/atlas

Geneva Graduate Institute: Centre on Conflict, Development and Peacebuilding

The Centre on Conflict, Development and Peacebuilding (CCDP) at Geneva Graduate Institute focuses on conflict analysis and peacebuilding, examining the factors and actors involved in violence within societies and states. It also explores policies and practices for reducing violence and enhancing peacebuilding and development initiatives at various levels. One of CCDP's research projects explores the role of digital technologies in international peacebuilding.
www.graduateinstitute.ch/ccdp

German Institute for International and Security Affairs

The German Institute for International and Security Affairs (SWP) advises the German government and parliament on foreign and security policy. As a major European think tank, SWP conducts independent research and interacts with the EU, NATO, and UN entities, maintaining academic rigor and confidentiality in consultations. They maintain a dossier on digitalization related to the broad diversity of challenges within the field, including regulation of digital technologies, cyber security threat, human rights and international law, and the tension between worldwide technological progress and regional political change.
www.swp-berlin.org/en/

German Marshall Fund: Alliance for Securing Democracy

The German Marshall Fund (GMF) of the United States is a nonpartisan organization advocating for a strong transatlantic alliance based on democracy, human rights, and international cooperation. The GMF engages in critical issues like democracy, security, and technological innovation, fostering diverse communities to promote transatlantic relations. The Alliance for Securing Democracy (ASD), a nonpartisan initiative under the GMF, develops strategies to deter and raise costs against antidemocratic interference within institutions. Uniting experts across technology, finance, elections, economic coercion, and cybersecurity, the initiative fosters collaboration to understand and counter threats through innovative frameworks. With staff in Washington D.C. and Brussels, the Alliance strives to strengthen resilience against multifaceted external and internal forces undermining democratic norms, including against authoritarian regimes seeking to control emerging technology. The ASD seeks to ensure that democracies are harnessing those technologies to enhance democratic institutions and freedoms.
   https://securingdemocracy.gmfus.org/

German Marshall Fund: Digital Program

The GMFs Digital Program is committed to ensuring that technology plays a pivotal role in promoting democracy, security, and prosperity not only in the United States and Europe but also globally. In collaboration with a network of experts, policymakers, and stakeholders, they devise practical solutions for complex technological policy issues.
   www.gmfus.org/innovation-work/gmf-digital

Global Center on Cooperative Security

The Global Center on Cooperative Security, an independent nonprofit organization, adopts innovative, equitable approaches to counter violent extremism. With a diverse, international team, it has implemented over 300 projects in more than fifty countries, bridging policy and practice to connect affected communities with decision-makers. As part of its focus on multilateral security policy, they produce comprehensive policy analyses on a range of issues including global security policy and artificial intelligence.
   www.globalcenter.org/

Global TechnoPolitics Forum

The Global TechnoPolitics Forum is an innovative organization focusing on the intersection of technology and geopolitics. It facilitates dialogue, conducts research, and builds communities for consensus-building, offering intellectual foundations and insights at various levels with a commitment to analytical rigor and policy pragmatism. The transformative influence of technology is a central component of the Forum's programs, with initiatives related to digital governance, blockchain, smart cities, misinformation and social media, surveillance, and robotics.
   https://technopolitics.org/

Google: Data Commons

Google's Data Commons initiative aims to bridge the gap between public data availability and usability. By organizing data from various sources, including governmental and international organizations, and enabling natural language access through AI advancements, Data Commons synthesizes a comprehensive graph, facilitating easier data access for diverse users.

www.datacommons.org/

Human Rights Watch: Technology and Rights

The Human Rights Watch Technology and Rights program actively defends human rights in the digital age, documenting governmental and corporate restrictions on online speech and investigating the impact of digital surveillance tools on activists and minorities. It advocates for laws and policies promoting privacy and digital inclusion, helping to hold both social media platforms and governments accountable.

www.hrw.org/topic/technology-and-rights

Humanitarian OpenStreetMap

Humanitarian OpenStreetMap Team (HOT) is an international group dedicated to humanitarian action and community development through open mapping. HOT's data revolutionizes disaster management and risk reduction, and supports the UN's Sustainable Development Goals.

www.hotosm.org/

HURIDOCS

HURIDOCS (Human Rights Information and Documentation Systems), an NGO established in 1982, aids human rights groups in managing and utilizing information for positive change. It develops methodologies and tools for efficient evidence, law, and research management, maintaining a steadfast commitment to its cause despite evolving technology.

https://huridocs.org/

ICT4Peace

ICT4Peace, founded in 2003, focuses on using information and communication technologies (ICTs) for peacebuilding, crisis management, and humanitarian operations. It advocates for cybersecurity and peaceful cyberspace, collaborating with governments, international organizations, and nonstate actors, and was launched with support from the Swiss Government.

https://ict4peace.org/

Igarapé Institute

The Igarapé Institute, an independent think-and-do tank, performs research and utilizes new technologies to propose solutions for public, climate, and digital security. Awarded Best Human Rights NGO in 2018, and best think tank for social policy, the Institute collaborates with the public and private sector and civil society to design data-driven solutions. Though headquartered in Brazil, they operate internationally, with projects in over twenty countries.
https://igarape.org.br/en/

Institute for Strategic Dialogue: Digital Analysis Unit

The Institute for Strategic Dialogue (ISD) has been addressing extremism since 2006. Its global team leads innovative policy and operational programs, partnering with governments, communities, and businesses to combat threats to democracy and cohesion, turning research into evidence-based action and training. Within the ISD, the Digital Analysis Unit has developed exclusive tools that adhere to social science data standards and offer detailed insights into the dynamic entities, strategies, and technologies responsible for disseminating hate, disinformation, and extremism on the internet.
www.isdglobal.org/

International Peace Institute

The International Peace Institute, an independent nonprofit organization, strengthens inclusive multilateralism for global peace and sustainability. It conducts research, convenes international events, and provides strategic advice, offering recommendations to the UN, member states, and various organizations, with a broad academic and international staff.
www.ipinst.org/

JustPeace Lab

The JustPeace Lab, a decentralized, net-based think tank, offers innovative ideas, training, and consultancy services. It conducts studies and facilitates exchanges with think tanks and research institutions, disseminating findings online. It aims to investigate, test, and expand the use of novel technologies, tools, and methodologies in order to discover improved solutions for creating peaceful, secure, and just societies.
www.justpeace.ngo/lab

Longview Philanthropy

Longview Philanthropy provides donor education, tailored research reports, grant recommendations, and progress reporting. Its services are expertly vetted, donor-specific, and free of charge, ensuring support in philanthropic endeavors. One of the areas that Longview provides grants in is artificial intelligence. They recognize that despite improvements, there are risks with transformative AI, and therefore fund projects seeking to improve the safety of AI.

www.longview.org/artificial-intelligence/

Meedan

Meedan, a global nonprofit technology organization, develops open-source tools for digital media annotation, verification, archival, and translation. Collaborating with various sectors, Meedan supports journalism, digital literacy, and information accessibility, fostering an equitable internet.

https://meedan.com/

Mila

Mila is a leading academic research center for deep learning. Established in 1993, it collaborates with Canadian universities, focusing on ethical AI development. Mila is recognized for its multidisciplinary AI research community and significant contributions to AI technology and society.

https://mila.quebec/en/

New America, Slate, and Arizona State University: Future Tense

Future Tense, a collaborative initiative of New America, Slate, and Arizona State University, examines the long-term impact of emerging technologies on society. It explores the transformative potential of technologies like robotics and augmented reality, questioning their democratic governance and ethical implications.

https://slate.com/future-tense

New York University: Center on International Cooperation

The Center on International Cooperation at New York University, a leader in applied policy, connects politics, security, justice, development, and humanitarian issues. For over two decades, it has strengthened cooperative approaches among various entities to prevent crises and advance peace, justice, and inclusion. The Center uses innovative, data-driven approaches to prevention and peacebuilding, which form part of the New Agenda for Peace.

https://cic.nyu.edu/

Open Data Watch

Open Data Watch works at the intersection of open data and official statistics, supporting the production and management of statistical data. Focusing on policy advice, data support, and monitoring, it aids in developing open data resources like the Open Data Inventory, addressing global challenges like the UN's Sustainable Development Goals.

https://opendatawatch.com/

Organization for Economic Cooperation and Development: Digital Government Project

The Organization for Economic Cooperation and Development (OECD) assists governments in formulating and executing policies by offering policy guidance and suggestions on how to incorporate these fundamental principles into reforms within the public sector. The OECD's Digital Government Project investigates the optimal utilization of ICTs by governments to embrace principles of good governance and attain policy objectives. Its recommendations seek to develop and implement digital strategies that bring governments, citizens, and businesses closer together.

www.oecd.org/gov/digital-government/

Organization for Economic Cooperation and Development: Open Government Project

The OECD Directorate for Public Governance Open Government Project assists governments with strategies and initiatives that revolve around the principles of transparency, integrity, accountability, and stakeholder participation. Some of the main policy areas concern the promotion and protection of civic space, the right to access information, and public communication and the media, including the rise of mis- and disinformation.

www.oecd.org/gov/

Oxford Internet Institute

Established in 2001, the Oxford Internet Institute (OII) is a versatile research and teaching department affiliated with the University of Oxford specializing in the social science of the internet. The OII engages in groundbreaking research, leveraging extensive expertise to develop new theories and methodologies. Its academic faculty and diverse graduate students collaborate across disciplines to address society's significant challenges, aiming to positively influence the digital world's development for the common good. Noteworthy contributions include early insights into "fake news," the definition of "big data," and pioneering research influencing technology and wellbeing. The OII's teaching programs, graduating approximately eighty students annually, produce alumni who excel in policymaking, technology development, civil society, and academia.

www.oii.ox.ac.uk/

Partnership on AI

Partnership on AI (PAI), a nonprofit collaboration, aims to ensure AI advances societal benefits. It convenes diverse stakeholders to develop tools and recommendations, influencing public policy and understanding. Staffed by experts, PAI facilitates dialogue and research in AI and sociotechnical development.

https://partnershiponai.org/

PeaceTech Lab

PeaceTech Lab, initially the Center of Innovation at the United States Institute of Peace in 2008 and an independent nonprofit since 2014, harnesses technology, data, and media for peacebuilding. It assembles diverse experts, including data and social scientists, engineers, and creatives, to develop solutions promoting global peace.
www.peacetechlab.org/

Poynter: International Fact-Checking Network

The International Fact-Checking Network at Poynter, established in 2015, unites fact-checkers globally to combat misinformation. It enhances fact-checking through networking, capacity-building, and collaboration, providing essential resources and support to fact-checkers and contributing to accountability in journalism.
www.poynter.org/ifcn/

Sentinel Project

The Sentinel Project, a Canadian nonprofit organization founded in 2008, collaborates with at-risk communities to prevent mass atrocities. It employs preventive measures, innovative technology, and direct partnerships, focusing on mitigating violence and facilitating peacebuilding and public education on mass atrocities.
https://thesentinelproject.org/

Simon Institute for Longterm Governance

Based in Geneva, the Simon Institute for Longterm Governance dedicates itself to mitigating global catastrophic risks. It emphasizes international cooperation and bridges the gap between technical innovation and policy, focusing on AI risks and advocating safe development through multilateral governance.
www.simoninstitute.ch/

Simon-Skjodt Center and the Dickey Center: Early Warning Project

The Early Warning Project, a joint initiative of the Simon-Skjodt Center for the Prevention of Genocide and the Dickey Center for International Understanding, uses data and forecasting methods to identify countries at high risk of mass atrocities. It aims to improve early warning systems and prevent genocide and mass violence.
https://earlywarningproject.ushmm.org/

Stanford Internet Observatory

The Stanford Internet Observatory, a multidisciplinary program, researches abuse in current information technologies, particularly social media. It aims to create a novel curriculum on trust and safety and translate research into practical applications, utilizing data analytics and machine learning.
https://cyber.fsi.stanford.edu/io

Stanford University: Peace Innovation Lab

The Peace Innovation Lab at Stanford University designs methods for positive pro-social behavior using technology. It explores the intersection of business, technology, and peace, developing ways to promote positive interactions and addressing the evolving field of peace innovation.
www.peaceinnovation.stanford.edu/

Techaide

TECHAiDE, partnering with various organizations, enhances education and economic opportunities in Africa through ICT solutions. Its team's local language skills and understanding of rural challenges enable effective ICT deployment in harsh environments.
https://techaide.global/

The GovLab

The GovLab aims to enhance the effectiveness of institutions, including governments, through open, collaborative, and data-driven approaches. It focuses on leveraging data, public engagement, and technological advances to innovate in governance.
https://thegovlab.org/

The Public Good Projects

The Public Good Projects (PGP) specializes in large-scale media monitoring, social and behavioral change interventions, and cross-sector initiatives in public health. Employing evidence-based, tailored approaches, PGP collaborates with various experts to promote global health and equity. PGP leverages science and technology to address the most urgent public health challenges of our time.
www.publicgoodprojects.org/

Toda Peace Institute

The Toda Peace Institute, an independent, nonpartisan institute, conducts research and promotes dialogue to advance peace and policy solutions. It focuses on cooperative

security, digital peacebuilding, climate change, and Northeast Asian peace and security, among other areas.
https://toda.org/

United Nations: Centre for Humanitarian Data

The Centre for Humanitarian Data, managed by the UN Office for Coordination of Humanitarian Affairs, enhances data use and impact in the humanitarian sector. It focuses on data services, science, responsibility, and learning, supporting staff and partners in humanitarian locations. In line with the UN's data-focused strategies, the Centre addresses growing data demands and challenges in humanitarianism amid calls for sectoral reimagining.
https://centre.humdata.org/

United Nations: Crisis Risk and Early Warning Unit

The Crisis Risk Dashboard, developed by the UNDP and the wider UN system, is a data aggregation and visualization tool for contextual risk analysis. It consolidates various data sets, enhancing evidence-based assessments through visual representations such as maps and graphs. The dashboard includes global, regional, and country-specific versions.
https://sdgintegration.undp.org/crisis-risk-dashboard

United Nations: Commission on Science and Technology for Development

The UN Commission on Science and Technology for Development is a subsidiary of the Economic and Social Council (ECOSOC) and has hosted annual intergovernmental forums on science, technology, and development since 2006. It focuses on following up on the World Summit on the information society outcomes, involving national governments and civil society in discussions, and advising the UN General Assembly and ECOSOC on related issues.
https://unctad.org/topic/commission-on-science-and-technology-for-development

United Nations: Futures Lab

The United Nations Futures Lab fosters strategic foresight across the UN through a network of distributed capabilities. It aims to improve long-term decision-making, addressing uncertainty and leveraging opportunities for impactful change in governance and policy.
https://un-futureslab.org/

United Nations: Global Pulse

The UN Global Pulse, the Secretary-General's Innovation Lab, facilitates inclusive innovation across the UN, collaborating on solutions and supporting transformation toward a more effective, digital UN. It experiments with data, digital tools, and foresight methods for global impact.
www.unglobalpulse.org/

United Nations: Innovation Cell

The UN's Department of Political and Peacebuilding Affairs' Innovation Cell, launched in January 2020, explores and pilots new technologies and practices in peacebuilding. It responds to the UN Secretary-General's call for innovation, fostering an ecosystem for collaborative, human-centered design in peace and security.
https://dppa.un.org/en/innovation

United Nations: International Telecommunication Union

The ITU, a UN agency founded in 1865, facilitates global communications connectivity. It allocates radio spectrum, develops technical standards, and improves ICT access worldwide, playing a crucial role in global communication and striving to connect underserved communities.
www.itu.int/en/Pages/default.aspx

United Nations: iVerify

iVerify, a fact-checking tool from the UNDP, addresses global challenges of misinformation, disinformation, and hate speech. Supported by the UNDP Chief Digital Office, it identifies false information to prevent and mitigate its spread, contributing to peace and security.
www.undp.org/digital/iverify

United Nations: Office of the High Commissioner for Human Rights

The UN Office of the High Commissioner for Human Rights (OHCHR), the principal UN entity for human rights promotion and protection, assists governments in fulfilling obligations, speaks out against violations, and provides a forum for human rights discussions. It focuses on research, education, and advocacy, collaborating with various partners to promote human rights globally. In its digital space and human rights project, the OHCHR convenes expert consultations and issues reports to delve into contemporary trends and issues arising from the digital landscape, affecting the right to privacy and other human rights.
www.ohchr.org/en/topic/digital-space-and-human-rights

United Nations University: Centre for Policy Research

The UN University Centre for Policy Research conducts policy-focused research and capacity-building on strategic global issues. It offers objective, practical solutions for immediate implementation, leveraging deep knowledge of the UN system and a broad partner network. It presents research related to the current thinking on the ethics and global governance of AI.
https://unu.edu/cpr/

United Nations University: Electronic Governance

The UN University Operating Unit on Policy-Driven Electronic Governance in Portugal is a think tank dedicated to electronic governance. It explores digital governance's impact and fosters the use of digital technologies for public operations, citizen involvement, and sustainable development.
https://egov.unu.edu/

United Nations University: Maastricht Economic and Social Research Institute on Innovation and Technology

The UN University's Maastricht Economic and Social Research Institute on Innovation and Technology focuses on comprehensive innovation for sustainable development. Collaborating with Maastricht University, it addresses interconnected risks and opportunities of innovation related to climate change, digital transformation, inequality, and the future of work.
www.merit.unu.edu/

University of Texas at Arlington: Claim Buster

ClaimBuster, developed at the University of Texas at Arlington, creates AI models for automated fact-checking, aiding journalists and the public in combating misinformation. Accessible via an API, it represents a significant step toward automated fact-checking.
https://idir.uta.edu/claimbuster/

University of Toronto: Citizen Lab

The Citizen Lab at the University of Toronto is an interdisciplinary project that researches the intersection of information technologies, human rights, and global security. Founded by Ron Deibert, it combines various academic disciplines, investigating digital espionage, internet filtering, and the impact of technology on freedom of expression and privacy.
https://citizenlab.ca/

University of Washington: Center for an Informed Public

The University of Washington's interdisciplinary center, Center for an Informed Public, involving the information school, human-centered design & engineering, and the school of law, translates research on misinformation into policy and practice. It fosters collaboration across various sectors and communities, engaging with the public directly to educate consumers of information to make informed decisions.
www.cip.uw.edu/

Uppsala University: Department of Peace and Conflict Research

The Department of Peace and Conflict Research at Uppsala University focuses on understanding peace and conflict dynamics. It houses the Uppsala Conflict Data Program, providing extensive, free data for conflict research. The department is recognized for its cutting-edge, externally funded research and programs.
www.pcr.uu.se/research/

Vital Wave

Vital Wave, founded in 2005, collaborates with governments and international donors to implement large-scale digital solutions for global development. It offers end-to-end services, utilizing its implementation capabilities and methodologies to advance sustainable digital solutions.
https://vitalwave.com/

Women in AI Ethics

Women in AI Ethics, initiated in 2018, addresses AI's ethical challenges by promoting inclusion and representation of women and marginalized groups. It publishes an annual list of influential women in AI ethics and offers resources for increasing diversity in AI/tech fields.
https://womeninaiethics.org/

Index

Aadhaar 128–129, 131, 133, 142, 144, 147
Algocracy 205–206
Algorithmic governance 3, 4
Artificial Intelligence (AI) 1, 3–4, 7, 9, 13–14, 16–22, 25–27, 40, 43–44, 55–57, 60–61, 63, 65–68, 83, 109–110, 132, 141–143, 150–151, 154–156, 167, 171–172, 185–192, 194, 198, 202–204, 209
Asylum 5, 17–18, 22–25, 30, 56, 62, 64–67, 85
Automated risk assessment 63–64, 68
Automation bias 6, 26, 166, 199

Bertillonage 28, 30, 32, 70
Biodata 8, 48, 134
Biometrics 4, 46, 197
Borders 18, 22–24, 56

China 4, 35–38, 58, 73, 83, 99, 104, 109, 114, 118, 126–128, 133, 136, 192
Chinese Dang'an 114–116, 118, 126, 132
Clearview AI 17, 24–26
Cognitive security 77–78, 199
Conflict prevention 161, 166, 173, 175
Civil liberties 12, 16, 18–19, 25, 39, 98, 105, 109–110, 142, 150–151, 167, 188–189, 192, 199

Data analytics 163, 165, 188
Data double 203, 208
Data privacy 22, 34, 189
Data protection 55, 62, 65, 67, 97–98, 100, 107, 141–144, 150, 152–155, 157, 189
Datafication 202–203, 209
Digital citizens 8, 202–205
Digital literacy 103, 185–186, 194
Digital rights 48, 55–58, 60–61, 63, 129, 133, 141, 147
Digital twins 170–171, 180
Disinformation 74, 77–79, 185, 187–188
Driverless government 2, 15

Ethics 7, 14, 87, 123, 172, 177, 197
Eugenics 31–33, 70, 85
European Digital Rights (EDRi) 55

European Union AI Act 55–56, 58, 63, 65

Facial Emotion Recognition (FER) 72–73, 75–76, 81
Facial Recognition Technology (FRT) 17–20, 25, 35–38, 40, 57, 141, 143–144, 150–151, 156
Funopticon 124, 136

Geolocation trackers 133, 142
Governance 4–7, 9–10, 13–14, 30, 67, 79, 97, 108, 113, 124, 127, 141, 151, 155–156, 158, 161–162, 172, 176–177, 188, 190, 192, 195, 197–198, 206
Government surveillance 100, 103, 106, 123–124, 192

Human rights 12, 37–38, 40, 55, 62–63, 65, 67, 73, 97, 107, 157, 166, 170, 189, 201

Large Language Models (LLMs) 43–44, 83, 132, 171, 204
League of Nations 158, 161

Machine learning 43, 74–75, 79, 163–165
Mass surveillance 12, 56–58, 105, 125
Migration forecasting 66–67

Natural Language Processing (NLP) 74–76, 79, 81, 121

Peacetech 170, 172
Predictive technologies 98, 109, 166, 173, 175, 186, 191
Privacy 1, 7–9, 16–17, 19–22, 24–25, 34, 36–39, 45, 55–57, 59–62, 67, 87, 98, 100–101, 103, 105, 107, 119, 121–122, 124–125, 127–128, 141–144, 147–149, 151–155, 157, 164, 176, 188–189, 191, 200–201, 206, 209
Prosopography 118, 132

Red Scare 117–118, 132
Roboprocesses 14, 80

Russian Third Department 113–114, 116, 118, 125, 132

Sentiment analytics 4, 17, 23–24, 74, 163
Skynet 35
Social credit system 126–128, 132–133
Social media monitoring 66, 74–75, 109, 150, 191
Social scoring 56, 58
State–citizen relations 2, 85
Surveillance 11–12, 16–20, 24–26, 29, 35–40, 48, 55–61, 66–67, 73, 75, 97–107, 109, 117, 123–126, 130–131, 134, 141–144, 146–153, 156–157, 159–160, 166–167, 173, 175, 186, 188, 191–192, 195, 202
Surveillance tools 16–17, 19, 39, 98, 106, 109, 124, 146, 150

ThinThread 119–121
Tsar Nicholas 113–114, 135

United Nations 4, 162–163, 168–169, 173, 185, 189–190, 193

Wearables 41–43, 45, 48, 136